HAMTRAMCK HAUNTS

HAMTRAMCK HAUNTS

Charlotte L. Cavanary

Library of Congress Number:		2002094759
ISBN :	Hardcover	1-4010-7537-1
	Softcover	1-4010-7536-3

This book was printed in the United States of America.

To order additional copies of this book, contact:
Xlibris Corporation
1-888-795-4274
www.Xlibris.com
Orders@Xlibris.com
16527

CONTENTS

Dedicated to my family, here and abroad.

HAMTRAMCK HAUNTS

A Memoir

Growing up in the shadow of the Great Depression, World War II, and a heart-wrenching family happening that affected (positively and negatively) an entire generation.

CHARLOTTE L. CAVANARY

Haunt: 1. To frequent, to visit intrusively.
2. To inhabit or frequent as a specter.
3. To recur to (the mind, etc.) frequently and spontaneously; as, haunted by vague dreams.
—v.i. to persist in staying or visiting

TODAY'S THOUGHT

We do not live alone. God
has invested every life
with the power of influence. As
we fashion our own lives, they
become forces to shape the lives
of others. The things we say and
do, the choices we make, the
loyalties we show—these things
forge themselves into a pattern
for someone else, perhaps for
many to follow.

—UNKNOWN.

Clipped from the *Detroit News* when I was in college and tucked
into one corner of the dresser mirror in my bedroom.

ACKNOWLEDGMENTS

A debt of gratitude to my husband Edward, who was initial proofreader, and to Mrs. Rietta Howard of the Senior Center for Lifelong Learning, who supported my efforts during several "semesters" of my attendance at her "Writing Your Personal History" sessions at the University of West Florida in Fort Walton Beach, Florida. And, special thanks to Rev. Edmund Wolschon, who encouraged me to write after receiving a letter from me describing an overnight camping trip at Tau Beta Camp.

CHRONOLOGY

12 April 1909: Andrew Kasperowicz, age 18, arrives on the SS Hanover, at Baltimore, Maryland. He is taken in by Frank Czekiel, his half brother, living in Detroit.

25 April 1918: Andrew Kasperowicz enlists in the U.S. Army, is stationed at Camp Custer, Michigan.

September 1921: Andrew Kasperowicz returns to his home village of Gibulicze, Poland, to claim the hand of Josephine Wróblewski. His dowry: $3,000 U.S.

25 October, 1921: Marriage of Andrew Kasperowicz and Josephine Wróblewski in Grodno, Poland.

December 1921: Andrew and Josephine Kasperowicz immigrate to Detroit, Michigan, via Ellis Island, New York.

23 September 1922, Eleanor Kasperowicz is delivered stillborn, first child of Andrew and Josephine.

1923 or 1924, Edward Kasperowicz, second child of Andrew and Josephine, is delivered stillborn.

21 August 1925, Loraine Kasperowicz is born by caesarean section at Providence Hospital, Detroit. Baptismal name: Charlotte.

September 1930: Charlotte attends kindergarten at Dickinson School on Norwalk Street, Hamtramck.

October 1930: The Kasperowicz family moves to 3291 Trowbridge, the house previously owned by the Borucki family. Their son Stanley remains in the U.S. studying for the priesthood while the rest of the family, parents, and two sons, return to Poland.

September 1931: Charlotte begins first grade at Our Lady Queen of Apostles parish school in Hamtramck.

26 March 1932: Leonard Kasperowicz arrives via caesarean section at Providence Hospital, the fourth and last child of Andrew and Josephine.

2 February 1933: A serious house fire at 3291 Trowbridge leaves the occupants temporarily homeless.

Summer 1933: Andrew Kasperowicz has a near-death experience while undergoing kidney surgery at Wayne County General Hospital. A blood donor saves his life, but Andrew loses one kidney.

June 1939: Charlotte finishes eighth grade at Our Lady Queen of Apostles parish school.

September 1939: Charlotte begins Girls Catholic Central High School located at 60 Parsons Street, Detroit.

May 1942: Josephine Kasperowicz is hospitalized at Wayne County General Hospital for treatment of Involutional Melancholia. Charlotte becomes surrogate mother to her 10-year-old brother and housekeeper of the family home.

June 1943: Charlotte graduates, an honor student, from Girls Catholic Central High School.

Summer of 1943: Charlotte meets a Hamtramck born serviceman, PFC Bernard J. Zacharias, falls in love, and experiences a devastating heartbreak.

September 1943: Charlotte begins her freshman year at Marygrove College, an all woman's school in Detroit, Michigan.

June 1947: Charlotte graduates with a Bachelor of Arts Degree in Sociology from Marygrove College.

September 1947: The first job is as Group Worker at the Polish Aid Society, a settlement house at 6000 Dubois Street in Detroit. Miss Irene Mayes is the director and also a graduate of Marygrove College.

January 1949: Charlotte begins part time graduate school at Wayne State University's School of Social Work. A stipend from the United Community Services allows for full-time attendance later that year.

June 1950: Graduation with a Master of Social Work degree from Wayne State University.

1950 to 1957: Social Worker, Program Director and Acting Director at the Polish Aid Society—Harper Community House.

27 March 1957: Andrew Kasperowicz dies at age 68 at the Veteran's Hospital in Allen Park, Michigan.

April 1957: Josephine Kasperowicz returns to her home on Trowbridge Street, her condition stabilized with psychotrophic medications.

July 1957: Charlotte, at age 31, invests in a studio apartment at the River House Cooperative, 8900 E. Jefferson Avenue, Detroit, moving from the family homestead.

April 1958: Charlotte is hired as a Medical Social Worker by the Wayne County Department of Social Welfare.

August 1959: The GRAND TOUR of Europe and "Behind the Iron Curtain" in Poland.

October 1959: Meeting my life's companion, Edward Cavanary.

26 June 1962: Wedding bells ring for Charlotte and Edward at Annunciation Church in Detroit.

1 July 1963: The Cavanarys move into their home at 28330 Ranchwood Drive, Southfield, Michigan.

1963 to 1993: Thirty years of happy living on our acre and a third.

17 July 1989: Josephine Kasperowicz succumbs to pneumonia at age 92 at Harrison Community Hospital, Mt. Clemens, Michigan.

July 1993: the Cavanarys relocate to northwest Florida and begin "retirement" at the Gulf Terrace Condos, 4000 Gulf Terrace Drive #250, Destin, Florida 32541.

EPILOGUE

The first entry in a spiral notebook where I began longhand writing of my personal history is dated December 19, 1989. My intention was to have it completed and presented to my brother on his 60th birthday, March 26, 1992. Well, he's had his 70th birthday this past March 2002 and I'm still adding bits of memories to various chapters, but plan to self-publish my memoir in book form this year.

CHAPTER 1

Polish Roots

A sudden shower from a dark gray cloud overhead dampened the grassy path where we stood. Opening my umbrella I lifted it to shield us before we moved on. Cousin Teresa and I had just arrived in this corner of "Polish Siberia" to search out my family's home village near the Belorus-Polish border. Many ancestors, especially from my mother's side of the family, lived around this section of northeast Poland.

It was September 1993. Fall was showing its colors early. The panoramic vista held my gaze, and I was awestruck. Clear blue patches above promised sunshine that would soon warm this stretch of meadow. Small rises in the fields met a rim of pines and oaks that defined the far perimeter. Brilliant scarlet and gold punctuated the backdrop of dark greenery. A cool breeze ruffled the overhead canopy of foliage.

Although I had visited Poland several times prior, this was my first visit to Gibulicze, the village where my mother and father were born. I breathed deeply. It was then that I understood my mother's yearning to return to Poland.

Mom had returned to Poland once, in 1974, fifty-three years after leaving her small village of Gibulicze as a young bride to start a new life in Michigan. She was unable to visit her home, however. Poland had been under communist rule since World War II and this section had become part of Russia after the World War II border shifts. Access to the country's small villages was limited. I accompanied her on this trip, and our goal was to visit her brother, my Uncle John. He was Mom's youngest brother and had left the

collective farm in Gibulicze for city life and a factory job in Elbląg
on the Baltic Sea.

Elbląg, a small town on the Baltic Sea, an hour east of Gdańsk
(Danzig), is about 250 miles west of Gibulicze. A very small village,
it became even more remote as we learned of visa requirements and
strict rules regarding visits. Specific dates of stay were required as
well as the names and addresses of the people we visited.

Recalling my mother's past leanings to return to her homeland,
I had proposed that she and I plan a reunion with her brother
John, her only living sibling. We saved her money, and in just over
a year, we had the $800 round trip air fare. We planned a two-
week stay, leaving on Mother's Day 1974. Mom was 77, and her
health was fair, but she was apprehensive as well as excited over her
first and only air travel and meeting with her brother.

Our flight reached Warsaw's Okiecie Airport at 7 a.m. The
terminal building was a low hangar-like structure, unbefitting of a
city that was the capital of a country. Our luggage was subject to a
search, we learned, after claiming our two suitcases from a conveyor
belt. The Polish customs official was a buxom matron in a dark
green khaki uniform. "Open that one," she barked. She pointed to
the almost new black Tourister bag that my mother had borrowed
for the trip. It was packed with her house dresses, underwear,
hosiery, slips, and nightgowns.

I was relieved that my suitcase, which was right next to Mom's,
escaped searching. It was filled with new items, gifts of clothing,
panty hose, special foods like instant coffee and peanut butter, and
cosmetics for my relatives. The items were not contraband, but
may have raised an eyebrow and some questions.

We recognized Uncle John, a tall man, lean and white-haired,
above us on a balcony. He was accompanied by his son-in-law, also
named John, and they waved to us. The bonds that existed before
the family separated fifty years prior, reemerged, and brother and
sister embraced and pondered what fate had brought into their
lives, this meeting, a momentous event in their personal histories.

We traveled to Elbląg from Warsaw in a tiny auto, a Syrenka,
that was son-in-law John's proud possession. The suitcases sat

securely strapped to the roof, as the trunk held a spare container of fuel. The trip was 180 miles. On the way, my mother's Americanization surfaced when she asked for a hamburger. Alas, there were no Burger Kings in Poland in 1974. Later when we strolled by a bakery with pastries displayed in the window, Mom exclaimed, "Look! American Ponchki!" Ponchki are jelly doughnuts. She forgot that they had originated in Europe. My mother's first cousin, Jan Gibulski, traveled by train from Stettin to this reunion. He was the best man at her wedding in 1921. What stories those three told. Uncle John, a German prisoner during WW II spoke of long journeys without food or water. Once, he said, at a pump, a German soldier knocked his metal cup out of his hand, thwarting Uncle John's attempt to get some water to drink. Jan Gibulski, a short man with ill-fitting partial dentures, was now a gentleman farmer. He provided us homemade farmer's cheese, some fresh eggs from his chickens, and some whole dried pears from his orchard. These pears were a tasty dessert after they were reconstituted by simmering in boiling water.

John then spoke of his oldest son, Walter, who was killed by a land mine in a field near their village in 1941. He was 13. He had picked it up and carried it, placing it on top of a large rock. When he set it down it exploded and killed him instantly.

Cousin John Gibulski survived ten years of a grueling existence in a labor camp in Siberia. Niece Teresa, Uncle John's daughter, related that, during WWII, she had to wear an arm band with a "P" on it (for Pole) and walk on the street, as the sidewalks were reserved for the occupying Germans. Uncle John's wife Mary described leaving their village. It was in 1957. The entire family— Uncle John, his wife Mary, and their four children, Edward, Stanley, Teresa, and Eleanor—was struggling and chafing under the Communist rule. They were disgruntled and disenchanted with collectivism in Gibulicze. Uncle John learned that his wife's sister, with her family, was living and working in Elbląg. Uncle John was determined to leave the land and seek employment in a factory in Elbląg. Aunt Mary's sister accepted and took them into her four-room apartment in the middle of town. Uncle John's family left everything behind—the 10 acres of farmland, their homestead with its low picket fence, the memories of a lifetime, their relatives. They had even killed their pet duck for a meal, and because no one wanted to eat it, they left the roast behind, still in its pan in the oven. Uncle John's oldest daughter, Jeanne, was married and had decided to remain with her husband in nearby Grodno.

As Uncle John and cousin John continued with their stories and sang folk songs, their language reverted to their regional Belorussian. My mother heaved a sigh upon hearing what life had become in the village. "I won't see Gibulicze again," she said, as she concluded that she would live out her days near her children and grandchildren in America. And she did not.

But I did, during my trip in 1993.

I found that the family farm and the homestead in Gibulicze, had become occupied by uncle John's sister, Eva, and her husband, once uncle John's family had fled to Elbląg in 1957. Eva had died in August 1964. Her husband, Jan Bujko, then married Bronia, a younger woman who bore him a son. Bronia Bujko, with her now adult married son, lived at the farmstead during my visit in 1993.

This small village was the backdrop for my mother and father's childhood. My mother recalled many of her early experiences which affected and marked her adult life. In my own "growing up" in Hamtramck, Michigan, there were also defining moments and events leaving indelible scars that haunt me still. When I began recalling my own younger years, some memories were easy to bring up, some wrenchingly painful. But they were all significant in my coming of age.

Gibulicze—WW I

JOSEPHINE, AGE 16, WITH SISTER EVA

My mother spoke often about WW I and how it affected Gibulicze, near Grodno, close to the Russian border in eastern Poland. In 1914, she was a young woman of 17, the oldest daughter in a sibship of five. When war broke out in Europe, soldiers from the Russian Army were quartered in their house. She spoke of her attraction for one of the soldiers. She recalled that he once rested his head on her shoulder. My grandmother squelched any further romantic involvement, however. She forbad any further progression of this budding romance, announcing that this kind of relationship was forbidden. He was a stranger and might have a wife some place, she told my mother. But most importantly, he was "not one of them."

My mother recalled the sounds of battles going on nearby. Gunfire and cannonballs exploded in the fields nearby. Artillery charges whistled overhead, and bursts and explosions lit the night sky.

All the villagers were forced to dig trenches around the perimeter of the area for the troops that came through. When the Russians left, or retreated, the Germans replaced them. The local villagers all learned conversational German. My mother often recited sentences and words that had become necessary to conduct the activities of daily living at that time. She especially knew all the profanity used by the occupying troops. I don't know how long these farm folk had to live with this kind of disruption.

In 1917, following the Russian Revolution, the Bolsheviks found their way into this village so near their border. Their occupation was the worst of all. These invaders were considered uncivilized. During the day, their shirts looked like the night shirts worn to sleep in. In my mother's memory, the Germans were feared but the Bolsheviks were worse. Unmannered and rough, they demonstrated little regard for the people of the land.

My mother's older brother Alexander had emigrated to the U.S. in 1913 to avoid military service under the czar. During the Russian occupation, my mother lost a girlfriend who died after being struck in the back with shrapnel from an exploding bomb.

Alexander Wròblewski, my grandfather, died a tragic death on July 4, 1918.

The circumstances leading to his death are tragic in themselves. Alexander boasted to his brother, Mihał, that he was not going to turn in his rifle as required by the occupying army. He would hide it. But a reward was offered to anyone giving information about any villager harboring arms. Mihał, turned in his brother and collected the reward. Word got around that a search was underway to apprehend Alexander. My grandfather determined to hide in the barn. When he lit up a cigarette and cracked open the barn door, the telltale wisp of smoke rising up gave away his hiding place. He was arrested, bound with ropes that were attached to a wagon, and dragged behind on the ground to the Grodno jail. With other prisoners, he was transferred to the town of Sokòłka where all were beaten and eventually shot. My grandmother never knew where he was buried. In 2000, during a discussion of this dastardly deed with relatives in Poland, I learned that Alexander was allegedly buried in the Orthodox cemetery outside of Sokòłka. In 1993, while visiting the village of Gibulicze, where this tragedy occurred, I strolled across the unpaved muddy rutted road, bissecting this small rural enclave. I sat down beside my mother's cousin, Josephine Wròblewski Ciereszko, as she stirred a pot of cooking mushrooms. Her father was Mihał, the brother to whom my grandfather boasted about his decision to hide his firearm. She was a child of four in 1918 when the action took place. We talked about what I heard about my grandfather from my parents. Her response startled me. In her opinion, Alexander Wròblewski, my grandfather, was at fault. "He did wrong," she added firmly, justifying her father's betrayal.

But a man, the victim, was brutally beaten and killed, leaving a wife and four children without a means of support.

What remains amazing to me is that, 80 years after the incident, family members still talk about what happened. My mother defended her father saying that he had only pieces of a rifle. My father's memory, probably through hearsay, was that Mihał's son was so ashamed of what his father did, that he entered a monastery.

Very little can be verified after the passage of time, not even where Alexander was buried. If his burial place can be ascertained, there may be an opportunity for closure. His grandchildren would be able to come to terms with his untimely and unnecessary death.

My grandfather's death left my mother, her two sisters Eva and Pauline, and John responsible for operating the family farm. Her younger brother, John, who was then 14, learned to plow the fields, and the sisters planted the crops, fed the animals, and milked the cows. I'm sure my grandmother helped, but she was probably mainly involved in keeping house and preparing meals.

JAN WRÓBLEWSKI—1923—
BROTHER OF JOSEPHINE

GRANDMOTHER ANNA WRÓBLEWSKI
AND DAUGHTER PAULINE—1928

Meanwhile, my father was in America. At 18 years of age, in 1909, he had left Poland, perhaps to avoid being drafted into the czar's army. He boarded the S.S. Hanover in Bremen and arrived in Baltimore, Maryland, April 12, 1909. He went to Detroit to live with his half brother, Frank Czekiel. Frank had immigrated to America and settled in Michigan with his wife and daughter Mary in 1906 and had probably informed relatives across the ocean about the opportunities here.

Saving enough money for a one-way passage to the United States was a challenge, as my father revealed many years later when we were adults. The sale of two horses bought the ship's ticket fare. Were the horses the property of the gentryman who owned the manor where my father worked? Where did the sale take place? Time and memory obscured the particulars. My father revealed only snatches of this happening. He must have planned an escape strategy that would assure his success.

Leaving Poland under Russian rule was risky as we heard from Stella Landers, a cousin whose grandmother, mother, and aunt finally emigrated to the U.S. safely just prior to WW I. Stella tells of her aunt Basia, at age 18, attempting to cross the border in the company of her male cousin who was also 18. She was caught by the police and imprisoned. The male cousin visited the jail, standing outside, under the cell window, calling to her, assuring her that he was waiting. However, as it turned out, he was able to leave the country alone, and Basia later completed her plans with her sister and mother. This trio, the Sarosieks, settled in upstate New York.

The Census of 1910 records my father as 18 years old, a laborer, and a boarder living with Frank and Leocadia Czekiel and their children, Mary and Frank. Their address is listed as 739 Medbury, Detroit, Michigan. His name is listed as Andrew Gasperowicz.

He was the youngest child of Julia and Anthony Kasperowicz. Born on December 14, 1889, in the village of Gibulicze, he joined an older brother Kazimierz and five half siblings from his mother's first marriage. Her first husband, Augustyn Czekiel, died, leaving Julia and their children. Anthony was 25 years old and Julia 32 when they married. When my father was born, she was 41.

My father's childhood was marked by hardship and hard work.

As soon as he was able, at about age 11 or 12, he left home to work as a stable hand at an estate in eastern Poland. He soon earned the position of driving the horse-drawn carriage that took the lord of the manor to town.

We know that my father learned to read and write, and that he received instructions in the Roman Catholic faith. My father was fluent in Polish and Russian. My mother and father used both languages when they spoke to each other at home. Catholic hymns, especially Christmas carols and Easter songs, were sung during the appropriate seasons by my parents.

The first passport photograph of my father portrayed him as a well developed, sturdy young male with a full face, fair hair, and light eyes. A heavy, dark turtleneck sweater encircled his neck. This photo is now gone, lost to the moves and cleanings of his personal papers. When I came across it, I studied it long and hard. I had never known my father looking so young and virile.

My father spoke of his early jobs from time to time. He spent many summers on an excursion boat that sailed between Detroit and Cleveland. As a room steward, he was assured a bed and meals, and often tips. He also worked in downtown Detroit at the Ponchartrain Hotel, now replaced with a glass and steel structure. I am unsure as to his position, but he often revealed work as a sous chef, assigned to making sandwiches which brought correcting from the head chef as being rather crude.

My father recalled with pride his service in the U.S. Army during WW I. Citizenship was granted to men who joined. He was stationed at Fort Custer, Michigan, where he drove a horse-drawn supply wagon. I remember how his chin quivered and his voice cracked when he told of the recruiting sergeant giving him a once over. "You are worth a bullet," the man had said. Then he signed him into the country's service. Dad always regretted being held back from overseas duty. His unit was leaving for Europe, but he had to stay behind because of severe varicose veins. His discharge papers list his service as six months, from April 1918, to Armistice Day, November, 1918. An army photo of my father shows a hint of a smile and a thick wool, army uniform. Hatless, he had light hair, fair skin, and clear pale eyes.

ANDREW IN WW I UNIFORM

During these first years in America, my father kept in touch with his family in the old country, and they with him. He often inquired about my mother, who was a budding, industrious 12-year-old girl when he left Poland. In the fall of 1921, my father, then 31 years old, was still a bachelor. Having never forgotten Josephine, he returned to his village in eastern Poland with $3,000 in a money belt to ask for her hand in marriage.

My grandmother, Anna Wròblewski, called her daughter Josephine from the potato field, instructing her to get cleaned up as a suitor was waiting to offer her a new life in the U. S. She was the oldest daughter, now age 24. There must have been a stir in the village at this time. A home boy made good, now returned to claim the prize—a home town bride. My mother's circumstances were meager. She accepted the offer of marriage, preparing for life across the ocean. She borrowed a dress for the wedding ceremony. Vows were exchanged on October 25, 1921, at the church of the Franciscans in the city of Grodno. The two witnesses were Jan Gibulski, her first cousin, and Adam Ciereszko, a former suitor.

My mother and father traveled then to Warsaw to obtain all the necessary documents and arrange passage by ship. Many years later, my mother admitted having second thoughts at this point, turning away from my father, to walk eastward to her village. My father took her arm reminding her that she was now his wife with an obligation to go with him.

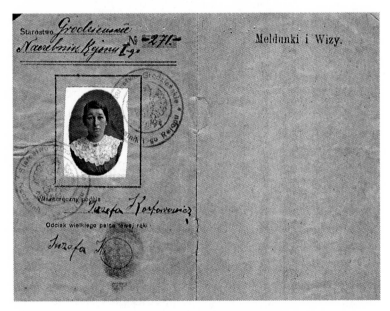

PASSPORT AND JOSEPHINE

The ship carrying them to the U.S. was the Acquitania. It sailed from Southhampton, England, arriving in New York December 9, 1921. The ship manifest listed their U.S. address as 2575 Superior,

Detroit, Michigan. My mother remembered these living quarters: two rooms above a garage. Before long, they purchased a two-story income house at 3364 Norwalk Street in Hamtramck Michigan, a small city within the limits of Detroit, joining many immigrants from eastern Europe who settled there in the early 1920s.

My mother missed and yearned for her large extended family, small village life, and surrounding verdant countryside. Her tribulations in the United States were compounded by a strange language, a faster paced city life, bothersome tenants, the Great Depression, and losing her first two children at childbirth. When conflicts arose her comment to my father was, "You wanted America. Now you have it."

When I was about three years old, in 1928, she expressed her longing and wish to return to Poland. My father replied, "You can go, but our daughter stays with me."

The words exchanged, made in anger, the reply, with a finality to it, ended with my father taking me outdoors. He located a field where a softball game was in progress. Just beyond, railroad tracks gleamed in the sunlight, and a Michigan Central passenger train chugged along, its forlorn whistle announcing its passing.

We were near enough to see heads through the windows. Was that my mother sitting, looking straight ahead, her chestnut colored hair in a bun at the back of her neck? Was she leaving me and my father? I said nothing of this vision to my father as we strolled back to the familiar fenced front yard when the ball game finished.

A fire department "rescue" truck occupied the entire space in front of the house. I was not allowed to enter but had to sit on one of the steps half way up to the second floor. A resuscitation was in progress. My mother had her stomach pumped after she was found unconscious in the kitchen with the gas jets turned on. It was the first of three suicidal attempts she made during her lifetime. I remember feeling puzzled and sad. Our daily routine resumed, my father kept his reaction to himself.

A half century later, I questioned my mother about that incident. She remembered, some hurt she experienced from an altercation with my father, followed by a feeling of desperation, seemingly with no solution.

I learned in early religion class, that it's a grievous mortal sin to take a life, your own or another, and eternally punishable. Life is a precious gift to be nurtured, protected. I considered the degree of hopelessness my mother experienced to be driven to take such a drastic step.

Marriage was a mixed bag of conflicting emotions for my mother. She learned to love, cherish, and care for her husband and children. But any setbacks, illnesses, difficulties, were thought to be unlucky streaks, a direct result of leaving her family. This was considered a punishment that could have been avoided had she remained in her native corner of Poland. It was during these hard times she told of harboring a fear of married life while growing up. An earlier suitor, Adam Ciereszko, was rejected for this reason. He later married my mothers first cousin, who, was also named Josephine Wròblewski.

BRONIA SAROSIEK, ALBINA SAROSIEK BIELAWSKA AND ALBINA'S HUSBAND PAWEł AND SON PAWEł (1923) THE TWO WOMEN—JOSEPHINE'S AUNTS

Birth

Charlotte Loraine Kasperowicz
Date: August 21, 1925
Place: Providence Hospital, 14th Street at West Grand Blvd.,
Detroit, Michigan

In 1925, Calvin Coolidge was President, Charles Dawes, Vice President. The best film of the year was Charlie Chaplin's "The Gold Rush." In music, "The Vagabond King" by Rudolph Friml opened in New York. Popular songs of the time were "5 foot 2, Eyes of Blue," "Always" by Irving Berlin and "Sleepy Time Gal" by Joseph R. Alden.

In Detroit's Providence Hospital, Dr. Priborsky, a well-respected obstetrician, delivered the third child of Josephine and Andrew Kasperowicz, by caesarean section.

Two previous pregnancies, full-term babies, a girl, Eleanor, born September 23, 1922, and a boy, Edward, born in 1923 or 1924, did not survive the birth process. A midwife attended these deliveries at home. When she was unsuccessful, a doctor was summoned. He delivered the first baby, but could not save her life. My mother told of the advice she received at this time from her sister-in-law, our Aunt Katarynka Czekiel. This aunt had delivered six children without any problem. Allegedly, she comforted my mother by observing that first pregnancies sometimes pose difficulties, but that she would not have the same thing happen next time. So when the second baby was due, a midwife was called again, and once more could not deliver the child. This time, a different doctor came to make the house call, advising the grief-stricken parents a live birth could be assured in the future.

The hospital stay during and after my birth was a meaningful and positive experience for my mother. The efficient and confident nurses made a lasting impression on her. Except once. One morning the rolling cart brought the newborn infants for feeding to each mother's bed. This time, the baby at my mother's breast fussed, squirmed, and refused to take the nipple. When the nurse arrived, she discovered the wrong baby was brought to my mother, in fact, it was a boy! The mix was corrected, but I had a "free meal" elsewhere. I had not discerned any difference.

Losing the first two full-term children was traumatic and an unforgettable experience for my mother. She relived the loss all through her life. When my brother and I were youngsters, we accompanied my mother periodically when she visited their graves at Mt. Olivet Cemetery. We covered the distance on foot from Trowbridge Street to Six Mile Road and Van Dyke. She would search for the grave marker in the section reserved for non-baptized babies, sobbing quietly when she finally located the spot.

My mother was 28 years old when I was born. My father was 34.

Parents and Other Family Members

and Family Friends

Several early memories surface from the first 6 years when I was the "only" child, the JEDYNACZKA. Our tenant, Mr. Lucjan Szkudniewski, gave me that moniker. He lived in three rooms in one of the two flats on the first floor of the income house we owned on Norwalk Street. That family quickly grew to four children in that span of time. They all continued to live in those three rooms for a number of years after we moved to Trowbridge Street in the fall of 1930.

3364 NORWALK BACK YARD WITH
MR. LUCJAN SZKUDNIEWSKI, DOWNSTAIRS TENANT

I recall being cuddled and hugged a lot by my mom and dad and given "raspberry" kisses. This is a kiss planted on the bare belly button with an audible exhaling of warm breath that tickles and brings giggles of delight. I also witnessed playful pinches of my mother's ample breasts by my father and of her giving my father caresses and kisses on his head and face as he rested on the couch.

Dad worked as a "laborer"—a blue-collar worker in one of the auto industry factories. He left the house while it was still dark, traveling by Baker Street car as he did not drive a car, nor did he ever have the desire to do so. Our house was in a "settled" section of Hamtramck, Michigan. The elementary school, a yellow brick structure, was right across the street. Dickinson School's playground had a high cyclone fence going around three sides. It was barren: gravel covered the surface that could be seen from our second story front porch.

Mom was a short, plump woman with an oval face, deep blue green eyes, and a long nose characteristic of her family of origin. Her hair was chestnut colored which she wore in the then fashion among immigrant women, parted in the center and the long strands coiled into a bun in the back. Large tortoise shell hair pins held the roll in place. Daytime dress was a print cotton house dress over which she tied a pinafore apron. No makeup was worn except on special occasions when some loose powder was patted on the face. Those first five years at 3364 Norwalk, mom's daily routine was caring for the house and overseeing the growth and development of her daughter.

Laundry was done by hand. In the basement were laundry tubs and a wash stand with a hand operated wringer. Mom used a washboard. The soapy scrubbed article went through the wringer into the tub on the other side holding clean rinse water with bluing. It became my job to operate the wringer. A wicker clothes basket held the damp clothes ready for hanging with clothes pins on the clothes line. In the winter this meant a long haul up the stairs to the attic. Other times she used a clothes line that extended from the second story back porch to the top of the coal shed.

The Door-to-door Photographer

The door-to-door photographer led a pony into the back yard of our house on Norwalk Street. He proposed a photo of me sitting on the saddle. I was about three years old. He took the picture, returned a few days later with the proofs. My parents viewed them outdoors in the bright summer sunlight, disappointed in the glossy unfinished proofs and refused to have them developed. I remember the outline of a young child perched on a pony's back. I don't recall how my disappointment was expressed, but my allergy to horses may have had its origin here.

**JOSEPHINE, CHARLOTTE,
AND ANDREW KASPEROWICZ**

Meat Markets

Several meat markets catered to the Polish and eastern European residents of Hamtramck. My mother preferred Jaworski meat with Kowalski as a second. But she shopped some of the other meat establishments on Joseph Campau too. I remember going into one small store front that had fresh sawdust on the floor and freshly smoked sausages (kiełbasa), hams, salamis, and bacon slabs hanging from iron hooks on the back wall. The aroma enveloped me as I gazed into the glass-fronted display cases. More processed lunch meats: New York ham, tongue loaf, blood sausage, bologna, among others, could be sliced up for sandwiches. I was especially drawn to a red paprika covered, small slab of bacon. My mother told me what was under that bright coating but did not buy it.

Of course, the "butchers," male and female, wearing white aprons, standing behind the counters, eagerly reached into the cases, when a customer made a choice. The long loaf was placed on the slicing machine and manually pushed across the blade, the thin slices falling onto a wax paper, then folded and transferred to white butcher paper, weighed, wrapped, with the price written with pencil on top.

Shopping at the meat markets on Joseph Campau was a pleasurable experience of my early years.

Other Family Members

We often visited dad's half brother, Frank Czekiel, his wife Leocadia, (my mother called her KATARYNKA), and their six children, all much older than I. They lived on Alice Street, within walking distance of our home on Norwalk Street. Also, we called on close friends of my parents: my Godparents, Mr. Walenty Keller and Mrs. Zofia Adamicka. They were also first generation Poles who lived in the neighborhood with their U.S. born children who became friends. Virginia Keller, several years older than I was, kept in touch for many years, through her marriage and her mother's widowhood. Mr. Keller died when I was about 5 years old. It was the first funeral I attended. I accompanied my father to the church and the cemetery. My Godfather's casket was lowered with ropes into the freshly dug burial pit, and I was one of the mourners tossing a handful of dirt on the lid of the casket as it as it moved to the bottom.

My godmother, Mrs. Adamicka, her husband, and three adult sons lived about three blocks from our house. There were frequent visits back and forth. My memory of her is of her purchasing a doll for me. I was about eight years old, "counter" shopping at the local Woolworth five and dime store. She greeted me asking me to choose a doll from the display shelves. I decided on a cloth bodied doll, about 24 inches tall, with auburn hair, a bonnet, slip, dress, ankle socks, black Mary Jane sandals, and blue glass eyes with long eyelashes that opened and closed. It was the only doll I owned and played with as a little girl. In 1965, the doll was still on one of the closet shelves in the house on Trowbridge Street. The sale of the house in "as is" condition, included some furniture, tools, and the one and only doll of my early girlhood.

3364 Norwalk Street

Early recollections of the first 5 years of my life on Norwalk Street remained with me throughout my many years of growing up, maturing, and reaching the golden years. Seared into my memory is of a male visitor to our second floor four-room flat. A robust man, he demonstrated how he chewed glass. I must have been a speechless and awestruck four year old, gazing at him, and listening to the audible grinding of his molars across a chunk of glass. I don't recall his swallowing that mouthful. And I don't remember what was the response from my mother and father. I think my father would smile and shake his head in disbelief, considering it a demonstration of a questionable ability, having little retail value.

Another memory is of my parents' compassionate treatment of an elderly homeless woman. It was a stifling hot summer day when an aged woman dressed in black asked for a place to spend the night. Our back porch suited her and in the morning she came inside to use the bathroom. I remember her floor length voluminous skirt and her weather beaten wrinkled face as she moved inside. A musty stale body odor accompanied her. I associated this odor with age for many years.

More Childhood Memories

There was a summer family outing to Belle Isle Park when I was about three years old. I remember a small amusement park near the bridge. My father lost his straw hat while riding the roller coaster. It probably flew into the Detroit River. He laughed good naturedly after he got off the ride.

My parents took me to another organized family picnic sponsored by the shop where my father worked. This one was on Boblo Island located on the Detroit River and reached by an excursion boat. I recall my first ride on a Merry-Go-Round. What a delight! Calliope music accompanied the movement—colorfully painted animals sliding up and down brass poles—while the entire carousel went round and round! A zebra, ostrich, lion, and horses circled while riders clutched the reins.

My mother and I watched a potato sack race arranged for the men. My father was holding on to the edge of the burlap bag, laughing as he hopped laboriously, then stopping as the other men in line moved ahead. I wanted my father to win, to come in first, not to give up. I was too young to give him any credit for taking part.

In a game for the children, I was instructed to retrieve pennies from a mound of sand. A slow starter, I played rather than searched. Others around me were faster and more aggressive, pushing the sand aside quickly and picking out the coins. Needless to say I did not gather the most pennies.

There was another trip, this one to a farm in Canada. It was an overnight trip with the visitors sleeping on the hay stacked in the barn. The air was scorching, driving most of the males to cool off in the river nearby. My father stripped down to his one piece sleeveless cotton union suit (underwear) then walked into the shallow water. He did not own bathing trunks, but it did not stop him from seeking relief from the oppressive heat.

Another summer Sunday with my father, when I was about four years old, took us by street car to Belle Isle Park. We crossed the bridge leading to the park and found a shady spot under a tree near a playground area. I climbed on the swing while my father sat down on the grass, his back against the tree. I clasped the long chains attached to the wooden slat but did not know how to get any movement except by pushing with my feet. The swing drifted back and forth as I sat, my father sound asleep in the warm afternoon air. Several older children approached claiming the swing I was sitting on. I got off, crestfallen, ran to my father, waking him and expecting him to "intervene" so I could get my swing back. All the swings were now occupied with laughing boys and girls moving high forward and high backward.

He shrugged off my pleas, and we headed back home much to my disappointment. Several years later I finally mastered the momentum and body push needed for getting a swing moving.

Uncle Frank and Aunt Katarynka

"Wuja" (Uncle) and "ciocia" (Aunt)—Frank and Katarynka Czekiel lived in a modest frame, two-story house on Alice Street. My parents and I walked the 10 blocks, usually on a Sunday afternoon, for a visit to our closest blood relatives in this country. The six Czekiel children, Mary, Frank, Eddie, Antek, Joey, and Frances were all older than I. Frances, born in 1918, was seven years my senior, and was now a preteen.

Mary and her husband, a Frenchman, named Deslippe, lived in a three-room flat on the first floor of the three-family house. The larger flat upstairs, occupied by my uncle's family, was minimally furnished with well-worn furniture. But there was an upright piano in the living room that Frances played by ear. Also, they owned a standard size collie that looked like Lassie, called "Lady." I liked to pet her and listen to the piano playing by my cousin "Freda."

Visits to this household felt strained, as if they were glad to see us, but the visit was disruptive to their routine. Aunt Katarynka hurriedly prepared a snack which was haphazardly laid out on the bare wooden kitchen table. This, after one of the boys rushed out to buy bread, cold cuts, and soda pop.

I considered cousin Mary very attractive because of her white porcelain-like complexion and her well-endowed figure. She was a hairdresser at a beauty salon in downtown Detroit; her husband a car salesman. I considered him handsome because of his tightly waved black hair peppered with gray. They had no children. Years later I learned the reason. They made occasional visits to our home on Trowbridge Street, which I always thought were special.

Uncle Frank Czekiel

Uncle Frank was tall, lean, slow moving. I'll always remember his crystal blue eyes, silver hair, receding hairline, and a round bald spot on the crown of his head. When he spoke and smiled, his facial and mouth movements were very much like Clark Gable's. In the early 1930s Uncle Frank purchased an automobile. It was a black "Tin Lizzie" roadster. Parked at the curb in front of our house on Trowbridge Street, it made a handsome sight. We all got in for a ride sitting on the black leather upholstered seats. There were no windows on the sides. Mom wanted to learn to drive then and there. Was Uncle Frank going to be able to teach her? Unfortunately, her wish was very unrealistic as we could not afford to purchase a car. The grip of the Great Depression was tightening. Then Uncle Frank and his family moved to Medbury Street in Detroit. This house and another one, both two stories, sat on one lot. Next to the houses was a city playground and a block away was the baroque church of St. Stanislaus and an elementary school.

With unemployment affecting their family, Uncle Frank next purchased a farm in Macomb County, where he and three sons, now adults, attempted to operate a dairy farm. (More about that farm in a later chapter.) Aunt Katarynka refused to move to this farm, Uncle Frank divorced her, later marrying two more times in his older years. Mom considered each of these women as "low life." We speculated about where he found these "treasures" and were relieved when these marriages ended. Uncle Frank lived alone and with his daughter Frances until his death in the 1951. Aunt Katarynka was cared for by widowed daughter Mary and later by daughter Frances.

Aunt Katarynka

Aunt Katarynka communicated with her whole body, seeming to never sit down, her arms gesticulating through the air as if they were chopping wood. Her clear blue eyes darted from one object to another as quickly as she changed topics. Hers was a broad face, with high cheek bones. Her thin, straight gray hair was usually covered with a scarf—a babushka tied under her chin.

It was her nonstop conversation that earned her the name Katarynka. My mother compared her continuous conversation to the musical instrument carried by the organ grinder who occasionally strolled the neighborhood streets with his pet monkey on a leash. Katarynka is the Polish word for a barrel organ. Aunt Katarynka's dialogue was not unlike its rhythmic sound, which in her case was propelled by her hands and arms, head bobbing up and down, emphasizing each word.

She was built close to the ground. Her short legs were barely visible beneath the layers of her faded and wrinkled skirt and petticoat. She was never without an apron and a long, loose sweater that enveloped her short square form.

This simple peasant woman came to this country in 1906 with her husband Frank and infant daughter Mary. She seemed to be in a time warp throughout her life here. Her success was bearing six children, maintaining a household, and functioning with a very limited understanding of English. She was concerned with the basics only: food and shelter.

My mother endowed her with powers and knowledge that were above and beyond the energy that permeated her animated talking. When my baby brother was a toddler, Aunt Katarynka patted his head vigorously and hugged him repeatedly. If he cried or fussed after this display of interest, my mother blamed Aunt Katarynka. She pressed too hard on his tender head, or maybe she cast a spell with her mutterings, influencing his cantankerous behavior. Looking back on those happenings, I concluded that it was just talk.

A dramatic scenario completed her exit from this earth in 1970. As her casket was slowly inched through the church doors to the hearse, Mary, her oldest daughter, sobbing, fell across the top of it, grasping the sides, crying, "Mama, Mama!"

I read the memorial card giving her date of birth and death. She lived to be 95. Her name was really Leocadia.

My Parents

When we moved to Trowbridge Street, my dad worked at the Riley Stoker Company located at the foot of Joseph Campau Street at the Detroit River. Cast iron stokers were produced for furnaces on ships and in factories, carted and shipped on railroad cars that moved alongside the factory's long low red brick building. My father was the cast iron chipper and cast iron shipper. Before constructing a wooden crate for the stoker, my father chipped off any protrusions or rough edges. Bits of iron slivers often lodged in his hard-skinned fingers. My task was to remove these metal irritants with a needle as his vision was not acute enough. I was willing to perform this task and pleased for him to ask me, since for most of his life he was very independent.

Even with limited knowledge of English, he grasped the meaning and importance of the movement in the factory to unionize the workers. I could tell that he thought over the implications of this step when he announced that he would vote in favor of the union. The AFL-CIO represented the employees after a momentous election in the late 1930s.

I remember the vision of my father returning from work on a hot summer afternoon. He was walking east on Trowbridge Street, 6 blocks from the Baker Street car, with his visor cap pushed back on his head, his well-worn suit coat over one arm, his hand holding a rolled up copy of the *Polish Daily News*. His gait was slow due to the heat and weariness from an 8-hour day of physical labor in a shop with no air conditioning. His face was coated with perspiration and grime that collected in the creases around his nose. Yet he looked with anticipation to climbing those few stairs so he could finally get inside his home. My brother and I were playing on the front sidewalk as he approached. I was glad to see his familiar figure walking toward me as it was like a completed circle, the family would be all together, another day was ending, supper was next, and he would read the paper while I did my homework. He always took his shirt off first and bent over the wash bowl in the bathroom to wash his face and neck. To keep cool, he often ate supper in his undershirt and work trousers. I appreciated having my father come home each day shortly after I came home from school. He left home before I arose for school but did return well before supper. It is a ritual that I replicated after marrying a school teacher who could be depended upon to come home each afternoon by 5 o'clock.

I also remember him sitting on his own handmade wooden stool painted brown next to the stove in the kitchen. He pulled on the draw string to open the small white cloth pouch with Bull Durham loose tobacco, carefully tapped the sides to release the golden bits onto the thin tissue-like cigarette paper held in his other hand. Some tobacco always dropped to the floor, as he rolled, licked the edges of the paper clamping the ends of the cylinder so no more tobacco sifted out. Then he struck a kitchen match to light his "smoke." After his hands shook and fingers stiffened, he smoked Lucky Strikes, then finally stopped after his health declined. I can still visualize my father backing up to the edge of the kitchen door frame to rub an itch on his back by sliding back and forth to get relief.

My father delivered discipline in two sizes: via the trouser belt or the razor strap. His anger came quickly for misbehavior. The belt buckle was released, the entire belt pulled out in one sweeping motion, and the necessary number of strikes applied to the rear end. For a major infraction, he rushed to the bathroom to pull the 2-inch wide leather razor strap off the hook next to the washbowl. That one really stung. Slaps often substituted for the straps. I was mortified when, at age 16, something I did, or said resulted in the last slap I ever received from my father.

A tiger cat we owned brought a different kind of "discipline" from my father. The cat did not always get "let outside" when the need arose. This day the cat used my father's pillow to drop his "litter." My father, in a fury, picked up the offending animal, rushed out to the back porch (we still lived on the second floor), and tossed the squirming furry bundle across the yard onto the roof of the garage. The cat survived, but I don't remember him in the house after this treatment. (This was before litter boxes became popular for use inside the house.)

When I was in elementary school, my father replaced the soles on my shoes, and later on my brother's. He used a square of thick tanned leather hide, that he cut to size and shape with a short sharp knife. Then he hammered on the new sole onto the bottom of the shoe, using short nails he held between his lips. The shoe set on a cast iron shoe last that had replaceable pieces for different sized shoes. I was very self-conscious of the tell-tale pale tan color and the uneven knife cuts along the edge of the sole that proclaimed re-soled shoes. Some years later dad found special leather shoe edging dye which he dabbed on, to help disguise the procedure.

My mother was industrious and hard working. Short and sturdily built, she tackled all the work in managing a demanding household: cooking, washing, shopping, sewing, canning. She helped Dad with some of the other jobs, too, like washing walls before painting, scrubbing the porches and hosing down the walks and yard and working with him on joint activities. These usually had to do with food preparation. They both got involved with canning: preparing the cabbage for sauerkraut, slicing green tomatoes and onions for relish, cutting up hot yellow peppers, fruits: peaches and pears, and once they attempted to make wine. They carried the small barrel with the prepared grape juice up to the attic where it was to ferment. But a hot spell warmed the air in that space so much that the whole batch just overheated and spoiled.

There was a supportive relationship between my mother and dad while I was growing up, a teamwork approach that I observed and accepted as required in marriage. My father would pitch in with tasks such as pulling freshly washed and dried bed sheets to square the ends. My mother held one edge of the muslin sheet, and my father grasped the other end. Together they pulled the fabric taught to straighten the folds. Then they creased the sheet in the center and folded it. I can still picture them standing on the second floor kitchen linoleum, my father leaning up against the door to the dining room, my mother stepping back and forth near the sink, as they tugged on the hems of the bed sheet.

Mom tried to make jelly and strawberry preserves, but often the paraffin did not seal properly, and some jars went to waste. We all loved her yeast coffee cake that she made for all holidays and sometimes in between. The aroma of vanilla and yeast dough permeated the house. Her preference was white or golden raisins for this Polish treat called Babka. The first wood burning stove had an oven without a thermostat or thermometer, so she had to guess when the temperature was hot enough for baking. Often the cakes came out with scorched bottoms that needed scraping before being sliced. I liked to pick off the raisins that stuck out of the crust, even though they were cinder-like.

The behemoth of a stove, a Garland, was moved from Norwalk to our second-floor flat on Trowbridge. It was a wood-burning affair, with an oven that did not have a thermostat. I know now that a portable thermostat was available for baking. For many years, housewives in Hamtramck relied on wood-burning kitchen stoves. They provided a quick warm up on chilly mornings before the furnace was fired up enough to send steam into the radiators. A handful of dry wood, ignited quickly beneath the round cast iron covers of the stove top that permeated the air with warmth. Water in a tea kettle came to a boil in a short time if it was set on the stove. A soup pot could simmer for hours, relying on the steady heat of the glowing embers inside the cast iron grates. Our stove had a warming compartment with sliding doors above the surface used for keeping certain foods from cooling too quickly before eating. A bowl of mashed potatoes was kept there while the main meat dish was frying. This type of stove required a round metal exhaust pipe to carry the wood smoke from the stove to the chimney. When my parents finally purchased a gas stove, I remember how concerned they were about it having no such exhaust pipe. It took some time for them to be convinced that it was not necessary.

The whole family loved her homemade tomato noodle soup. She used a chunk of chuck beef with bone, canned tomatoes, a can of Campbell's Vegetable Soup, wide egg noodles, and real sweet cream. The flavor was unique and unmistakable. Nobody else in the family could ever duplicate it.

Another unique treat that she made were apple pancakes, made with sliced apples that were tossed into a flour-egg-milk combination and fried like blintzes, thin, with the apples just barely cooked. Another quick luncheon dish that was our favorite had fried sliced onions, to which cooked fine noodles and beaten eggs were added to make an omelette-like concoction.

After I was grown and married, my visits to my mother's house were not complete unless she had a stack of potato pancakes ready on the stove. Hers had fairly large pieces of onion that made them different from those served in restaurants.

Mom was very hospitable. Before we owned a refrigerator or even an ice box (circa 1930's) or a telephone, visitors and relatives arrived, it seems, without advanced notice. So the "larder" needed to be replenished. She would send me to buy soda pop, cold cuts, and sometimes sliced white bread so the table could be set with sandwiches and drinks. Mom enjoyed feeding guests who often sat around the kitchen table.

At holidays, the dining room table was covered with the "good" table cloth, a pale pink damask cloth with a self-fringe and matching napkins. It seems we always had that special table cloth. Now my brother has it. It was stored first in a drawer of the buffet, then was kept in the black metal steamer trunk.

For the baptism of my brother Leonard in the summer of 1937, Mom purchased a new Noritake china dinner service for twelve at J. L. Hudson's downtown. From then on it was set out on that damask cloth for special occasions and holiday company dinners.

Mom's idea of a company holiday dinner revolved around tried and true Polish favorites: fresh and smoked kiełbasa, gołąbki (stuffed cabbage), chicken soup with homemade noodles, breaded pork chops, city chicken, and whenever possible, a whole ham. The clear, glass-footed cake stand had center position with a Sander's Buttercream layer cake. "Klops" were a weekday favorite. This was essentially a small-sized individual meat loaf or an oversized oval meat ball that Mom made from ground beef, pork and veal, egg, bread crumbs soaked in milk, and the inevitable chopped yellow onion. She formed these "klops" by flapping them up and down in her cupped hands, then frying them. These were good with ketchup or mustard. They were moist on the inside, crusty on the outside, mealy, and filling.

As Mom became more Americanized, other foods appeared: chop suey and cup cakes and layer cakes made with baking powder rather than yeast. About her chop suey, I remember that it always turned somewhat soupy, but it was a treat nevertheless. Spaghetti was discovered via Chef Boyardi. Pasty and overcooked, this canned novelty was to become a childhood staple in our house. Mom was always willing and eager to learn new and better ways of preparing food, but I remember her by the old familiar standbys.

Toys

A very early Christmas gift was a child's dresser set. It was pink "Bakelite" (forerunner of plastic). The comb, brush, and mirror made me feel quite grown up. Then there was a scrawny doll. What it looked like when new, if it ever was, I fail to recall. (Dad had a knack of locating "used" articles that could be purchased for much less than when new.) This rag doll, with no clothing, I tossed over the second floor back porch railing onto the cement walkway below. I was too young to do stairs, so I don't know that it was ever retrieved.

Then there were mud pies that Clara Szkudniewski and I fashioned by patting damp black soil into fluted shiny metal "pie pans." They were recycled in this way after consuming the original filling, a very sweet fondant type confection, probably purchased for a penny at the candy store across the street next to the playground.

Always a memorable occasion was a walk to the Hamtramck shopping area that we just called, "Going to Joseph Campau." Dad took me, to Federal's Department Store where a child-sized wooden rocking chair was chosen for my use. The legs, arms, and runners were wrapped with strips of paper for the transport home. Dad carried it back to the house and it was unwrapped giving me many hours of pleasure. A fondness for rocking chairs remains with me still.

A small porcelain "Betty Boop" type doll, about two and a half inches long, was a possession easy to dress and house. Scraps of left over cloth from Mom's sewing projects were cut into circular skirts. Another smaller round of material, with a hole cut out of the middle became a floppy hat when positioned on the doll head. Kitchen matches came in a cardboard box that slid into a slightly larger sleeve became a bed and/or house for this doll.

Paper dolls, cut out from the Sunday Comic Section, were a source of a family of dolls. Blondie was a favorite character that I liked to dress in different outfits that were attached by pressing back small tabs.

An early family photo shows me (about age 3) standing on an upholstered stool, mom and dad on each side. I'm pouting as I thought of myself as "too big" to be placed up on a stand. I hold a small purse on a chain with a round faced play clock attached to the front. That purse was a favorite for a long time.

A favorite play area was the back yard and the coal sheds that also stored broken articles "too good to throw out."

A discarded alarm clock gave me hours of diversion during summer months when the weather was mild and I was allowed to rummage through the shaded cool interior of the shed.

How Something Changed My Life
or Five Blocks North

In 1930, at the age of five, I experienced the first of four events that changed the direction of my life. We moved from 3364 Norwalk Street in Hamtramck, Michigan, five blocks north to 3291 Trowbridge Street. My father purchased this house, a two-story frame income property, from owners, the Borucki's, who were returning to Poland to operate a mill on a farm. The income came from renting out the six-room lower flat.

We hear about programs in cities that allocate homes in middle-class neighborhoods for purchase or rent by lower economic class persons or sometimes welfare families with the idea that rubbing elbows or keeping up with the Joneses will influence and affect the living standards of the new residents, helping them climb the ladder of acculturation and assimilation. This is what I believe happened when we moved to the house that backed up to a commercial strip.

The two-story frame building stood on a narrow city lot next to an alley we shared with several commercial enterprises. These shops were owned by families who lived above or behind store fronts. The groceries and meat markets had brick smoke houses in the yards. All these families had acquired a few more comforts than my parents. Some were second-generation Poles, still able to speak their native language, but also fluent in English. Their acquisitions and seeming success certainly affected me.

Our upstairs flat on Norwalk Street had only four rooms. The two families who rented the downstairs flats were unemployed and on the county welfare program. Our other neighbors were also of modest means. Two houses to the west, the Czekaj family lived in abject property: four total orphans, three sisters under the age of 16, and an infant brother struggled, their living quarters exuding the sour smell of neglect. Other neighbors were dealing with alcoholism and health problems. Sirens often rang in the

night announcing ambulances that may remove a neighbor's
husband to dry out at the county hospital for the indigent. The
Mom-and-Pop grocery in the middle of the block operated
minimally as the mother's goiter condition progressed. So when
we relocated, Dad was still a landlord, but our tenants and
neighbors were very different from previous neighbors of the past
five years.

Moving was upsetting my mother. All the furniture was on
the truck. The four rooms were bare. My mother held a broom in
her hands, sweeping the kitchen floor. She was crying, grieving
over the loss of familiar corners. Perhaps my father made the decision
to invest in another income venture without consulting my mother.
So relocating, even five blocks north meant another adjustment.
There would be new neighbors, a different parish church, a location
near a busy intersection (Conant and Caniff), and next to an alley
that separated our house from the commercial strip. A three-car
garage filled most of the backyard that was completely cemented,
eliminating any possibility of a garden. We inherited two roomers,
middle-aged bachelors, who assured an immediate income of $7 a
week each. The downstairs renters paid $25 a month. They were
very good friends of the previous owners but were strangers to our
family.

The tenants below us in our new house on Trowbridge Street
had two school-aged sons who paid no attention to me, but their
mother allowed me to play with their toys during the day. I
remember a shiny black iron toy train engine that I moved over
the circular track.

This family was replaced by the Wesołowskis, who owned a
dry goods store around the corner on Caniff Street. Their automobile
was parked in our three-car garage and was used for Sunday trips
to Elizabeth Lake in Oakland County, about 25 miles north of the
city. Their daughter, Eleanor, was a teenager studying voice. She
attended an all-girls high school known for its high academic
standards. She was an avid reader. Her discarded pulp fiction
romance novels ended up on the basement floor. The printing was

on porous, almost gray, coarse paper, but the intriguing covers drew me to examine these early paperbacks.

It was my first encounter with people who not only bought books to read, but replaced them with new ones and cast away those that were read! Later, after locating the city library and getting a library card, my choice of reading material was more appropriate to my age, however, I believe this early experience with literacy had a ripple effect that lasted all my life. Until that time, the only book in our house was the prayer book used in church on Sunday. When a book club advertised in the newspaper, I sent for the free hardcover volume of "The History of America in Pictures." It was the first book that arrived and stayed in our home. Getting out of the no-obligation-to-purchase more books took some effort and correspondence.

Across the side alley on the corner of Conant and Trowbridge Streets lived the Baranowski family: parents and three children. Their flat-roofed dwelling had a confectionery with living quarters in back. Lillian, who was a year or two older than I, bought song sheets with words to all the popular tunes of the day. Many afternoons we sat on their backyard swing rocking back and forth, shadowed by the tall catalpa tree, memorizing these ditties. "The Boulevard of Broken Dreams" was an early favorite. Inside, they owned a player piano that was pumped by foot. Happily, I applied the necessary energy to keep the piano rolls moving. What fun to vocalize and follow the printed words with musical accompaniments. When their flat roof needed a fresh coat of tar, we smelled the fumes of the hot pitch while it was applied.

The Jeloneks owned a beer garden on Conant Street, halfway between Caniff and Trowbridge Streets. Our second-story kitchen window overlooked their backyard with its lone Tree of Heaven (Ailanthus) that shaded some of the pavement of the alley. My first sight of their daughter Eleanor, who was a year older than I, was of her wearing a stylish navy plaid, pleated skirt, its hem midway between the knee and hip, and a navy cardigan sweater with the sleeves pushed up above the elbow washerwoman style.

Well! When Eleanor started to attend the prestigious all-girls high school in Detroit, Girls Catholic Central, that was where I wanted to go, too. My enrollment experience at that school requires a separate chapter.

FRONT OF HOUSE AT 3291 TROWBRIDGE STREET

Our new home was also more decorated. We acquired most of the furniture in the seven rooms as the previous owners left most of their pieces for us. The dining room set was a dark walnut veneer. A room-sized rug covered the living room where a gray velour couch and arm chair stood. A narrow library table completed this room. Two beveled glass French doors closed off the living room when it was not used. Central steam heat came from coal furnaces in the full basement. Every room had a radiator. Lighting for the living and dining rooms was from a hanging chandelier set above in the middle of the ceiling. The switch was on the wall for the lights in the kitchen, dining and living rooms, bath, and hallways. In the bedrooms, a pull chain operated the single-bulb fixture hanging from the ceiling. As a child growing up I remember walking on linoleum rugs in the kitchen and in the dining room and eating at the kitchen table covered with a patterned oilcloth tablecloth.

Dad chose the linoleum rugs from patterns available in the local hardware store at the corner of Caniff and Conant next to the Pietraszewski Pharmacy. A 9-x 12-foot linoleum rug covered most of the kitchen floor, with an edge under the stove and dish cabinet. My father bought it in a roll so he could carry it home on his shoulders. When he laid it out, part of the curve remained for several days before flattening out. What fun it was to examine the new pattern! There was always a border design, then circles within squares, squares within triangles, all in muted colors. When the designs wore off from walking, and sometimes a hole wore through the thin composition backing, it was time for a new one. The old one went up in the attic, acting like a layer of insulation on the floor.

Mom washed the linoleum each week with a wet mop she squeezed out by hand, covering the damp surface with sheets of newspaper which she removed after a few hours. When I started working in 1947, my father finally agreed to have inlaid linoleum installed. He marveled at the wall-to-wall installation and the metal strips that were placed to hold down the edge in doorways.

Mom purchased oilcloth from the five and dime store on Joseph Campau, usually Woolworth's or Kresge's. I liked to help my mother choose from the variety of designs on the rolls before us. Sometimes there were flowers, and sometimes in a plaid or checkerboard pattern. One and a quarter yards covered the rectangular table. New and smelling new, it served for several months before the pattern wore off from daily wiping after meals. Also, it took several days for the edges to straighten out from the initial curling under. Oilcloth was used on the kitchen table only. The dining room table was reserved for special occasions and holidays at which time a damask cloth with matching napkins was used.

The house on Trowbridge Street had a large attic and full basement. My brother and I played in both places while we were growing up. A favorite diversion for me was examining all the articles that were stored in a large black metal trunk, the "kuferek" that stood near the window of the attic. My parents brought it with them in 1921 when they came to the United States from Poland. Mom had to find the key hanging from a thick gray cord. An elaborate brass lock flopped down after she opened it, and then the heavy lid had to be lifted before we could remove its contents one by one.

The first item was a black fox fur shrug, lined with black satin that fit around the shoulders and fastened with a cloth-covered fastener at one edge. Also, mom stored her dark brown homespun wool skirt. It was part of her travel outfit that she wore on her trip to the U.S. in the late fall of 1921. There was also a fawn-colored vest, probably from the wedding suit that my dad wore. There were several handwoven, long linen towels with black and red cross-stitched embroidery and fine crocheted edging. Heavier linen tablecloths had a grayish tone and herringbone pattern. Rolled up was a cloth belt with pockets, the money belt my father wore under his outer clothing when he traveled to Poland to court and marry my mother. In a silk handkerchief, I found the long twist of chestnut colored hair. My mother stored it in the trunk after she cut her hair in the early 1930s. My father tossed his abdominal truss into that space after using it in the past for a hernia condition. Also, his partial denture with three teeth spaced around a pink upper plate that no longer fit following subsequent tooth extractions.

After my brother's baptism in 1937 at age five, his white satin suit with short pants and white leather shoes found a safe place inside that black metal container.

The choicest item that I enjoyed examining from the mothballscented interior of that trunk was an elaborate pin cushion. It was shaped like a modified five-pointed star, covered in turquoise velvet with rounded points decorated with loops of colored beads. It was about six inches across and about three inches thick. I pondered over its purpose, function and origin.

There were other stored items in that large attic. Our renters, the Wesołowski family who owned the dry goods store, kept a large flat cardboard box with family photos at one end of its cavernous area. No key was needed to view the tens of wedding photographs, communion and christening photos. It mattered not that they were all strangers to me, but I reveled in the women's clothing. Bridal outfits of satins and laces, veils held by lacy, pearl encrusted crowns, bouquets of flowers that covered the entire lap and cascaded to the floor. Some brides were seated, some were standing. A few dresses looked to be from the flapper era of the twenties, short in front, falling to a train in back. I paid little attention to the men in the photos, but generally they were in formal attire.

Most of the articles in the attic were pieces of furniture no longer used by my family. My own dark maple crib that rocked was pushed under the sloping sides of the roof. A baby buggy made of tan wicker, used for my brother, was dismantled partly. The top that shaded the baby was a makeshift rocker in one corner that was my den.

Inside a tall, round storage carton we kept depression glass luncheon sets. There were three colors: gold, green, and pink. Each color had a service for four: cup and saucer and a luncheon plate. They were premiums received when we ordered coal from the Mistele Coal Company. Of all the items left in the house when it was sold in 1969, I regret most leaving behind the Depression glass in that round storage carton next to the red brick chimney in the attic.

Whenever my brother and I had costume events, we checked our appearance in the crackled mirror of an old dresser that stood next to the window. It was made of very dark wood. The drawers were lined with red flannel cloth. Two doors below had carvings on the front.

Our costumes were blankets that became royal capes. The crowns were fashioned from cardboard, covered with gold crepe paper. Pompous parades took place around the red brick chimney that passed through the center of the attic. I was always the queen and my brother, six years younger, was the prince.

The attic was stifling in the summer. Hot air penetrated nostrils, so little time was spent there except to retrieve some needed article. Unheated, it was frigid in the winter. In between, about once a year, I helped sweep up the thick gray dust that accumulated on the wood floorboards. To keep down the dust, we brought a bucket of water and newspapers. Shredded paper was soaked in the bucket, then scattered over the surface. Then a long-handled brush moved the damp paper with the dirt clinging to it.

We played in the basement all year. It was warm and dry in the winter and cool and damp in the summer. We shared the space with two large coal furnaces, two coal bins, two sets of wash tubs, shelves for canned goods, a gas two-burner stove top with a brass kettle for boiling clothes, a curtain stretcher and clotheslines. When the furnace was operating, I remember tossing potatoes onto the hot coals, lifting them out when they were charred black, and scraping off the burnt layer before eating the steaming creamy pulp.

Once after a downpour, the basement flooded with about two feet of water. The drains in the floor backed up, and after the water subsided, there was silt and a lot of soaked items to remove. The basement, too, needed a regular cleaning. When the furnaces stopped heating the building for the winter, a layer of ash settled on the cement floor. Mom and Dad brought in the garden hose, hooked it up to the faucet in the wash tub, and sprayed the floor clean, sweeping the surplus water into the floor drain. Now the basement windows were opened to let in the warm, fresh air to dry the pavement.

One memory I have is of roller skating on that basement cement floor. I'm sure the rumbling noise must have been heard all the way to the second story! I used the supporting iron posts to swing around circling the open areas. Roller skating outdoors on newly paved asphalt streets was the real treat! It was quieter and smoother, and muffled the sound of metal wheels on the skates.

It was in that basement that I sneaked my first cigarette, hand rolled from my father's Bull Durham tobacco pouch. The hot smoke smarted my eyes and scorched my nose and throat. It had no further attraction for me after that one attempt.

Early Soaps

In my present bathroom, on the shelf beneath the vanity, sits a bar of Fels Naphtha Heavy Duty Laundry Soap, still in its wrapper of red printing with a dark green logo. It is the lone reminder of cleaning agents of my childhood.

During the 1930s, it was the product to use on household laundry before the first Maytag washer occupied the space next to the cement washtubs in the basement of our house on Trowbridge Street. Mom used a washboard that leaned against the inside of a round, galvanized washtub that was sitting on a wooden stand with a hand-cranked wringer. Steaming hot water covered towels and sheets, the caramel colored rectangular bar was rubbed directly on the surface of the article, which was grasped, then pressed up and down the corrugated metal washboard, before getting the water squeezed out in the wringer. My two-and-a-half year-old brother was attracted to this caramel-colored wedge that was left in the wire soap dish hanging on the bathtub. Yes, it looked good enough to eat. His mouth got soaped even before he learned swear words! A doctor came to the house, and a sobbing, fretting mother was assured that this, too, would pass.

We used other soap for bathing and washing, chosen because of advertising on the radio and in the Sunday comics. Palmolive promised a smooth complexion since it was made from the oils of olive and palm. The soap and wrapper were a distinctive green. Sweetheart soap, was oval in shape, white with flowery bumps all over, encased in a box. A deep voiced male announcer on the RCA radio speaker advised Lifebuoy would eliminate body odors (BO), pale red, its smell had a faint hint of carbolic acid.

Camay Soap, gentle and feminine, had a cameo face stamped in the center of the rounded rectangle. But used most often in our household, was Ivory. Not only was it 99 and 44/100 pure, but it floated! The Lava Soap bar, gritty and gray, stayed on the basement washtub to deal with the grime and dirt under fingernails. Dad's shaving soap, a small cream-colored round, fit into the bottom of his shaving mug. Moistened with water, a round short soft-bristled brush was swirled in the mug to produce suds that the brush transferred to a whiskered chin. Our dog had his special soap, Pine Tar Soap, available only at Pietraszewski's Drug Store. It was black and allegedly effective in the control of fleas.

Slivers of soap, too small to use, were stuffed into a soap saver. This was a small metal, cage-like container attached to a handle that hung on a hook next to the kitchen sink. Whisked and agitated in the dishpan, it lived again.

Soap powders came in boxes with bold colors: Gold Dust Twins smiled from an orange and black background. Mom liked Oxydol and Rinso for heavy duty laundry, Ivory Snow and Lux Flakes for delicate items. Are Lux Flakes still manufactured? No other cleaning agent had such fine translucent bits that would suds up in a washbowl. When the toilet bowl was scrubbed, Lysol disinfectant got the job done.

Murphy's Oil Soap, a gentle vegetable-based thick amber liquid, was Mom's preference for use on anything wood or varnished. For windows, my mother used a cake of Bon Ami (hasn't scratched yet—written next to a newly hatched chick). With a damp cloth rubbed onto the white cake, a film was left on to dry, then removed with a dry cloth until the surface gleamed and sparkled.

Detergents, spray cans, foams, and 2000 flushes are part of our life now, but I want my nieces and nephews and their children to have a glimpse of life as it was in the years when Grandma and her family managed a household during the Great Depression and just afterwards.

Getting Around Hamtramck

Daily life depended on foot power, not motor power, when I was growing up. Most of the services that we needed were within walking distance of our home—the school, church, bank, utility companies, bakeries, dry goods stores, department stores, the five and dime, confectionaries, and watering holes. All could be reached within a 5-to 20-minute walk. And most residents of Hamtramck did just that.

Owning a car was a luxury affordable to very few people in our neighborhood around Trowbridge Street. We accepted walking and public transportation. My father never expressed a need or desire for a motor car. The expense was his first obstacle. After purchasing the house in 1930, we seemed to get poorer and poorer as the Great Depression deepened. My father's job was reduced to 20 hours a week. The renters on Norwalk Street lost their jobs. My father's health deteriorated. He felt a car unnecessary and an expense he simply could not afford. Besides, he may have been a little wary of his ability to operate a motor vehicle.

Mrs. Jelonek, Eleanor's mother, had a dark blue Packard, with fold-down seats to accommodate her family of six children. This was an anomaly. The Wesołowski family, who lived downstairs, also owned a car. Both families were affluent enough to have cottages to visit. The Jelonek's was at Walled Lake, about 20 miles northwest of the city. The Wesołowski family made regular runs to Elizabeth Lake in Oakland County.

Because we didn't own a car, we often caught the Baker Street car that ran through the city. This necessitated a hike of about six blocks. We walked to Miller's grocery store, a short block through the alley to the corner of Conant and Caniff. Pietraszewksi's Pharmacy was catercorner from Miller's. Above the pharmacy were the offices of the dentist, Dr. Guzowski, and the local doctor, Dr. Kłosowski, and the living quarters of the pharmacist, his wife, and their daughter.

Several merchants in our corner of Hamtramck lived above or behind their places of business.

The Dry Goods store, next to Bill's Confectionary on Caniff Street, was owned by the Wesołowski's. They lived in the six-room flat downstairs in our two-family house. Jax Bar, next to the confectionery, belonged to Mrs. Miller's brother. He and his family lived above the Miller grocery store as did the Miller family.

We walked to all of these establishments as well as to the larger stores: Kresge's, Woolworth's, Neisner's Five and Dime, and Grants, all on Joseph Campau Street, past Klinger, Moran, Gallagher, McDougall, Charest, and Mitchell. We made frequent trips to the specialty shops on Joseph Campau. Several Polish bakeries, Mom-and-Pop meat markets, a hardware store, Cunningham's Drug Store and the Federal's Department Store received our business and provided employment to many individuals in the area. The owner of P.C. Jeżewski's Pharmacy became mayor of Hamtramck replaced later by Dr. A. Tenerowicz.

For six cents, the Baker Street car would take us to downtown Detroit, just behind Crowley Milner's Department Store. With a penny transfer, the Crosstown street car traveled east, then south to Jefferson Avenue and Belle Isle Park.

I did a lot of walking with my chum Jane Ciwinska during elementary school. Her parents were Polish immigrants like mine, and our fathers were both blue-collar workers. I spent many afternoons at their one-story white frame house on Belmont Street, one block away. We used a set of aluminum play dishes that she owned for our snacks. Her mother served hot tea with milk and slices of bread spread with butter and honey. What a treat! We often walked to school together along Conant Street. When I spotted her from our second story window, I would join her as she reached the corner of Conant and Trowbridge.

Our walks took us to the theaters in Hamtramck and to parks in the vicinity. Belle Isle Park located on the Detroit River was a destination for an all-day trip on foot. We couldn't wait to reach East Grand Boulevard with its unique stately mansions. As we walked, we took turns, "I like that one." "I want that one." They were red brick, gray stone and painted stucco in the Tudor style. Some featured turrets and stained glass windows on the side, beveled glass on the double front doors, round stone pillars, wide porches, some wrapped around the sides of the building, wrought iron railings and fences, landscaped front lawns with Camperdown elms, all on spacious lots so unlike the modest wooden dwellings built on a 30-foot frontage in Hamtramck. What fun and fantasy we created for ourselves!

Jane and I frequented the neighborhood theatres, Martha Washington Theatre, Conant Theatre, Farnum Theatre, and then the Fox on Woodward Avenue and the Fisher Theatre on West Grand Boulevard. One Sunday afternoon we left a Deanna Durbin movie with the music in it circling in our heads. We took the short cut through the alleys behind the Farnum Theatre located on Joseph Campau south of Holbrook Street. In unison we sang the first line of the signature tune: "Opera, sur le opera, la, la, la," our voices rising to reach the high note. The melody lingered and was repeated over and over until we reached our respective homes.

When we got old enough to ride bicycles, Dolores Wójcik and Eleanor Jasinski (who borrowed a bicycle) joined us for trips further from home. We cycled across the Ambassador Bridge to Windsor, Canada and to the Shrine of the Little Flower in Royal Oak, at Woodward and Twelve Mile Roads, also to Cranbrook Gardens in Bloomfield Hills, to Palmer Park at Six Mile Road and Woodward and to River Rouge Park. But it was those strolls home from Belle Isle Park along East Grand Boulevard that were the grandest and most memorable.

The Stork

My baby brother was born in 1932, when I was 6 years old. My parents told me that my mother would be going to the hospital for the delivery of her son (somehow she was certain it would be a boy). It would require an operation and a hospital stay of 2 weeks. I remember imagining this addition to our family. In my mind's eye, he would come into this world wearing a navy blue sailor's outfit like the boy pictured on the Cracker Jack box. I believed this infant was inside my mother fully dressed.

My mother prepared for the new baby by sewing diapers of white flannel on the Singer sewing machine. In addition, she purchased other small garments that would be used for the newborn. He was the fourth and last child in our nuclear family.

On Good Friday, March 25, 1932, my mother and father left for Providence Hospital located at that time, on W. Grand Boulevard and 14th Street and leaving me with Mary Czekaj. My brother was delivered into this world the following day. Mary stayed with me all day Friday since my father would be home on Saturday and Sunday.

That Saturday I experienced the first of many changes brought on by the addition of a brother. Until then, my mother helped with my Saturday night ritual bath. She made sure the water was the correct temperature and washed my back. Now I was alone in a tub of water in the bathroom. I called my father, who came in half heartedly to swab my back with a soapy washcloth. From then on I was on my own during bath time.

After a 2-week stay in the hospital, an ambulance brought my mother home. She was carried up the front stairs by stretcher with the baby in her arms. He was rosy-cheeked and had big blue eyes. Our roomer, Stanley Trochomowicz, declared this newcomer would surely grow up to be a doctor. His prediction, by the way, turned out to be correct.

My baby brother's first bath at home was an elaborate production. Mary Czekaj helped set the table in the kitchen with a white enamel pan, lots of towels and blankets and the door to the dining room closed to keep in the heat from the black cast-iron kitchen stove. I don't recall subsequent baths being carried on in the same manner, but I noticed my mother giving special attention to the baby's uncircumcised penis. She applied olive oil to the foreskin following drying.

My mother was still very weak, stooped over when she tried walking, due to the healing incision. She did breast feed my brother along with supplementary feedings of bottled milk enriched with Karo syrup.

My mother's choice of a name for my brother was Leo, but the opinion of the nurse at the hospital was that Leonard was a more popular name, Leo was old-fashioned. My parents were pleased that at last they had a son. My father and the doctor agreed that after two caesarean sections my mother's child bearing days should end, so the doctors performed either a tubal ligation or a hysterectomy at the time of my brother's birth. From what my mother confided, I don't think that she had been consulted first. The Catholic Church considered such operations unacceptable methods of birth control, even if the procedures were performed in a Catholic hospital!

Everybody wanted to pamper, feed, change, coddle, rock, kiss, hug, and fuss over the new baby. I remember a tan wicker baby buggy inside the house. A heavy strap was attached to the handle and Mr. Trochomowicz, while sitting at the kitchen table, would push and pull the buggy, sending my brother inside it on short rides across the kitchen floor.

When summer arrived, my parents assigned me the job of strolling my brother outdoors. The novelty wore off quickly as I found that this duty interfered with my play time. When he became a toddler, I was to look after him. I wanted to be free of this responsibility, particularly after school and on the weekends when I wanted to be with my friends.

One Saturday, my brother, who was about three years old, and I went to the corner confectionery for ice cream cones. The stools in front of the marble counter were screwed into the floor but the seats revolved around and around. My brother held on tightly while taking a running start. The centrifugal force sent him reeling onto the floor. He landed on his arm, which he held, crying in pain. He continued to cry after we returned home, so my parents took him to St. Francis Hospital on Evaline Street. He came home with a cast on his right arm. Petrified, I hid under the bed, fearing judgement and punishment for his injury while under my care. Several hours later, all was quiet, and my parents never mentioned that it had been my fault.

3-YEAR OLD LEONARD WITH FATHER ANDREW

My brother was all boy. He was always busy playing with pipes, cars, boats, boxes, airplanes and, the likes. But, when my girlfriends and I played while he was around, he would always run over, interfering with our games, listening and intruding. I was helpless and ineffective in stopping his behavior, and feelings of resentment welled up inside me.

I also resented the different expectations that my parents seemed to have for a son in our culture. They were much more permissive with him than they had been with me. Reviewing the times, I now realize there were many extenuating circumstances. My brother had developed and survived pneumonia as an infant. A disastrous fire traumatized my mother when my brother was just a year old. Shortly thereafter, my father was hospitalized with serious kidney problems. The Great Depression plunged our family toward bankruptcy. Survival took precedence over "amenities" like minding, keeping up with school assignments, and maintaining good grades.

My first experience with the arrival of babies happened when my family lived on Norwalk Street. Our four-room flat upstairs had no access from the front. A door opened onto the front porch, but to reach the upper flat required going around to the backyard and climbing up the open stairway. Three steps from the sidewalk led to the two flats of three rooms each on the first level. In one lived my first playmate, Clara, with her mother and father, also Polish immigrants, the Szkudniewskis. About a year or two younger than I, she had a gentle disposition, freckled face, and striking strawberry blond hair. When I was about three years old, in 1928, Mr. Lucian Szkudniewski called me downstairs to reveal the circumstances of her sister's arrival. He pointed to the window in the entry door to their flat. It held a piece of cardboard, allegedly covering the hole made by the stork when he delivered his bundle to the expectant parents.

Indeed, I remembered this revelation whenever a panel truck drove by on the street with "Diaper Service" on the side and a depiction of a white stork, with wings spread out, suspended from his beak, a newborn, in diapers.

There is another aspect to the stork story. After a trip to Poland, I was showing photos of storks' nests on top of old chimneys. My niece, Ann, a teenager in the late 1970s, looked on with interest. She remarked, "I thought that storks delivering babies was a myth." She thought that the entire tale of storks delivering babies was made up; even storks were fictional.

Religion

Both my mother and my father were raised in the Roman Catholic faith practiced in Gibulicze, their small village in Poland, where religion permeated all aspects of daily life. As a child and a young woman, my mother participated in all her church rituals, including feast day celebrations, holidays, and pilgrimages. She sang hymns from memory and recited church prayers. She walked three miles barefoot to the parish church in Grodno that her family attended so as not to muddy her boots on the road.

Religion and prayer provided comfort for my mother throughout her life. Her fears, apprehensions, and worries were easily aroused. They were part of her personality and remained with her, even intensifying later in life. Preaching from the pulpit gave additional direction, admonition and instruction along with frequent fire and brimstone threats. I believe I was more influenced by religious instruction and Sunday sermons than my parents had been. Recognizing venial sins and mortal sins with their consequences was central to the preparation for receiving the Sacraments. For 16 years of schooling, religion was part of my curriculum. My mother's reaction to natural disasters and catastrophes was tied to fate and luck. She felt a personal type of persecution by forces beyond her control. But prayer, litanies, and religious hymns alleviated her discomfort. A certain rhythm crept into her recitation of the Rosary prayers. Religion and its rituals were palliative for my mother.

Dad was anti-clerical, but a believer nonetheless. Each night I heard him reciting the credo in Polish before retiring, but he only attended church on Easter and Christmas, and whenever he had stayed away too long from organized religion.

When I became an adult, my dad disclosed the roots of his anti-clericalism. An experience in the old country led to his attitude that the men of cloth have feet of clay and knees of jelly. Little escaped the villagers' eyes. A preacher, who was admonishing his congregation from the pulpit on Sunday, was seen the night before kneeling with a woman. My father henceforth considered the clergy much more realistically human, with human inclinations and failings. He would not take seriously preaching about moral behavior.

Another story that he related illustrated the peasants' pragmatic approach to the basic beliefs of the church. His was told like a riddle: God made the first man from the clay of the earth, then propped him up against the fence to dry. Who built the fence? I believe this riddle questioned the veracity of the Bible's depiction of creation.

Above all, my father believed in following your own conscience.

My parents instilled these beliefs in me from the time I was a young child. Polish was my first language. Before I could read or write, I learned to recite a short sentence in Polish that said, "I was born on this earth to know God, to serve Him and to be happy with Him in everlasting life." I knew this like other children knew "Patty Cake, Patty Cake."

My parents had a porcelain statue of Jesus, about 6 inches tall, with his hand pointing to his heart. I knew this statue as a "Bozia" (God), and I had to pay it respect and obedience. Indeed, my parents often reminded me that "Bozia grozi"—God threatens—when I misbehaved.

The porcelain statue stood in the center of Mom's mini altar on top of the china cabinet in the dining room. In front of it was a votive candle in a red glass holder supported by a lacy brass-footed base. My mother lit the votive candle at various times to petition a favor, usually one of healing an illness or one of safety and protection from dangerous or severe weather. Less often she had the votive flickering in thanksgiving for a prayer granted. Two vases of blue-black Goofus glass flanked the statue of Christ. All of these items sat on a linen runner that was embroidered with flowers and trimmed with a handcrocheted edging.

In addition to the votive candle, it was important to have a blessed beeswax candle. This was available and purchased on the feast day of St. Blaise, February 2nd, when throats were blessed in church as a precaution against coughs and colds. We used this thick candle, a deep ochre color, during electrical storms. When it was lit and set on the dining room table, it was supposed to protect the house and its occupants from injury.

Religion reinforced the code of behavior that my parents expected of my brother and me. And religion meshed with the pageantry and food of holidays: Christmas, Easter, All Souls' Day, Ascension, and Assumption. Our celebrations were as much culinary as religious. Christmas Eve began with the breaking of the wafer. As we sat around the laden table, my father would hold a small, thin rectangle of baked unleavened dough with a nativity scene stamped on it. He would break off a corner and give a wish as he held it out to each person at the table. His chin quivered with emotion as he made his way around the table during this solemn traditional procedure.

The first course was a meatless soup of sauerkraut and dried mushrooms imported from Poland. Over the years, I learned to associate the pungent odor of cabbage mixed with the earthy aroma of the mushroom with Christmas Eve. We then feasted on cold pickled herring, baked pike, mashed potatoes, pirogi (dumplings made and filled with cheese and sauerkraut), and plenty of hearty pumpernickel bread.

For dessert, we chose from a spread of poppy seed cake and almond paste roll and hard candy in wrappers imported from Poland. Mom always served tangerines, mixed nuts, and a fruit compote of cooked dried prunes, apples, figs, and raisins.

There are more special foods that I associate with Christmas Day. A whole boiled ham that had simmered for hours the day before sat on a large oval serving platter. Homemade horseradish accompanied this meat for several days. We also ate chicken soup with homemade noodles, lettuce with sour cream dressing, homemade Babka, always with white (golden) raisins and again, a lot of sweets.

After dinner, we sang Polish Christmas carols, religious ones, that told the nativity story. They centered on the infant Jesus, the blessed Virgin Mary, the shepherds, the angel, and the three kings. These carols were very melodious, and my mother and father knew the words and sang them during holiday time. I heard these carols during services at our parish church and learned them in grade school where we were required to sing in the choir after we reached the 5th grade. As I advanced into middle school—6th, 7th, and 8th grades—I learned English Christmas carols. It was then that "Jingle Bells," "O Little Town of Bethlehem," "Angels We Have Hear of High," and "I'm Dreaming of a White Christmas" became favorites, too.

At our church, inside the sanctuary, the altars were profusely decorated with balsam fir evergreen trees and with an elaborate nativity scene with life-sized figures of the Holy Family and the shepherds with their animals. After Midnight Mass, the figure of the Baby Jesus was placed in his straw-laden manger at the front of the center aisle, just in front of the main altar. Worshipers had to kneel in order to kiss the outstretched little arms or the raised feet of the figure of the Holy Infant.

Shortly after entering the 1st grade, I learned about Santa Claus and his North Pole workshop. I wanted to believe that if I hung a stocking, on Christmas morning it would be filled with gifts. So I borrowed one of my mother's long cotton stockings, and I hung it on the outside door knob of the kitchen door, hoping for the best. My parents must have been amused at my naivete. Nothing happened, but at school Santa Claus made a visit distributing candy canes and chocolates. It was known that the Skupny Brothers Funeral Home, located across the street from the school, donated the candy every year.

Easter also involved religious songs, church services and special foods. My family commemorated the 40 days of fasting and abstinence with seasonal rituals. Every Sunday afternoon parishioners gathered to sing Gorzkie Żale or Bitter Sorrows, a melancholy retelling of Christ's passion, suffering and death, all in verse. On Friday of each week during Lent, Stations of the Cross were conducted. This service required a lot of standing up then kneeling down and reciting of prayers. Holy week services had special observances on Holy Thursday, Holy Friday and Holy Saturday. Thursday: all-night adoration of the Blessed Sacrament; Friday: attending Tre Ore services, held from noon to three; Saturday: Blessing of Food baskets; and then Resurrection Mass on Easter Sunday morning, scheduled for 5 a.m.

At 3 p.m. in the afternoon on Holy Saturday a "Blessing of the Food" ceremony took place in the church. Each family prepared food baskets with hard boiled colored eggs, fresh homemade kiełbasa, tiny bowls with salt and pepper, small round loaves of rye bread (purchased specially for this occasion at the local bakery), a jar of horseradish, and a footed glass with butter. My mother used a spoon to turn this mound of butter into what looked like a rose with petals. The priest recited special prayers thanking God for this bounty, and then he walked up the aisles of the church sprinkling the baskets that lined the floor. These baskets, festooned with ribbons and the finest linen cloth, exuded aromas that permeated the entire church. This food was the first to be consumed on Easter morning after Resurrection Mass. This custom continued in the church well after I was married, but the group that gathered for the ritual in our suburban parish church grew smaller and smaller over the years.

Attending the 5 a.m. Resurrection Mass as children meant getting up and wearing a white dress and wreath of greens on the head. Students from the elementary school all walked in the procession around the inside of the church as the figure of the Resurrected Christ was carried on a special throne. Men from the Holy Name Society usually had this honor.

Religion continues to be important in my life. Prior to Vatican II, mixed marriages between Catholics and non-Catholic were discouraged and made very difficult. If a young woman started to date, keeping company with a non-Catholic was frowned upon. In the parish where I grew up, the pastor allowed mixed marriages, but the ceremony took place in the rectory, not in the church. I'm relieved that Pope John XXIII lightened up and promoted Ecumenism. It is a welcomed turnaround to a Catholic who expected eternal damnation for missing Mass on Sunday or eating meat on Friday or having an impure thought.

1ST HOLY COMMUNION PHOTO OF CHARLOTTE

Birthdays

Birthdays were not a significant enough event to celebrate with a party or gifts in our family until I was sixteen. Before that time, in grade school, one practice that was popular was to receive or administer hand whacks across the bottom equal to the number of years you lived. Therefore, the older you were the more you received. Since my birthday came in August, I escaped this painful celebration.

In those good old days, children received given names after the saints of the church. In this ethnic corner of Michigan, I would meet many classmates named Helen, Irene, Eleanor, Mary, Hedwig, Jane, Cecilia, Josephine, Anna, Stella, Theresa, or Genevieve. Some saints had greater prominence in the church calendar. St. Joseph's Feast Day, March 19th, was a biggie. St. Stanislaus had his day on May 8th. Our pastor was Rev. Stanislaus Wasilewski, so he treated us to a day off school on his Saint's Feast Day. St. Sylvester got New Year's Eve, which was called Sylvester's Night.

Searching out my baptismal name, Władysława, after St. Ladislaus, I discovered he was a Hungarian king. I still have a Holy Card with his likeness. His feast day was on June 26th. Again, since it was after the school year, not much was done.

American customs began to creep into our family life as school, radio, newspapers, and new neighbors began to influence our daily activities of life. My sixteenth birthday was celebrated with a party to which both boys and girls were invited. My girlfriends, Dolores, Eleanor, and Hedy arranged a surprise party at our second-floor flat with my parents' permission and cooperation. They invited friends from the church youth group and other former classmates. It was August 21, 1941. But the surprise aspect was negated when early that day my mother led me to one of the bedrooms where a large decorated sheet cake sat on the top of the bed. I remember wishing that this could have been a real surprise and was disappointed that my mother did not go along with the surprise idea.

We moved the chairs out of the dining room to get more floor space for dancing. Our electric Victrola played 78 RPM records from our small collection, and other people brought some of their own to play—Glen Miller, Artie Shaw, and Benny Goodman. BIG BAND sounds were favorites. Dancing couples circled the table, then moved to the living room and onto the front porch where the night air was fresh enough to cool off and the location secluded enough to escape the adult chaperones. But the happenings there did not escape my eagle-eyed mother. She held me responsible and I later received a scathing lecture because of what she observed—cuddling and hugging while some girl sat on a boy's lap!

This was the only mixed party in our home before my mother's illness. I attended many gatherings and dances at the Skoney home and at Lalewicz's and Wykowski's finished basement recreation rooms during high school and as a young adult. I remember a birthday party at Dolores Wójcik's basement where we played the final dance record of the evening in total darkness. If there was any cuddling or hugging, it could not be seen!

Duck Soup and Down Quilts

I recall another special Sunday fare: duck soup. My father walked to the Farmers' Market in Hamtramck on Saturday to pick out a live duck from dozens quacking away in a wire cage set upon wooden saw horses. A ruddy cheeked matron with a scarf wrapped around her head and an apron around her ample middle stood behind the cage. She tied a short cord around the duck's webbed feet. My father chose the bird carefully. It couldn't be too old. He checked its age by the size and color of the pin feathers next to the tail. If they were too yellow and thick, he picked another bird. When he found the right bird, he positioned it inside a black leatherette tote bag with its head free.

My father killed the duck outside the kitchen on the back stairway landing. He placed it firmly between his feet. He held the duck's bill down against its neck and quickly cut it across the top of its head. When the blood began to drip, he directed it into a bowl that held about a half cup of white vinegar. This was to prevent coagulation.

My parents plucked the feathers and saved them in a paper bag to add to the collection from other meals. When enough were gathered, my mother sat on a stool in the coal bin in the basement and stripped the feathers by hand, saving the soft part and discarding the stiff central spine. She stuffed them into pillows and comforters.

We cooked the duck in a soup pot. After it cooked for a while, my mother added wide noodles, prunes, and golden raisins. Just before it was finished, she added the blood mixture to the broth, giving it a sweet and sour taste, a hint of the vinegar aroma and the distinctive brown gravy color.

Penny Candy

Kresge's Five and Dime Store on Joseph Campau Street in Hamtramck, had a wraparound candy counter in the center of the store. What an array of colors and scents greeted a customer who walked by! I was 3, then 4, then 5 when I tugged at my mother's house dress hem, whining for some sweets.

There were banana-shaped and banana-flavored mouth-sized morsels that I liked. There were sugar-encrusted orange slices and chewy, green-leafed spearmint ones, each with its own characteristic taste and aroma. Also, through the slanted glass, I wanted the small white waxy shaped miniature bottles that held red, green and purple flavored sugar water. I quickly bit off the bottle cap, drank the colored liquid, then chewed the soft, white wax like gum.

Hard candies were okay, especially the raspberry shaped ones with a bit of raspberry jam inside. One of the bins had hard candies from Poland in it. They were usually wrapped in paper. The picture on the wrapper indicated the flavor: grape, lemon, orange, etc. A whole section of the counter was divided into bins of chocolate candies. That's where the aroma really got to anyone in the vicinity. Hershey's kisses in their telltale silver wrapping beckoned, along with chocolate-covered cherries, caramels, and butterscotch morsels.

Colorful corn kernels, called chicken feed, were pale yellow and deep orange, all shaped like individual kernels of corn. Any shopper could buy these by the pound. A sales lady scooped and weighed them and then placed them in a white paper bag. My mother usually relented and chose small amounts of two or three kinds of candies that I begged for. These were quickly disposed of as we walked back to our Norwalk Street flat.

After we relocated to Trowbridge Street, I ran by myself to the corner confectionery, owned by the Baranowski family. It was easy to choose the penny candy, displayed low in the glass-fronted showcases. I always picked my favorites—Squirrels, Chocolate soldiers, Mary Janes, Walnettos, spearmint leaves, orange slices and hard candies like suckers and jaw breakers.

Saturday and Sunday matinees at the Conant or Martha Washington theatre cost 10 cents, and the trip usually demanded an extra 5 cents for candy. We made our choices carefully so that the candy would last through two features, the serial, the cartoon, and the newsreel. The only candy that did this was the Holloway sucker. The flat, hard chocolate-colored caramel on a stick dissolved very slowly. There was always a thin sliver on the stick after the theatre let out, just enough for the long walk home. I also bought Cracker Jacks some time because of the small prizes found inside the box. Ju-Ju Bees were sticky and came in different flavors. Bit-O-Honey had crunchy almonds scattered throughout the thick taffy-like bar. But it was the Holloway sucker that gave the most for the money.

I remember boxed chocolates, gifts to us children on special occasions. Once the box was opened, I would remove a candy, test it by pushing my finger through the bottom. If it was a soft cream, I replaced it into the paper cup and searched further for a caramel or a nut center.

My heavy consumption of sugar took its toll on my baby teeth and my permanent teeth. I did not start regularly brushing until after entering elementary school and my teacher talked about dental health. The benefits of flossing were not yet known. Even my baby molars developed serious decay. As time went on, I developed cavities in every tooth in my mouth. Some teeth needed two and three fillings. I take conscientious care of my teeth now, consuming very little sugar, sweets, or candy. I drink coffee black and tea unsweetened. I plan on keeping my remaining capped and crowned teeth as long as I live.

Illnesses and Remedies

What a flood of memories swamps me! The first five years of my life were relatively free of any serious illnesses. Constipation was a bothersome occurrence that my mother remedied with a dose of castor oil. To make it palatable, she mixed a tablespoon in a half cup of cold black coffee or with a half glass of orange juice. I could see the globules of oil floating in the liquid as I held my nose to swallow it without smelling the telltale aroma. (When I tried drinking black coffee as an adult, my first association was that it had Castor oil in it). If that did not bring results, then my mother resorted to a soapy water enema.

When I began attending elementary school, I suffered from frequent coughs, colds, boils, impetigo, bloody noses and a goodly amount of scrapes on my knees and elbows.

We tried Old World remedies first. If those did not work, we would then consult a pharmacist. We summoned the doctor last. Mother always resorted to a mustard plaster for chest colds and coughs. She formed a paste of dry mustard and water, spread it onto a cloth square, then placed it on my bare chest to do its work. I remember screaming "enough" as the heat intensified quickly, and then I pleaded and urged Mom to administer the antidote, a coating of white lard that relieved the burning. Mom's fingers were rough skinned, and her hands large and strong.

My mother treated head colds by getting a pail of very warm water in which I soaked my feet until perspiration broke out over my whole body. The next step was to get into bed with a hot water bottle wrapped in a towel for keeping toes toasty warm. Then, propped up on a pillow, I sipped a cup of very hot milk laced with chopped fresh garlic and a dollop of sweet butter. When I got to be a teenager, the remedy was advanced to a "GRZANKA"—a hot toddy—strong hot tea laced with honey and whiskey.

My mother always had Vick's Vapor Rub, an ointment that she administered liberally on the chest and dabbed under each nostril. Sometimes she placed it in hot water for inhaling of the vapors, and sometimes she smeared it onto my neck and wrapped it with a warm flannel cloth, usually a recycled diaper.

Mom also made cough syrup: a concoction of chopped onions, sprinkled liberally with sugar and set in a cup on the warm stove shelf. When the sugar dissolved and the onion juices blended with the sugar syrup, she gave me a spoonful that I swallowed with a grimace.

For toothaches I got a jigger of straight whiskey that I held in the area of my mouth where the offending tooth was aching. The drug store substitute was Oil of Cloves. She soaked a cotton swab in it and inserted it into my tooth. Most of the time it was a cavity that caused the pain, and extracting the tooth was the permanent solution.

Boils. Do kids still get boils? I had a painful boil erupt on the knuckle of my little finger of my left hand. Mom's remedy was to get a couple of leaves from a common lawn weed, I think it was plantain. She wrapped these leaves around my finger, securing it with some gauze and string. The infection was drawn out without further problems.

I remember a rash that I developed on my face. For this I was instructed by my mother to watch for the windows to fog with humidity, and to use that moisture to spread onto the skin. Voila! It worked.

My mother soaked cotton balls with Camphor Oil to cure earaches. In class I remember noticing classmates with the telltale cotton plug in the ear, denoting ongoing treatment.

At age six, I developed a bothersome tick. My index finger would jump up, and my hands and arms would jerk behind my back. There was no old world remedy for this puzzling phenomenon, so my father took me to Ford Hospital. A Doctor Mason examined me after I changed into a hospital gown. I never heard what his diagnosis was, but his treatment was a daily dose of Cod Liver Oil and a confinement to the house for a spell. This medicine was in a heavy dark amber syrup and was much more palatable than any previous home remedies.

There was one more home remedy: this one requested by a

doctor, and it invoked a Rite of Passage. When I was fourteen, about 1940, Dad had a gall bladder surgery. His convalescence was complicated by a ruptured abdominal incision. Dr. Walkowiak made house calls. He arrived and examined the gaping opening on my dad's abdomen. He did not have materials for this situation in his black bag. He turned to me and said, "Get me a sanitary napkin." My skin pricked with the flush of heat and embarrassment. Retreating to my bedroom, I reached into the back of the closet where the Kotex box was hidden behind folded clothing. My father was to witness and have direct contact with this intimate personal female object that signaled a rite of passage into womanhood. I avoided eye contact with both my father and the elderly doctor. The doctor covered the wound with the pad that cushioned the area adequately and taped it securely. He gave some final instructions and left. The wound healed without further complications.

Places, Weather, and Objects of Significance

For the first five years of my life, the place of significance was the second floor four room flat in the "income" house owned by my parents in Hamtramck, Michigan, on Norwalk Street. Access was by going through the backyard, up an open stairway on the porch shared by two other smaller flats (3-room shotgun type). A kitchen, dining room, living room with a door to a front porch, one bedroom, and a bathroom. This was an improvement made by my father. He also had a cinder-block foundation put in that gave the building a full basement. However, heating was still by a coal "parlor" stove with isinglass windows and nickel trim that stood in the center of the dining room. The kitchen was where everything took place. The black cast iron cooking stove did have an additional two-burner gas cooking feature, but most of the time quick heat was obtained by throwing some wood kindling into the left side. In one corner of the room stood a galvanized 40-gallon water heater that required lighting a gas burner under it to heat water for a bath. The kitchen table was rectangular with a drawer for cutlery. It stood under the two kitchen windows that looked out South and the back porch. The unfinished wooden top was used for rolling out noodles, kneading yeast dough, cutting out "chruściki" and "pirogi."

At mealtime the table was covered with an oilcloth square purchased by the yard from rolls at the five and dime. It was such fun to get a replacement: the design was new and bold and well defined. Usually mom chose a floral design. When new, the cloth smelled distinctly and the edges curled under for a while.

A tall wooden cabinet with two doors had glass so that dinnerware was visible on the shelves. Two drawers below held kitchen towels. On top of this cabinet sat a tin oval bowl with painted roses on the old gold sides. It was mom's sewing container and button holder. She continued to use it throughout her life. Now it belongs to niece Kim who also acquired the Singer sewing machine. The sewing machine was purchased new about 1927 or

1928. It stood in the kitchen with a velour runner on the top when it was not being used. Mom bought unbleached muslin for sheets and pillow cases that she sewed and then bleached outdoors in the sun. Patterns for dresses posed some problems so she often took apart a dress that did fit properly and used it as a pattern for a new one. One year during the depths of the Great Depression mom cut down one of her dresses for me to use as money was very scarce and did not stretch to allow for a new dress.

Mom learned to crochet after she came to the U.S. She quickly became very proficient. She made curtains and valances. Long narrow panels hung from the top of the doorframe between the kitchen and dining room as a divider. The panels tapered at the ends to a point from which dangled a "teardrop" stuffed with cotton to retain its shape. The curtains on the window were also crocheted with fringed bottoms. Gradually these articles were relegated to boxes in the attic as mom took on "American" styles in furnishings for the house.

Another object of significance was the first crystal-type radio requiring ear phones that a neighbor showed to all who wanted to experience this new wonder. Well, not too long after this, dad purchased an RCA radio with an electric phonograph player in the top section. This was a notable piece of furniture, a mahogany veneer object, on four tall legs. A small dial moved showing the numbers of the stations and a tiny light bulb illuminated the opening. One sat in front of this new piece of equipment on a wrought iron bench. The seat was padded and upholstered in burgundy velour. The first two records were housed in albums that fit into special slots next to the record player: Paul Whiteman playing "St. Louis Blues" and Maurice Chevalier singing "Louise." Mom added a Polish Krakowiak and a polka featuring clarinet music. We danced around the dining room table and listened to records for many years. The records were played with a needle. Two small metal cups held used and new needles.

I remember only the summers of those first five years. That's when my playmates were Clara and Stella Szkudniewski, daughters of the family who rented that lower flat in our house. Other children my age were the Czekaj girls who lived a couple houses to the left.

There was a hot spell that brought our bed, or rather the mattress out onto the floor of the upstairs porch for sleeping. It was just too hot indoors. What an adventure to stretch out under the open sky and stars, even for one night!

The backyard, with two apple trees, bushes and flowers, and a small vegetable garden, was significant to me. Along the left fence grew clumps of lavender irises, a bleeding heart bush, and an old-fashioned rose bush with very peppery smelling deep pink blossoms. The apples were usually wormy but did make good apple sauce. Other annual flowers planted in that yard were taken to church on August 15th, Feast of the Assumption of the Blessed Virgin Mary or as it was known in the Polish Parishes, Our Lady of the Herbs. It really was the time to thank God for a bountiful harvest. The bouquets brought to church for blessing often held sprigs of wheat and oats.

Tonsils and Adenoids

"You'll be eating a lot of ice cream after your tonsils are out," one of the older neighborhood children told me. At six years of age, ice cream was the ultimate treat. So without a fuss, I made the trip with my father to the Professional Building on Woodward Avenue near downtown Detroit. The procedure was planned in the doctor's office. Yes, I could count, and the nurse asked that I repeat after her, as she placed the ether mask over my face. One-one, two-two, three-onto twenty-six, twenty-six. Twenty-seven, twenty-seven. Twenty-eight, twenty-seven. Twenty-nine, twenty-seven, and I was under.

Dad hired a taxi for the trip home. Still woozy from the ride and the ether, my stomach rebelled with a vomiting spell. Oh, a new sensation, as the warm fluid rose up my gullet, through my mouth and my nose!

Swallowing the vanilla ice cream posed a problem again as the squishy, creamy mass pushed up into my nasal cavity where my adenoids used to be. What a bother!

The soreness in my throat soon abated, and healing progressed satisfactorily. My parents were now convinced that a tonsillectomy reduced throat inflammations and eased breathing. I was, however, still susceptible to colds and fevers and later developed allergies.

My brother Leonard, at age 10, had his tonsils out. He was also circumcised. My father arranged this with Dr. Kłosowski, who hospitalized my brother at St. Francis Hospital. Neither the doctor nor my father prepared Leonard for this double surgery. When my brother came home, he confided his discovery to me. Needless to say, his frightened reaction was appropriate. I reassured him that I recalled he was not circumcised right after birth and this was considered minor surgery.

The Big Fires of February 1933

It was a frigid, cloudless night that 2nd of February, 1933, the height of the Great Depression. Temperatures were low, dropping into the single digits, then below zero. Both coal furnaces in our basement were burning full blast, sending up steam into the radiators of every room in the lower and upper flats. We were all asleep when in the middle of the night, our downstairs tenant, Mr. Wesołowski, knocked hard on our kitchen door shouting "Fire!"

I became aware of lights going on in all the rooms of our upstairs flat and the sound of rushing footsteps. My father dressed quickly and left by the front staircase to call the fire department. The fire alarm box was on a utility pole at the corner. There were no telephones in our house. Mom was breathing heavily as she scurried around looking for some clothing to put on. As she rushed from room to room, she told me to get a coat to wear over my bed clothes and shoes to put on my bare feet. My mother wrapped my brother, who was one year old at the time, in a blanket and held him in her arms.

The three of us went into the kitchen. My mother opened the door and looked down the inside stairwell. Thick brown smoke rolled up the passageway and moved into the second level. My mother gasped. She yelled to me, "Shut the door!" I panicked, frightened by all the commotion, and left the door ajar.

We turned around to go through the house and leave by the front exit. As we rushed into the frosty air, the flames and smoke billowed up the side of the house where the basement windows had shattered from the heat.

Our neighbors next door took us in as we all waited for the fire trucks to put out the flames, but they did not come. We waited and waited, and still, they did not come. The fire station was on Caniff Street, just west of Joseph Campau, only about eight blocks away. Meanwhile, the flames burned brighter and higher, crackling into the crisp freezing night.

Somebody learned that all the Hamtramck Fire Department equipment was on Joseph Campau Avenue where both the Woolworth and the Kresge stores were ablaze. Finally, the adjacent city of Highland Park sent its fire trucks to put out our fire. The firemen traveled about ten miles to get to our address. The men brought the blaze under control by daybreak. We had to move to our house on Norwalk Street and live with the downstairs tenants, the Szkudniewskis. Now there were nine people in that three-room flat.

I had to walk an additional five blocks to school for a week or so while the damage to our house was assessed. My school work habits were completely disrupted by the crowded surroundings. It seems we were continually dodging each other as we moved about those three small rooms. I wondered each day when and if we would ever return to our home.

Going back to our house on Trowbridge was a traumatic experience. Water from the hoses formed a solid sheet of ice on the siding and on the sidewalk in front and next to the house. In the charred basement there was a gaping hole above the furnace where the floor burned through to the dining room above. The buffet fell through the opening and was now standing on the basement floor.

Most of the damage to the second floor, the stairwell, and the attic was from smoke. The heat of the flames blistered wall paint and varnish, but the smoke permeated and stained everything it touched. The Singer sewing machine that I remembered from Norwalk showed the remnants of that fire. One drawer had been pulled half open, allowing the smoke to penetrate the contents. There is an outline of a button, a safety pin and a spool that lay on the bottom. The area around is a dark brown, and the wood where they rested lighter in color. When I gave the machine to my niece Kimberly, I made a point of pulling out that right-hand top drawer. The smoke-stained wood on the inside still showed the outlines of those items, 50 years after the fact!

The smoky odor that returned when the humidity was high reminded us of that frightening event for many years.

Mr. and Mrs. Wesołowski lived downstairs at the time. They owned the dry goods store and kept a lot of empty cardboard boxes in their half of the basement. With the furnace so near, a spark from the hot dropping ashes could have ignited the paper nearby. The source of the fire was quite clearly where the boxes were stored. The heaviest damage to the basement and floor above was in the area in front of the furnace that heated the first floor. My mother blamed the Wesołowski's carelessness for this loss and affected our attitude toward them. Their insurance on the contents of their flat covered replacement of most of their furniture and possessions. Our insurance was only on the building, so repairs were done to most of the interior of the first floor. We watched as the two wooden pillars in the living room were replaced by a stylish plaster archway. New oak floors and woodwork gave the first floor flat an updated look. Upstairs our belongings required a lot of washing, airing and refinishing.

Experiencing the disruption and loss as a result of a fire sent shock waves that lasted many months as my family struggled to resume the daily activities of living. News of the fire reached the nuns who taught at the school I attended. One of the sisters made a home visit to our family to present me with a small box with an apple and several nougats in it. Just before Christmas that year, the doorbell rang. One of the city firemen presented us with a gift box containing three woolen scarves. My mother relived that fateful night many times as the months went by. She was saddened and sorrowful over the near catastrophe. Our finances were also affected by the loss of rental income from the lodgers and from the downstairs flat. The repairs and rebuilding took several months.

Meanwhile, this disruption and loss affected my not-so-robust physique. I developed frequent nosebleeds that had my mother worried. Somewhere she got the advice that what I needed was to spend some time in the fresh air. How and what she did to accomplish this is another chapter.

The Kidney Operation

In 1933, my father developed a serious and painful ailment: kidney stones that had to be removed. Without medical insurance a patient paid for surgery, hospital bills and doctor fees from savings or became a "county" (welfare) case. The Wayne County General Hospital at Eloise, Michigan served these "indigents." My father sought the advice of a local attorney, Victor Kulaski, who was familiar with the procedure. Ownership of our house, an asset, still not paid for, was transferred to uncle Frank Czekiel.

The first surgery to remove stones from one kidney was completed successfully. The second surgery was scheduled for two weeks later with my father staying on at the hospital. When the second surgery got under way, the doctor noted that the entire kidney would have to be removed. Meanwhile, the anesthesia began to wear off. My father woke up to be told that he required a blood transfusion in order to survive the second surgery. He recalled having no sensation in his lower legs as he continued to lose blood. But another patient volunteered his blood and as they lay side by side for a direct transfusion, this Good Samaritan told my father he would pray for him.

I remember one visit to the hospital with my mother and baby brother. Mom located an old man with even an older car willing to drive us to the hospital some 25 miles away. My father's bed was in a huge ward. We walked between single white iron beds passing one bed with a man who was lying on his back, very still, his head on the pillow, his mouth, wide open, and not a breath coming out. I tugged at my mothers dress, telling her what I saw. Indeed, when we called a nurse, she confirmed our observation. The sheet was pulled over his face and he was whisked away on a Gurney.

We returned home late, as our driver had a flat tire that he fixed himself as we stood on the Michigan Avenue roadside. He struggled with a rubber patch that had to be applied to the inner tube and get it back into the same tire as he had no spare.

My father recovered, admitting that he owed his life to a compassionate stranger who gave his blood and offered prayers.

Fresh Air and Uncle Frank's Farm

I was 7 years old at the time of the fire in 1933. The Great Depression's grip was tightening. I recall a definite decline in eating habits as money dwindled. We always had bread, potatoes and soup, but a day did arrive when there was only bread spread with rendered pork fat. As the months passed, my health began to decline. A county health nurse in a dark blue uniform came to talk to my mother about the state of my teeth. I was able to get a diseased first molar extracted at no cost. Another molar was treated and filled with a red pigment after a school nurse checked our mouths. Nosebleeds, coughs, and an underweight body concerned my mother. She determined to change this, to get me to gain weight, and to be more robust.

Uncle Frank Czekiel's daughter, cousin Frances, now a rough and tumble teenager, regaled us with the benefits to be gained from the fresh air at her father's farm. Uncle Frank had recently divorced his wife, my Aunt Katarynka, (or maybe it was the other way around) and purchased this farm. The two oldest sons moved to be with him, helping to operate the dairy farm.

The farm was located in Macomb County, beyond the city of Mt. Clemens, about 25 or 30 miles northeast of Detroit. How to get there without a car was the question. Uncle Frank's dairy cows supplied milk to the creamery on Belmont Street on the next block. Their milk trucks made regular trips to collect those tall galvanized containers. My mother arranged for us to travel in the cab of that milk truck. We were to spend two weeks in August at Uncle Frank's farm. We would be dropped off in front of the property on the regular route that went through Ray Township and Uncle Frank's fresh air accommodations.

My mother, baby brother who was about 1 1/2 years old, and I climbed into that high cab before dawn. We were prepared for this sojourn. My mother used an old pillowcase to carry hard salami, loaves of bread, bed linens, towels, and clothing. We hauled this "luggage" aboard the truck where it rested at our feet.

Ah, yes, the bracing fresh air, the scent of freshly cut hay and the open fields of swaying grain surrounded us as we clambered down from the high milk truck cab. Ahead was the gabled farmhouse, set back, with a low porch across the entire front. The grass was tall in the area between the wrought iron fence that defined the roadside of the yard and the building. Wooden pillars and no railing made it easy to get up onto the veranda and then into the inside.

The rooms were very sparsely furnished and were obviously in need of deep cleaning. Kerosene lamps furnished the light, and a hand pumped well in the back provided water. An outhouse stood in the tall weeds between the house and the barn.

My mother was aghast at the conditions and could not contain her disappointment to us. An old decrepit cast iron wood burning stove was ashen gray and spattered with grease from neglect and abuse. Our first meal was a picnic lunch on a blanket spread out on the matted high grass of the front lawn.

Uncle Frank and his sons, Antek and Edek, were very cordial and accommodating. I watched as Antek milked a cow and poured the fresh milk out of a pail into a mug. He gave it to me to sample. It was warm, frothy, and very strange tasting. Then Edek gave me a ride on one of the work horses. It was a new adventure, as he guided the slow-moving animal around the barnyard as I sat on its bare back. It was a bit awkward to straddle the broad back wearing a dress, as I was not prepared for anything but fresh air!

Before we settled in for the night, my eyes began to itch, water, and swell. Then my nose began to run. What a predicament as we began to get ready for bed! The dusty bedroom had a bed, mattress, and dresser. My mother used her own sheets and blanket on the mattress of undetermined vintage. We extinguished the kerosene lamp and attempted to fall asleep. As soon as it was totally dark, Mom and I became aware of getting bitten while we were covered with bed sheets. Indeed, the mattress harbored bedbugs that would not stop biting us! So we took the blankets and sheets and spread them on the low front porch where we spent the rest of the night. Of course, now I was surrounded by the grasses, weeds, wild flowers, golden rod, and ragweed that abounded. In addition, that raw milk did not sit well in my digestive track and this meant frequent trips to the outhouse.

When morning came, we gathered up our belongings and returned home by the next truck. Now I was in worse shape than when I came for the cure in the fresh air.

My mother told Uncle Frank that my health took a turn for the worse with yet another affliction, hay fever! She attributed it to the yellow flowers—goldenrod that was all around the farm. Years later, while undergoing skin tests, I found out that it was the horse dander that caused the greatest allergic reaction.

My mother grumbled for many years about the hay fever I contracted at Uncle Frank's farm and cousin Frances' glowing picture of the benefits to be obtained at her father's farm.

My memory of this event is of my mother and her determination to find a way to improve my health through getting to fresh air at Uncle Frank's farm.

To this day and throughout my years of growing up into adulthood, I have been allergic to horses and most farm animals. I don't ride horses, I avoid hay rides, I sit high up on the bleachers at rodeos, I go to very few circus performances, and view horse races from the inside of the club house.

The allergy condition flared up again when I became a teenager and was treated by Dr. George Waldbodt, a respected allergist. Treatment began early in the year, no later than March, and included trips weekly for desensitization. The idea was that by ragweed time in the middle of August, my immunity was built up so that I could tolerate the high pollen count during that month.

This all began with seeking fresh air at Uncle Frank's farm.

Franklin Delano Roosevelt in Hamtramck

Dad and I started early to cover the ten blocks on foot to the corner of Gallagher and Leuschner streets. It was to be the itinerary for Franklin Roosevelt's visit prior to the election of 1935. Indeed, residents of this Democratic stronghold of blue collar workers, lined each of these two streets waving small hand held American flags. An open roadster held the presidential party. Seated behind the driver, bareheaded, with a long cigarette holder clenched between his smiling lips the president waved as the vehicle proceeded slowly past us turning west onto Leuschner Street. What a thrill to see the head of our country in person! His predecessor, Herbert Hoover, was decried as the one who closed the banks, but Roosevelt gave us the New Deal, the WPA, the CCC. He was our hero. Well, the city fathers were appropriately affected by this unprecedented visit to this city. From then on the name of the street was changed to Roosevelt Street. This was the only President I ever saw in person in my entire life. Once I did shake the hand of Michigan governor, G. Mennen Williams, while he was getting votes in Gaylord, Michigan, during a Winter Snow Festival. He was a popular and appealing politician with his trademark green and white polka dot bow tie, but the impact of that childhood Roosevelt viewing is with me yet.

Post Script

The Polish Pope, John Paul II visited Hamtramck after I moved away. The city fathers vacated almost a city block in the commercial area on Joseph Campau Street to erect a bronze life size statue of him in a small park setting.

The Laundry

A number of business establishments were clustered on both sides of Caniff Street near Conant Avenue. Just opposite Moran Street, on the south side, was a commercial laundry. The narrow store front was similar to the others nearby, such as the grocery store owned by the Surdacki family, the confectionery operated by the Pyczynski couple, and the dry cleaners across the way.

This building extended all the way to the back alley. Its tall round brick smokestack spewed black smoke from coal furnaces that heated the water for the washing machines somewhere in the rear. Pressing, ironing, folding, and wrapping was completed in a large open area facing the front of the establishment. Laundromat workers wrapped packages holding shirts and other laundry in brown paper and placed them on shelves behind the counter near the front door.

In the summer, the front door was propped open. As a child, I watched the pressers, who were all women, sit or stand next to baskets of damp clothing, reaching for and turning each item into a dry usable item. I heard the electric fans whirring and oscillating high above the heads of the workers. A cloud of steam followed a hiss as the pressing machine clamped down on a shirtfront.

Wide eyed I watched as those women toiled and operated heated metal appliances. They were perspiring and dried their foreheads and necks, turning now and then to catch a breeze from the mounted fans.

One special pressing appliance was a shiny cylindrical-nickel upright affair about 30 inches tall. With one pull-on gesture, its heat dried and smoothed the entire long sleeve of a man's shirt, leaving it without a wrinkle. A real labor saver, I concluded, noting the NRA sticker with the American flag on it, pasted to the front glass display window. Those windows were either frosted or steamed over from the humidity inside. The lower half of the windows had brown wrapping paper stretched across so the interior was only visible when the door was propped open in the summer heat.

Our roomers and many other single workers used this laundry for dress shirts, work clothes and personal items. When I began working, following college, the laundry's drop-off wash and fold feature was a great time saver. The cost of laundering bed linens, towels, and personal items was determined by the weight of the bundles.

After getting married, I used a small laundry in Berkley, Michigan, for our household laundry until we could afford to purchase an automatic washer and dryer. We bought a wringer washer from the previous owners of our house. I used it for selected items and enjoyed hanging the laundry outdoors on a clothesline using clothespins to attach each piece of the clothing item. After flapping in the wind, the cloth had an unmistakably fresh scent not duplicated by any fabric softener in a clothes dryer.

I recall the sweat shop conditions in the laundromat of those sweltering summers of the 1930s and how they affected the women working in the neighborhood commercial laundry. The working conditions in our local strip mall laundromats that offer drop-off service are now much more comfortable and civilized than those in the Caniff Street laundry.

The Beer Garden

When I sat at the table and looked out the window of our second-story flat, I could see below into the backyard of the Jelonek family. An alley separated our house from their fenced quarters, and walking on the pavement did not provide a view of the back of their building with the second-floor corner porch and the grass. There was an overhang that provided protection from the elements and was an ideal spot for games.

In 1934, shortly after the repeal of the Volstead Act, which prohibited the sale of alcoholic beverages, the Jelonek family moved into this location to open a Beer Garden. The backyard of their two-story, white frame building became the garden, with small tables sitting on the lawn. Beer and liquor were sold and consumed behind the tall wooden fence. A good crowd of men and women patronized this new form of neighborhood recreation. I could hear glasses clinking and a lot of voices punctuated by bursts of laughter. Candles shielded by hurricane globes illuminated each table. Cigarette smoke wafted through the night air, temporarily obscuring the gaiety and the bodies moving to and fro among the tables.

My family observed the camaraderie from our second-story vantage point. But the partying did not last. There were neighbors with school-aged children living on each side of the Jeloneks. The decibels increased as the evenings wore on, and eventually, the outdoor aspect of the Beer Garden was relocated inside the store front, which from then on was still called The Beer Garden. In fact, other establishments opened along the commercial strips in Hamtramck, and they also were referred to as beer gardens. Some displayed neon signs in the front windows, Jax Bar, Belmont Cafe, The Old Mill, but to the locals they were beer gardens.

When Jelonek's Beer Garden moved indoors, there was a change in atmosphere, attendance, and attitude. The area consisted of a bare wooden floor, tables that were painted black, bentwood chairs, and walls and ceilings of pressed tin. There were fewer women among the regulars, who were usually blue collar men dropping in after their factory shift. Pay day was especially busy when the men stopped in to cash their checks before going home. There was always a lingering smell of stale beer, spilled whiskey, and old tobacco ashes.

I'm sure someone counted the number of these beer gardens within the city of Hamtramck. Every block along Conant, Caniff, Joseph Campau, and on the streets in between had at least one corner beer garden and often another one in the middle of the block. They did have to stay a certain distance from a school or church.

The beer garden I remember was the one I could see, through the curtains, sitting at the table in the kitchen of the second floor flat on Trowbridge Street.

Church Bells

From 1931 until 1969, the year we sold our house on Trowbridge, our parish church was the Catholic Church of Our Lady Queen of the Apostles. Located on Conant Street, it occupied the entire block from Prescott to Harold Street. The first story of the red brick structure housed the church. The elementary school rooms were on the second floor. Three solid brass bells hung in the square belfry that rose above to form a third level. There were openings on all four sides. A parishioner could see the bells as well as hear them. Our house, just two blocks away, was within good hearing distance when those bells rang.

At noon and at 6 p.m., the bells rang melodiously reminding the faithful to pray the Angelus. If I was in the vicinity of the school and a nun was in view, I noticed her stopping, bowing her head, and quietly reciting, "The angel declared unto Mary . . ."

There were distinctive rings, denoting various occasions. When a single bell tolled slowly, the reverberations ending before the next rolling clang, a funeral was in progress. A more vigorous motion of one or two bells was a call to the parishioners to Sunday services at 8, then 9, 10:30 a.m., and the last Mass at noon.

The resounding brass bells always had a happy connotation for me. Their song was a call to gather, to worship, to partake. It was a reminder, without words, but with robust metallic strokes. The echo of those golden sounds permeated the walls and windows of each frame dwelling nestled in that corner of Michigan.

Mr. Filip was the church and school custodian, with the added task of bell ringer. Three of his four sons were students at the grade school during the time I attended. Mr. Filip was a short, intense man who was always busy sweeping, mopping, emptying baskets from classrooms. His family lived on the street next to the church, so he had a short walk to his duties.

The bells had a heavy rope attached to them, its end in a small cove in the church vestibule. Now and then, I saw one of the Filip boys pulling the rope. It was no secret that Mr. Filip occasionally sought relief for his tired muscles from a pint of Seagram's. When he overindulged, one of his sons filled in for him. Both Joe and Mitchell were of short stature like their father, so they needed to spring up to grasp the rope to get the bells to swing.

The most memorable bell ringing I remember occurred in 1939, in the middle of a summer afternoon. All three bells began tolling without a pause for what seemed about 15 minutes. My mother recognized this to indicate a death among the clergy of our parish. Our pastor, Rev. Stanley Wasilewski, was elderly when we joined the parish. It was his demise that those bells announced.

The other two churches in Hamtramck, St. Florian's and St. Ladislaus, also had their own church bells, but they were too distant from our house to be heard.

Trilingual Jackie

Nick Mistinitz, a Russian emigre, rented our four-room flat on Norwalk after we moved to the Trowbridge home. His wife and mandolin-playing, raven-haired daughter, and a dog named Jackie, filled those rooms. My father, the landlord, sometimes collected the late rent in person. Often I tagged along to listen to the mandolin music and to play with Jackie, a medium-sized Belgian police dog. Nick gave commands to the dog in Russian, and my father and Nick also conversed in Russian.

A year or so later, for a reason unknown to me, Nick and his family moved. Jackie, a payment for rent owed, moved to our Trowbridge address. Now we had a dog. My mother and father gave commands to Jackie in Polish and my brother and I addressed him in English. He willingly gave his paw and sat up. His buda (shack) was under the small back porch. Inside was an old rug for a bed and outside a metal pan for his water.

It was my job to feed Jackie and to give him his bath. My mother asked the butcher for raw pig hearts that I cut into pieces and fed to our new pet, tossing the pieces one by one, giving him time to catch each morsel and chomp on it before swallowing. Jackie relished leftovers from our meals and bones from chops and steaks as well.

During hot summer days, I hauled a round galvanized wash tub from the basement to the backyard. I set it on the cement pavement in front of the garage and in the sun. With the garden hose hooked up to the faucet on the side of the house, I filled the tub about half full. Then I lifted Jackie's front legs and plunged them and his front torso into the tub. His back legs and rear end remained outside the bathtub. After wetting down Jackie's black and tan coat, with a bar of black Cuticura Flea Soap in my hand, I worked up a foamy lather. Following a rinse with a low spray from the garden hose, I moved Jackie's rear half into the water for the same soaking, soaping, rubbing, and rinsing. Jackie remained still, tolerating the procedure until after the final rinse. Out of the tub, he shook vigorously, spraying me with the excess moisture that clung to his rich black, tan and white coat. I always placed a clean rag rug on the pavement just for him to use. He scampered to it and rubbed the sides of his snout, head and neck, then his sides, finally turning upside down on his back for a final drying off.

During the cold winter months, my parents allowed Jackie indoors to sleep in the warm basement and get his bath there.

Jackie was a people dog. He liked to sneak into our second floor living quarters and find a warm spot for a nap. He stayed away from the high-traffic areas, choosing to hide under the kitchen table where he hoped my mother or father would not see him and shoo him away. When it rained, my parents let him stay inside where it was dry. It was thunderstorms that Jackie feared most. He would scramble under a bed, move to the farthest corner, tremble, and curl into a ball until the thunder subsided. No amount of coaxing got him out of that position.

His guard dog demeanor was to lie across one of the back stairs that led to the second floor, bare his teeth and growl if an unfamiliar person approached. His greatest nemesis was a moving auto. If we left the front gate open, he would dash onto the street and bark at the turning wheels of a passing car. It was during one such occasion that he was hurt, limping home. He remained in the basement for several weeks where he dragged his rear leg until the healing process completed and he resumed walking on all fours.

Sometime during those years, Trowbridge Street made the front page of our local paper, the *Hamtramck Citizen*. Our street had the distinction of having the most dogs of any street in the city. Shortly after this dubious honor, a dog show was announced. Children of the neighborhood were invited to bring their canine pets to the Dickinson Elementary School for a judging. Not having a leash, I led Jackie, holding his leather collar, through the alleys, to Norwalk Street, five blocks away. It was a motley group of dogs, held by their young owners. All the other dogs were smaller than Jackie. Some had longer hair, and some were short haired. Most were mixed breeds. I don't recall the categories, or the criteria for judging. Jackie didn't even get honorable mention. But then I did not advertise his distinction of being able to respond to commands in three different languages!

Jackie was a beloved, faithful family pet for a number of years. In 1939, when I returned home from what was to be my last summer camp experience as a teenager, Jackie was gone. My mother made a very brief comment about a fatal collision he had with a car that he was chasing. Many years later, in the summer of 2000, my brother told a different story about Jackie's demise. He claimed that Jackie had succumbed to poisoning by one of our neighbors. Whichever way we lost our childhood pet, I was spared the unfortunate details of Jackie's last day.

Rough-hewn Wood

Ours was an intact family—father, mother, and two children. Most of our neighbors were also nuclear families with parents and children of various ages. The Siek household was one of the exceptions. This single-parent family was composed of a middle-aged mother and her two daughters—Lottie, who was about 20 years old, and Genevieve, age 5, who was about a year younger than I. Mrs. Siek had been married twice. Lottie was the offspring of the first union and Genevieve was the offspring of the second. I was never sure if Mrs. Siek had been widowed or divorced.

We considered Lottie Siek as the head of the family. She worked as an assembly line laborer at one of the auto factories. Her earnings supported this trio, however not exclusively. Periodically I passed a mound of corn mash, steaming and moist, that had been dumped in the alley against the Siek's backyard fence. Rumor had the Sieks operating a still somewhere inside their house. Their basement had tables set up where visitors drank glasses of an amber-colored liquid in exchange for silver coins that the ever-present Mrs. Siek swiftly scooped up. The suspected clandestine moonshine operation was never discovered to my knowledge.

In the 1930s in Hamtramck, Lottie was ahead of her time. Most of the time she wore men's clothes—blue denim shirts, black work trousers, and flat-heeled oxfords that reflected her job at the auto plant, as well as her responsibilities of maintaining the house and grounds of their property on Conant Street. Brusque and tough talking, her steely blue eyes squinted, her face twitched, and her mouth freely rolled out expletives. Her dark brown hair was straight and cut short in a shingle. A cigarette usually dangled from the side of her lips. She reminded me of Leo Gorcy, one of the Dead End kids in the movies.

Genevieve Siek and I became playmates, visiting each other's homes. The first-floor flat she lived in with her older sister and mother was very neat and clean, with only the required articles of furniture and no frills or decorations. Their lifestyle was frugal and lacked any extras. How frugal their daily life was, was illustrated to me during one of my visits to their home. I asked to use the bathroom off the kitchen. Genevieve instructed me diligently to use only four squares of toilet tissue from the roll on the wall. I complied but avoided using their facilities after that one experience.

Lottie owned, drove and serviced her own modest black Ford sedan. She was the only single female in our acquaintance with this ability and skill. In the summer of 1933 or 1934, she took me and her little sister on a memorable trip in the Ford to the Salt Water Swimming Pool in Rochester, Michigan, which was about 20 miles north of Hamtramck, to experience the taste and properties of salt water. We were also in the company of a unique group of sun worshipers. I remember musclemen and body builders' physiques with deep tan skin that glistened with oil as they reclined around the perimeter of the pool absorbing ultra violet rays.

One Easter I learned that Lottie had a talent and a skill, a socially redeeming quality, not previously known to me. She could create Pisanki, a folk art that used a wax-resist method of coloring Easter eggs. I watched the process with great interest.

The Siek kitchen table stood in the center of the room. Sheets of white butcher paper were spread on the top of the table and tools sat in front of Lottie: a burning beeswax candle in a small holder and clear glass jars of dye baths. With her rough-skinned hands and stubby fingers, she held a raw egg delicately in her left hand. Using a homemade stylus or kistka, which was akin to a pencil, she drew a thin stream of melted beeswax from a candle onto the surface of the egg. She applied traditional symbols and motifs—flowers that symbolized friendship and lines for long life—with the fine point of the metal stylus.

Lottie cleaned the final product, a decorated egg with many layers of wax and several dips into progressively darker dyes, after spending several patient hours creating it. She used a soft cloth or paper towel to clean small areas of the egg that contained wax that she softened by holding the egg near an open candle flame. She displayed her final creations, intricately designed and multicolored eggs, year after year.

I remember seeing a crystal bowl with several Pisanki in the china cabinet standing in the Siek dining room. How I envied their possessing this unique Easter commodity! And how I admired the deep rich colors, fine lines, and detailed shapes on each egg.

Forty years later, in the 1970s, the Polish seminary at Orchard Lake, Michigan, sponsored a Pisanki workshop that my husband and I attended, eager to learn and experience this unique folk art that I had first observed at the Siek house.

I believe other stories could be told about the Siek women by my brother. He recalled a male acquaintance (friend?) of Lottie who provided some steel I-beams for building an addition to the front of their home. These beams were stored on the vacant lot next to their house for several years before construction actually took place. The addition became a small banquet hall used for showers and small celebrations that were, no doubt, other sources of income for the Sieks. Genevieve left Hamtramck for California after completing two years of college, taking a job as a waitress in one of the big cities. I lost contact with Lottie and her mother after my own move out of Hamtramck in 1958.

The Organist

The pupils in the 5th grade at our Lady Queen of Apostles Church elementary school began the fall semester as new recruits of the choir. All the boys and girls gathered in what was the music room, a small classroom with seats such as could be found in a theater. Black hardcovered hymnals had songs for all liturgical seasons, printed in Polish and Latin with accompanying musical notes.

We learned to read music and follow the notes as the organist, Mr. Edward Banasiak, accompanied us on the well-used upright piano, which was the only other piece of furniture in the room. When he faced us there was a reasonable response to his directions, but when he sat down to play the piano, his back was to the restless youngsters, so a lot of mayhem began along with the singing.

Mr. Banasiak was a dapper gentleman, always impeccably dressed in a dark blue suit, white shirt and tie. He sported a neatly trimmed black mustache and his cheeks and chin had a hint of talc over his freshly shaven skin. His was a challenging chore to turn this motley group into a Vienna Boys and Girls Choir.

While the rest of the grades sat in the pews during daily Mass, the fifth graders were positioned in the choir loft at the back of the church. We stood during the entire service, shifting about the small area beside the organ and the organist whose back was to the group. The loft was set higher than floor level, about six steps up.

Most memorable were the hymns of mourning that we sung during Requiem mass: *Dies Irae*, and Polish hymns used at funerals. These were wrenching, emotional tunes that almost sobbed, calling on the Virgin Mary as the Queen of Heaven to have mercy on the repentant sinner who was seeking admission through the pearly gates.

Many of the parts of the mass were sung in Latin during a high mass. Also, Latin hymns were used regularly. We struggled with the correct pronunciation always patiently coached by our organist.

More rewarding, I'm certain, was the adult choir of mixed voices that the organist trained for singing at the Sunday masses. The young adults, male and female, auditioned before being accepted into this prestigious group and earned the esteem of the rest of the parishioners, who frequently attended the high mass in order to hear their beautifully blending voices.

Our organist had another duty. Just before the Christmas holidays, he made home visits to the registered parishioners. Nattily attired, wearing a gray Homburg and a gray tweed overcoat and gray spats over his oxfords, he came to the front door with the "Opłatek," the thin white rectangular wafer with a nativity scene stamped into the crisp texture. This was used just before the Christmas Eve dinner, shared with all at the table, while giving wishes. The Felician Order of nuns at our parish church baked these wafers, but the organist distributed them and collected the goodwill offering for them.

I believe Mr. Banasiak stayed at this church his entire career. He succumbed to an illness, leaving a wife but no children. I think of him whenever I hear Gluck's *"Song of the Blessed Spirits."* He played it on the organ at each of those Requiem masses while we hovered around that choir loft.

Church music, particularly Polish traditional hymns are melodious and memorable. The Christmas carols relate the story of the nativity from the viewpoint of the shepherds, the child Jesus, the angels, the Virgin mother, and the three kings. Easter songs are lofty and grand, proclaiming the miracle of the risen Christ. Songs of Lent are mournful, focusing on the pain, the cross, the suffering and the abandonment experienced by our Savior. Songs about Mary are the happiest, stressing her motherhood and her closeness to her son. The Litany to the Blessed Virgin Mary calls her the Heavenly Queen of Poland.

The organist brought all of the Church music to a group of rebelling youngsters. Ah, I remember it well.

Chop Suey Or The Americanization of Josephine

My mother and father continued to prefer their traditional Polish food most of their lives, as well as the Old Country religious customs that affected food choices. But my mother slowly adapted to American ways, expanding her culinary horizons after we moved to the Trowbridge address.

The first floor tenants moved out after several months. They were replaced with the Wesołowski family, second generation Poles. Mrs. Wesołowski was tall, very trim, and wore her permed, graying hair in a short bob. She was willing to provide recipes for some of the food we could always smell cooking.

Upstairs, our daily meals were usually predictable. A pot of soup, with stock made from a chunk of meat with bone, had pieces of root vegetables and made a hearty first course. This bowl of soup included all the globules of fat floating across the surface of the liquid. My father cut slices of crusty rye bread with a large knife as he held the loaf against his belly. He instructed us to eat everything including the fat. The boiled meat was served separately with mustard and horseradish.

Other food began to appear on the table—hot dogs, Franco-American spaghetti, and store-bought cookies (Lorna Doones and Fig Newtons). My mother began to bake layer cakes and cup cakes made with baking powder. There was less time given to yeast-raised breads. Then one day she learned to make Chop Suey from a recipe she received from our tenant downstairs.

My brother and I liked this change of menu. Combining the canned bean sprouts and canned mushrooms with small pieces of pork and slices of onion and celery, she stewed it all with some water. It was quicker than the long-simmering soups. We added soy sauce over the chop suey covering the rice and munched away. I recall the liquid was a bit soupy and had small globules of fat glistening across the surface. My mother, Josephine, either overlooked or eliminated the final process of thickening the broth!

Grown up and in the workaday world, I found authentic Chinese restaurants in Detroit's small Chinatown district on Third Avenue near downtown. Chung's became a favorite dining spot before attending the theatre or movies. Their chop suey was engulfed in a golden, gelatinous broth, thickened so all the ingredients were coated evenly with no surplus on the bottom of the plate. There was no sign of fat. Green tea, in a China teapot, was served in small heavy cups without handles.

In 1974, my mother and I traveled to Poland for a reunion with her only living sibling, her brother Jan. He met us at the Warsaw Airport with a car owned and driven by his son-in-law Jan Raplewicz. Our first stop was the Shanghai Restaurant near the city's center. We walked up one flight of stairs to a large room with Chinese lanterns hanging from the ceiling and tables covered with white tablecloths. The menu was printed in Polish so it took a bit of translation to find the Chop Suey listing. The entree was served in a round low soup bowl with a wide edge. Nearby the soy sauce was offered in a glass carafe. The ingredients were not too visible, buried in a golden broth, and yes, just a bit soupy. And round globules of fat clustered and shimmered on the surface of the liquid. The chef either overlooked or eliminated the final thickening procedure. With a smile, I wolfed down the meal before me.

My chop suey, made in a cast iron wok, stir fry style, often has green pea pods, fresh bean sprouts and fresh mushrooms added to the lean pork strips, onions, and celery. Now and then, due to some miscalculation in measuring the thickening agent, the broth is just a bit soupy.

The Creamery

"Refresh and cool off with Buttermilk," was the billboard message. My husband and I were touring southern Poland during July 1989, where I read this advice, translating it from the Polish for my spouse.

I recalled the creamery of my Hamtramck neighborhood. When we sat on the front porch of 3291 Trowbridge Street, the creamery buildings across the street filled the block from our street to Belmont Street, the next block south. The back building section, closest to our house, was one story. It was the horse barn. Each morning the horses from this barn pulled the milk delivery wagons as they clip clopped through the streets of our growing city. It was the fall of 1930 when we moved to this convenient location, but my mother freely expressed her opinion whenever the south wind put us downwind from the horse barn.

The rest of the creamery was a two-story yellow brick structure. The central section, with very tall garage type doors, opened to reveal the huge machines that washed racks of glass milk bottles, and other machines that held the bottles upright as the white liquid filled each container, then sent the bottle to the contraption that placed a round cardboard lid onto the top, sealing the vessel with printing on the surface indicating the kind of milk inside. What a fascinating process to watch for a 6-year old!

The front of the building faced Belmont Street. It had the offices of the owner-manager and his secretarial staff. When entering the front sales room, I saw the secretary at a machine that held a sheet of paper which moved up a notch as she pulled a lever to one side. Her fingers made a click, click noise while she tapped the keys, and a line of print appeared on the page. I was entranced!

My mission was to purchase buttermilk at the counter to the right. There were two spigots in the back wall, leading from somewhere in the creamery where other dairy products were made: butter, cottage cheese, and the bottled milk. One spigot had regular buttermilk and the other one had "special" with extra butter flecks enriching the flavor. They were both served ice cold right into your pitcher. A small pitcher cost 10 cents and a large pitcher cost 15 cents. A small square of thin wax paper was placed over the top for carrying back home. My mother had one white pitcher, considered small, with a blue flower on the front. I made many trips to the creamery on hot summer days for this delectable potion, which at our home accompanied Friday dinners of boiled potatoes and herring. This was a meatless staple for many years.

After seeing the typist, I tried to recreate this operation at home. Using a lidded metal tea container, I inserted a small sheet of paper creasing it so it looked like the one in the real typewriter, and tapped with my fingers on the table, simulating the actions of a real typist. It should not be surprising that I studied typing in high school and my first job after high school was as a typist. And I find a cold glass of buttermilk refreshing and cooling, like the one that came in a pitcher from the creamery on Belmont Street.

Recycling in Hamtramck and in Our Home

On many a Saturday, my father walked to the farmer's market at the corner of Holbrook and Conant Streets with a folded, leatherette shopping bag under his arm. He tossed heads of cabbage, bunches of carrots, eggs, fruits of the season, potatoes, and usually a live chicken or duck into this container. Very few paper bags were used either at the farmer's market or at other shops. Newspapers and cardboard boxes made good kindling in the kitchen stove or the basement coal furnace. Milk bottles and pop bottles were returned for a deposit and were reused by the creamery or pop bottling company. Sliced bread came wrapped in a heavily waxed paper which we were asked to bring to our home room in the parish church elementary school. Torn into smaller squares, we placed it under our feet and used it later to buff the linoleum under and at the side of our desk. The school janitor had a large building to keep swept, and washing the floors happened very infrequently. Glossy blue and yellow containers from Blue Valley Butter were collected in school to purchase sports equipment.

All the streets in Hamtramck had alleys accessible to garbage collectors, milk delivery wagons, coal trucks, and the junk collector. His horse-drawn wagon rumbled next to our house. He blew on a short tin horn to announce his presence. From the faucet at the side of our house he got water for his horse. The driver sat under a fixed cloth umbrella from where all business transactions took place. We called him Reksman (Ragsman). He was also known as "the shinny." He accepted any discard, for a few dollars he would haul away items like furniture, metal or appliances. We saved our old sheets and pillowcases because we needed them. They made great dust cloths. We recycled old towels into wash rags for the floors and walls by tearing them into smaller, more manageable pieces. Our floor mop was made of heavy, thick string. Sometimes we cut up worn-out long knit underwear with the buttons cut off to replace the string.

We shoveled ashes from the coal furnace into a round, galvanized tub next to the furnace and then emptied them next to the garage in the alley to be scooped up by the city cleanup trucks. Some houses in our neighborhood had another mound next to the ash pile. A steaming knoll of moist mash (from a basement still), often sat next to the wooden fence of the Siek residence. It's no wonder that I took to composting so easily after moving to my own home with a yard and garden. I layered grass clippings, leaves, fireplace wood ashes, vegetable and fruit peelings and reused this compost as mulch in my vegetable and flower garden.

We saved old clothes for another life in a rag rug. We removed and saved all the old buttons. We took the rags to a weaver in the area who made rag rugs that my mother used throughout the house. After they were on the floor, it was a source of entertainment to pick out a familiar piece of cloth that had been a dress, shirt, or blouse.

After I learned to weave, the rag rug technique became one of my favorites. I used it to make place mats and table runners, using some of my mother's dresses, housecoats, and nightgowns after she passed away.

Hamtramck Halloween

"Trick or Treat" was an American custom that I learned about as an elementary school student. October 31st was All-Souls Day and the eve of All-Saints Day, a holy day in the Catholic Church. So the good nuns and priests at Our Lady Queen of the Apostles Church emphasized the religious aspect of these two days. My friends, playmates and I, however, did not overlook the secular feature of Halloween.

When I was old enough to walk unsupervised to the commercial strip on Joseph Campau, I was determined to fashion a disguise to use on Halloween night. It was a homemade getup. Assembling a hobo outfit was easy—a blue kerchief over my head to hide my hair, smudges on my face with a charred cork, a faded flannel plaid shirt, and my father's work trousers. A broom handle with a cloth bag hanging from its end completed the masquerade.

The shops on Joseph Campau, the neighborhood confectioneries, the drug stores, and the mom and pop grocery stores were our targets. Many other costumed youngsters were on the street when a group of us started out.

P.C. Jeżewski Pharmacy was on the corner of Belmont and Joseph Campau Street. A clerk behind the counter tossed a package of Teaberry gum into our brown paper bags. What a disappointment we found when we opened the wrappers! The gum was stiff as cardboard and crumbled into bits as we put it in our mouths. P.C. Jeżewski had a good reputation as a pharmacist but not as a trick-or-treat source. We were tricked, not treated!

On one subsequent Halloween night, I wore a Dutch girl costume. It had long blond braids extending from a white Dutch cap and a small square print apron. I don't recall making a stop at the P.C. Jeżewski Pharmacy after my first experience.

School Days

I called it "kinnygarden" for many years. On my first day, my mother held my hand as I pulled to cross the street to the Dickinson School Kindergarten on Norwalk Street. The morning air was cool, so I was glad to get indoors to experience a whole new world.

I have no memory of the teacher, only what she imparted to the class members. We repeated nursery rhymes and played with toys. When I went home, I repeated *"Hey Diddle Diddle, the Cat and the Fiddle, the Cow Jumped Over the Moon."* In my mind's eye, I pictured a black and white cow leaping over that pale yellow disk in the night sky. *"Hickory Dickory, Dock, the Mouse Ran Up The Clock"* conjured up a vision of a tiny, gray, furry rodent scurrying up the front of a grandfather clock, then falling to the bottom to begin the process once more. Since my first language was Polish, which was always spoken at home, this was my first introduction to spoken English.

Make believe tea parties were fun in that classroom. Aluminum play cups, saucers and plates with a small tea pot sat on the black piano bench. I remember feeling very impatient as I waited my turn to use those popular items.

After moving to Trowbridge Street, we lived too far away to walk to the Dickinson School. I was disappointed and missed the stimulation and enrichment. My new parochial school had no kindergarten. Our new house came with a few toys, but they were not as stimulating as those I found in kindergarten.

In September 1931, I started first grade at Queen of Apostles School in Hamtramck. My mother fretted because of two major roads, Conant and Caniff Streets, that I would have to cross every day on the way to class. She accompanied me the first day, and we walked the two and a half blocks through two traffic lights. Crossing guards were stationed at each corner. My mother cautioned me about being watchful of the traffic and remembering to always look both ways at intersections.

The first grade classrooms were on the ground floor of the red brick school building, just inside the double doors that opened onto the shaded playground. This was the "little playground" for the first three grades of students. Mature catalpa trees throughout this area provided a cool play area for our "pauza" or recess each day. Skipping rope, playing "London Bridges" and other circle games became favorites.

Our teachers were nuns of the religious order of St. Felix, or "Felicians." Their habits were dark brown wool and reached all the way to the floor. Black veils covered their heads and hung to their hips. Their foreheads and sides of their faces and neck were enclosed in stiffly starched white cloths. Once in a while a wisp of hair worked its way out from under that stiff cloth. How we snickered upon discovering the secret of a sister's hair color.

The Felician order was founded in Poland and brought to the U.S. to teach the children of the immigrants who settled in large enough numbers to warrant having their own parishes and schools.

I looked forward to school, eagerly anticipating the acquisition of new information within the structure and scheduled times for each subject.

My first grade teacher was Sister Maurycja. She was past middle aged, experienced and competent. Early in the month I learned what happened when I would not abide by the teacher's order to keep silent during class. Sister called me to the front of the room and told me to hold out my right hand. She delivered several strikes with a wooden twelve-inch ruler to my upturned palm. I winced, feeling my skin smart, sting and turn a hot red. I kept my hand closed and hidden all the time after coming home, not daring to reveal the source of my pain. I would have received an additional smarting to reinforce the teacher's directive of no talking in class.

I recall learning to read and write in Polish, as well as English. Religion was taught in the Polish language and the hymns and prayers in church were also in Polish. Students whose parents were second generation Poles had a more difficult time mastering the 32-letter Polish alphabet and preponderance of consonants in the words. The first reader in Polish had depictions of the nose, the ear, the eye, a cap, a hand and other familiar objects that were familiar to the 6-year-old first graders.

In the 2nd grade Sister Kajetana, who was a tall, lean, serious nun, expanded on arithmetic and simple sentence structure. Her name suited her: it is related to a Polish word, kajdany, meaning shackles.

My parents took a keen interest in how I applied myself to my homework. In fact, they both stood over me as I sat at the kitchen table painstakingly forming letters across the page of a writing tablet. Often I would feign getting overcome with drowsiness so that I could be excused from further writing.

Sister Idalia, my 5th grade teacher, was a young, spirited, vivacious nun with dancing brown eyes and an infectious smile that won our devotion and attention. It was a pleasure to follow her guidance.

Each school day began at 7:30 a.m. in the home room where we gathered to march two by two to the church, which was on the first floor of the same building. Students of grades 5th through 8th stood in the choir loft singing appropriate songs during the mass. Our teachers accompanied us and provided ongoing monitoring, which sometimes required the removal of a student who misbehaved or did not conform to the expected behavior.

Expected behavior in the classroom included standing whenever the principal or a priest entered the room. The guest's greeting was "Blessed be Jesus Christ." In unison the class members replied, "Forever and ever, amen," in Polish.

Preparation for receiving the Sacrament of the Holy Eucharist and the Sacrament of Penance (Reconciliation) started in the second grade and was finalized in May. In the third grade, our daily routine changed once a month, on the first Friday of the month. After confession on Thursday afternoon, we had a clean slate to receive Holy Communion the following morning. We must, however, fast from midnight the previous evening. That meant nothing to eat or drink. So we ate our breakfast in the classroom after this morning mass. Because it was Friday, a day of abstinence from meat, my sandwich was always Philadelphia Cream Cheese between two slices of Silvercup white bread. A half pint of coffee lightened with Pet Milk and sweetened with sugar in a glass jar was my drink. I placed the jar on the steam radiator while the class was in church, so the liquid was still lukewarm when we returned for our meal.

The desks we occupied had a shelf under the top for storing books, tablets and pencil boxes. Many wads of gum were also affixed to the underside for later use, but often hardened there. On the right upper corner of the top was a round hole, an inkwell, that held a bottle of ink that was periodically refilled from a quart-sized container. The responsibility was assigned to an agile and well-coordinated member of the class. Hedy Jurewicz was chosen for this task.

When we were considered advanced enough to write with ink, a pen holder and metal nib with an ink blotter had to be purchased. Some writing tablets had pages with very fibrous paper, so an inked letter often spread. Writing with ink demanded considerable care as a round inky blob could easily drip down the nib and obliterate most of a word if the pen carried too much ink.

We looked forward to Wednesday afternoons when movies were shown in the old parish hall. The seats were long hard wooden benches. The projector sat on a table in the back. All the windows had covers of one-piece wooden frames with cardboard centers. Clamped at the sides of each window, they never completely shut out the outside light. I remember eating a pomegranate in the dark during one of the many silent features that we watched during most of grade school.

We saw mainly cowboy movies with a lot of white horses and white or black cowboy hats so we could distinguish the good guys from the bad. Laurel and Hardy features were very popular during these years as well as Buster Keaton and W.C. Fields. When talkies became available, newsreels were added. The projector was hand threaded and when one reel was finished, the lights went on while the second reel was added.

These movie sessions were always noisy and stifling hot, even in the winter months, but were a way to escape the classroom routine. The assistant pastor, a younger priest assigned to the parish, was in charge of the movies. All eight grades marched two by two to the Conant Theater to see three movies when they were featured there: *the Song of Bernadette*, *The King of Kings*, and *The Seal of the Confession*. The last movie was a silent one.

There was another diversion in the classroom involving direct application of foot power. Each student brought a waxed wrapper from a loaf of bread. It was placed on the floor next to his or her desk and rubbed back and forth with each foot until the scuffed linoleum gleamed with a high shine. The school custodian had responsibilities other than keeping the classroom floors waxed, but the good sisters found their own way of improving the environment.

One of the nuns chose to improve our physical condition with some exercises. She had the upper half of the windows lowered for this activity. To do this required a long rod with a knob on the end that fit into a metal indentation at the top of the window. It was the only way to lower or raise those high windows. We all stood in the aisle imitating her movements which involved arm raises and squats in place. I believe it was a quick way to air the room and gave us another break from the routine.

In September 1937, I faced being in one of the two big sections of the seventh grade. Sister Clotilda had a reputation of using severe disciplinary measures. Alas, my best friend, Jane Ciwinska, and my two other close friends, Dolores Wójcik and Hedwig Jurewicz, and I found ourselves assigned to Sister Clotilda's home room. Hers was a figure of massive proportions. She was about as tall as she was wide. A booming voice sputtered from a mouth set in round puffy cheeks. Wisps of gray hair worked their way out onto the sides of her forehead from behind the white starched wimple. In class, her waddling gait and overwhelming presence, spread all over the room: across the front, up and down the aisles, and along the back. As I remember, every student in her home room had his or her 15 minutes of shame and tears.

Jane Ciwinska was a gifted and brilliant student, memorizing verbatim all assignments. When called to recite, she stood next to her desk, and as she spoke, her short figure rocked back and forth in place. Well, Sister Clotilda stopped her recitation and ordered her to stand still and stop rocking. Jane could not. Flustered and embarrassed, she dissolved into tears and sobbing.

Another disciplinary incident involved Henry Kwiatkowski. Small for his age, he was recognized for blushing for no reason, his face a florid red, his underdeveloped frame shrinking like a cowering puppy. Some misbehavior on his part drove Sister Clotilda into a rage. She rushed down the aisle, her long heavy rosary beads rattling against the sides of the desks, her arms pumping. She lifted Henry bodily off his seat and carried him to the back of the room where black iron coat hooks were fastened to the wall. Raising him, she caught the collar of his coat jacket on the prong, letting him dangle as the class members stared in horror. He turned all shades of scarlet, finally breaking down, crying from humiliation and shame.

One day, Sister Clotilda chose me for an important errand. I felt privileged to be allowed to leave the school building on this personal mission. Sister gave me some cash and asked that I purchase a jar of Arid Deodorant from Cunningham's Drug Store, which was ten blocks away, at the corner of Joseph Campau and Caniff Streets. I returned to the classroom from this solitary journey, wondering how a semi-cloistered nun learned about worldly items like underarm deodorant. Sister Clotilda checked the jar, then decided she wanted the large size, sending me back to get the order right. After walking a total of forty blocks, I concluded that being the teacher's pet had its drawbacks.

Another event took place when Sister Clotilda caught me talking during class. As punishment, she ordered me to lay face down on the front seat of the first row of school desks. This was a humiliation I would not be subjected to. Rigidly, I stood next to this seat, dissolving into tears, adamantly determined I would never place my body on that wooden slat. I don't recall how long this standoff lasted. Eventually, Sister relented, satisfied that I was adequately contrite and sufficiently remorseful.

Sister Clotilda had one socially redeeming quality. She was an avid reader of modern literature. In 1937, *Gone With The Wind* was a best seller, but Roman Catholics needed permission from their confessor in order to read it. Father Wenanty Szymanski, assistant at our parish church, gave his okay for Sister Clotilda to read this novel. It sat on her desk many a day as I wondered about what were the forbidden passages between the hard covers.

Rev. Szymanski gave us a skewed spelling lesson one morning. We were to write down a four-letter word for what is found on the bottom of a bird cage. Did we dare to put on paper what was in our mind, that slang street word? The slips of paper were collected. Thankfully, we did not have to sign our names to this incriminating information. Not one 7th grader knew GRIT.

We don't know if Sister Clotilda's disciplinary methods changed during her long teaching career, but those she used when I was in her seventh grade home room were unforgettable.

My Friend Jane Ciwinska

In the first grade Jane Ciwinska and I became friends, our friendship solidified when we found we were wearing identical spring coats with matching tams to Sunday Mass. The fabric was a mustard colored wool. An attached cape collar was a singular feature. How we giggled in delight!

It seems I spent more play time at her house than she did at mine. Her sister Josephine, had graduated high school and had a job as a window display arranger for one of the five and dime stores on Joseph Campau. Jane's mother, a ruddy faced short woman, was a stay at home mom, busy with house chores when we played inside their single, small frame house.

Jane was quite a story teller. We were both getting instructions in religion, preparing for first Holy Communion. Jane depicted what hell would be like: the poor souls damned to the eternal fiery depths would see a grandfather clock with a swinging pendulum sounding the words, "ZAWSZE-NIGDY" (always-never), attesting to the perpetual nature of the sentence deserved for dying unrepentant.

Jane and I were still having conversations in Polish, our first language. She told the above tale in Polish. She was a bouncy youngster, with short brown hair and brown eyes, very natural and down to earth. We accepted each other, delving into activities typical of our age group.

When we reached puberty, Jane announced that her mother had a "facts of life" discussion, revealing "all about where babies come from." I was envious and desperately wanted to initiate such a dialogue with my mother. I already had some facts about the process, but how would my mother explain everything? Alas, there was a negativity expressed about pregnancy and sex which I could not permeate at the time.

Jane was adventurous, willing to experience the attractions outside our immediate neighborhood. We attended movies on Saturday or Sunday, hiked to and from Belle Isle Park and biked across the Ambassador bridge to Windsor, Canada and to landmarks in the next county. We toured the Shrine of the Little Flower and Cranbrook. At the Cinema theatre in downtown Detroit, we saw a memorable French movie, *The Ballerina.*

JANE, DOLORES, AND CHARLOTTE AT PALMER PARK

When Jane's sister, Josephine, announced she was getting married, I found it difficult to accept the wedding plan. It took place in Bowling Green, Kentucky, the quickie nuptial city used by couples in a hurry or those not wanting or not able to spend the money for a traditional feast. I missed seeing her as a bride dressed in white gown and veil—a fantasy I had when I first heard about the marriage.

The Ciwinski family moved to Ryan Street in Detroit, several miles north of their Belmont Street location, sometime during our high school years. I visited their new house, built bit by bit as money allowed. The interior was still unfinished, but I remember the kitchen had a counter with a corner cupboard that revolved using the space efficiently. The rooms had wooden partitions and slats but nothing else. Jane was perfectly okay with the unfinished condition of her living quarters. She was carrying on with her activities seemingly oblivious of the rooms "in progress" around her. We drifted apart as our lives moved to different paths.

A number years later, I recognized her sister Josephine walking on Woodward Avenue. We discussed Jane's marriage to Raymond Stasiuk, a classmate from Queen of Apostles grade school, and their move to a farm near Plattsburg, New York. They had two sons. Before marrying she was a lab technician at the Riley Stoker Company where my father worked. I wonder if she knew him. About 1997 or 1998, I sent her some of my notes on our walks to Belle Isle Park, but did not receive a reply.

Tau Beta Camp

"Can I Mom? It costs only $4 a week, so that is $8 for the two weeks. Eleanor and Dolores are going," I pleaded. Mom looked interested, so I obtained an application and the list of recommended articles that campers were to bring.

It was 1937. I was going to be 12 years old. I was anxious to experience what I heard from Dolores Wójcik about the wonders and adventures that awaited us at summer camp.

The camp was sponsored by the Tau Beta Community House, a settlement house (community center) established for this community of immigrants and their families for the purpose of aiding in acculturation. The Tau Beta Sorority, a Junior League-type of organization, sponsored and financially subsidized this project. There were scholarships available for anyone not able to pay the full tuition. Eleanor's (Jasinski) mother, now a single parent with seven children, could not afford the $4 per week fee. It was reduced to $2 a week, and Eleanor would work extra in the camp kitchen preparing meals.

So in addition to the classes that I enrolled in, which were knitting, cooking, sewing, and later Girl Scouts, now the Tau Beta Community House offered summer camp at an affordable cost.

Campers brought bed linens for a single cot, a blanket, towels, soap, toothpaste, toothbrush, and clothing for outdoors and for swimming. What fun it was gathering up the items and checking them against the master list! Mom expressed some separation anxiety about my venture into the unknown, but my enthusiasm was unbounded. I was going!

A full-sized Greyhound bus, with engine humming, was parked in front of the community house on Henley Street across from the Hamtramck City Library. We loaded our belongings and scrambled up into the comfortable ample seats that gave us a towering view outside the windows.

Columbiaville was about 60 miles northeast of Detroit. We rode through Mt. Clemens, a resort city known for its spas that had sulfur springs and the accompanying aroma of rotten eggs. We all held our noses remarking, "Phew, this must be Mt. Clemens."

Then the route took us through towns I had never been to before. Oxford, Michigan, made me wonder if they manufactured shoes there. Metamora was a strange sounding name to my ears. Dolores recognized it as the site of the Girl Scout camp that she had attended the previous year.

Finally we arrived at the campgrounds. Spacious rolling hills dotted with buildings and beyond a small lake with a short wooden dock and floating deck greeted us. The main lodge was where meals were served and indoor activities took place. Another building, two stories tall, was the residence of the administrators and the office of the camp nurse.

Small wooden cabins lined one side of the lake. There were five cabins, each holding twelve campers and one counselor. They were painted white with green shutters that folded down to cover the screen-only windows. For the summer, each shutter was propped up to allow air and light. Six cots sat in the large room to the left of the counselor's cubicle, and six more sat in the room to the right. The walls consisted of unfinished two-by-fours and unpainted wood boards. The floor was also natural wood. Our narrow metal cots had a rather thin mattress that worked well for our young frames.

The first activity after choosing our cot location and making up the bed was a get-acquainted circle game led by the camp director. She was not much bigger or taller than we were, was energetic and definitely in control of this exuberant group. She told us that she just returned from China where she was a teacher. Already our horizons were widening as we listened to her experiences in a country half way around the world.

Each day the camp director posted a schedule that listed the assignments for chores and the times of activities, assemblies and evening programs. We searched for our names to see what maintenance duty awaited. The duties were rotated. Most responsibilities revolved around mealtime—setting the table, serving the food, clearing the table or sweeping the floor. There were also the responsibilities of grounds clean up, and last and most dreaded of all, latrine duty.

Of course, latrine duty was not over until the lucky camper emptied a bag of lime into the circular openings inside the outhouse and swept all the wooden surfaces with a broom dipped in a solution of Lysol cleaner and water in a bucket. The smell was only briefly camouflaged by the carbolic acid odor. It was a duty that brought groans of repulsion.

I eagerly participated in canoeing, archery, and swimming. Miss French, a plump nurse, was our waterfront instructor and helped me feel comfortable floating, then doing the dog paddle, and finally the crawl stroke.

The other counselors were mainly school teachers with the summer off who wanted to earn additional income from this kind of job. We liked our cabin counselor because she had stories to read to us after the bugle sounded taps and bed time arrived. But this counselor did not escape our caper of short-sheeting her bed and sewing her panty legs together!

Our cabin was for sleeping only. Showers and brushing teeth took place in a separate building a short distance away and near the outdoor toilets. This was my first experience using a shower. Adaptation was immediate. Getting to the main lodge for meals was no problem as our ears and stomachs were alert to the loud dinner bell that rang to summon us to eat and to the other scheduled events.

Special events included hikes to town, scavenger hunts and special theme parties in the big lodge.

In the small town of Columbiaville, the ice cream parlor was a regular stop. The town had an abandoned mansion that was explored by us on one hike into town. What a sight! There were several bathrooms with very elaborate wash basins. They were probably marble in different colors. We admired the elaborate gold hardware. There was a lot of gingerbread woodwork on the three-sided porch and parquet wood floors in the rooms inside. A curved staircase reached to the second floor. I learned many years later that this gem was restored to become a trendy restaurant.

The scavenger hunts were both educational and very foreign to me. A knowledge of trees and leaf characteristics was necessary in order to collect a number of items on the list. I could identify a weeping willow easily but the different types of oaks, hardwoods, and pines were beyond my expertise at that age.

A masquerade was loads of fun as we had to be very creative and imaginative fashioning costumes from items available. First prize went to Lorraine Ura who smeared wet, greenish gray clay on her face to become a scary and believable witch. Her hat was fashioned from black cardboard and her hair was strands of dry grass bunched up and hanging to her shoulders. It was a sight I've never forgotten.

The assistant camp director, Miss Smith, conducted the daily general assembly right after we completed our duties each morning. We sat on long benches for the quasi-prayer inspirational sermon she directed at all of us, but we knew it was meant to curb some of the mischief makers in the camp. Then she led us in singing folk songs from various countries. I fondly remember learning *Marianina, Kookaburra, From Lucern to Weggis Fair, Frere Jacques, John Jacob Jingle Heimer Schmidt,* and many American favorites like *Old MacDonald Had a Farm, On Moonlight Bay, Clementine, On Top of Old Smokey, Row Row Row Your Boat, Ash Grove, Camptown Races, Swanee River, The Bear Climbs Over the Mountain, I See the Moon the Moon Sees Me,* and others.

Miss Smith was a career woman, an unmarried female about 40 years old. Slender, flat chested, with a deep voice and usually wearing a skirt and blouse, her most distinguishing feature was the fuzzy short pale brown hair on her upper lip. She made no effort to bleach it, so it was a point of focus for us as she conducted us through the lines of the new songs we learned.

During the second week of camp, we were to learn something else. Some of the Tau Beta Sorority members were scheduled to visit. Several long, sleek, shiny, luxury cars purred into the campground. The young women who emerged from these Detroit-made chariots were debutante daughters of wealthy automaker families. We took in their swishy hairdos, with streaks of platinum, cascading to their shoulders. With cashmere cardigans caped around their slender arms and clean saddle oxfords on their feet, they greeted us with smiles of perfect teeth.

Miss Halverson, director of the community house, accompanied them. She was a tall imposing woman who carried her authority with each deliberate step. Graying hair and a dour face added to her image as a person having an important administrative position.

We gathered around Miss Halverson as she sobered us with information that our $4 per week fee did not cover the real cost of operating the camp. Well! That bit of reality set me back on my heels. Until then I did not know I was underprivileged. I still wonder if we needed to be told this rather earthshaking bit of information. Okay, so these sorority sisters put on moneymaking projects to subsidize our fun.

Rev. Arthur Krawczak was a newly ordained priest and assigned to attend to our spiritual needs. On Sunday morning he offered a mass on a portable altar set up in the dining room. He probably traveled to this camp from Detroit. The non-Catholic campers had a service conducted by Miss Smith.

The resident dietician was a middle-aged woman of ample proportions. Her strong accent sounded German but was really Swiss. Besides giving us a varied diet of good food, she had a much more memorable talent. She could yodel, and we would coax her into demonstrating her talent on special occasions.

The resident maintenance man was usually dressed in blue coveralls and was also middle-aged. We immediately put one and one together to fantasize a romance between him and the dietician. After all, we saw them talking and laughing with each other.

The crowning experience during the two-week stay at camp was the "overnight." A small, selected group of campers would leave the cabins with bedrolls to sleep under the stars, out in the open, directly on the ground. I signed up for this trip along with Dolores Wójcik and Eleanor Jasinski.

How exiting it was! The two counselors, Miss French and our own cabin counselor began preparations by teaching us how to form a bedroll using our sheets and blankets. I never forgot this process. We loaded a large canvas tarpaulin, several boxes holding breakfast items, outdoor cooking utensils, and a shovel onto the back of a truck with our bedrolls.

The pickup truck bumped along the gravel back roads to an isolated farmer's field. As the sun sank in the west, behind a stand of oaks edging our campground, we arranged our sleeping gear on top of the tarpaulin spread out on the ground near a split rail fence. It was so quiet, we noted the constellations we could identify: the Milky Way, the Big Dipper, the Little Dipper, and the North Star. Millions of points of light twinkled above us as we lay on our backs. Inky blue depth surrounded the moon that rose above the adjacent cornfield. We all fell asleep under this great night sky.

When daylight came, I was aware of a mooing sound behind my head. Turning around I noticed a cow poking its black and white head through the split rail fence. The sky was now cloud covered and a fine drizzle settled on our faces and camping gear.

We scrapped our plans for breakfast in the rough and returned to the main lodge to prepare oatmeal. I wrote a letter to our parish assistant priest, Rev. Edmund Wolschon, describing this overnight excursion. He commented on my narration, giving me the first encouragement to write.

When I returned home, our kitchen looked so small. My mother had heard a lot about the kind of food I had hoped to get, especially at breakfast, now that I was home.

The last season of camp for us was when we were 14 years old, the cut-off age for Tau Beta Camp. That year, we convinced Irene Skoney to join us. Our appetites as teenagers seemed insatiable. I especially recall breakfasts. As soon as metal pitchers of hot cocoa were set on the tables, we passed them around and returned them to the kitchen for refilling as many times as needed to satisfy us. We disposed of platters of buttered toast. Even if the weekly charge was doubled, it would not have covered the food costs for the growing bunch that summer. When I returned home after that camp session, I reached the weight close to my adult weight. We all filled out during that last summer at camp.

While I was in college, I again spent three summers at camp. I worked as a counselor with several school teachers and nurses who chose to devote their vacations imbuing youngsters with the love of the outdoors. This was at the St. Vincent's Villa Campground on a private lake near Brighton, Michigan. My responsibility was the waterfront, which required a Red Cross Life Saver's certificate. I also coached archery and canoeing, led hikes, and supervised campfires.

Nom de Plume

The *Sunday Detroit News* devoted an entire page geared to young people and their interests. Through the newspaper a youngster could obtain a pen pal with the use of a nom de plume, a pen name. What fun to choose a pseudonym! I decided it should have alliteration. "Silver Sands" had the sound I wanted. I only remember the name I chose, not anything else that followed.

I do remember a contest asking how many words can be formed from given words. For this I purchased a 25-cent dictionary as a reference. This contest absorbed me totally for many hours as I flipped through the pages of the dictionary, looking for words of two, three, or four letters that could be formed from the letters given in the words in the newspaper. I waited patiently for the "gift" promised for what I believed was a formidable list. But what I received in the mail, was a form requesting a dozen containers of an ointment that I was expected to sell from door to door. My "gift" would be the profit from the sale of the tins of salve. Needless to say I was disappointed and did not enter any more contests. However, this contest sparked a lifelong interest in words and language. I like to tackle most crossword puzzles in the local newspaper although it takes two of us to complete some of them. Husband Ed has the better ability with many clues. I often use the Crossword Puzzle Dictionary as an aid.

Buying a Piano and Piano Lessons

Dad and I took the Baker streetcar to downtown Detroit to search out the big bargain advertised in the paper. A $25 used piano. We left after he got home from work, easily locating the address. It was about 1936, I was 11 years old, and I was determined to learn to play the piano.

The $25 piano was a wreck! It was weather beaten to a stark gray color without any kind of finish on the wood. The keys were yellowed and a number of them were without the ivory top. Clearly this was a bait and switch operation!

Despite our initial disappointment, Dad and I found another affordable piano. It was quite old, the dark varnished panels were crackled from age, but it came with a bench and the legs of the bench had metal claws over a glass ball at the ends. It came at a much higher price, $100 plus a delivery charge. For a number of years it stood in the dining room. A large wood framed mirror hung above it on the inside wall. Later, when we moved to the first floor flat in the same house, the piano stood in the front vestibule. The light was very poor in that entryway and the piano did not get used very much after I began full time employment.

My classmate, Alice Jara, had a much older sister who gave piano lessons in Hamtramck. Her name was Mrs. Thaddeus Majchrowicz. We knew her as Sophie. She was married to a successful attorney who became a judge in Hamtramck and later served as a representative in the U.S. Congress. The family lived in a tastefully furnished brick house on Gallagher Street. Her piano was a grand piano that stood in their spacious living room.

I walked to the lessons after school. After all the basics, I moved to classical music by Liszt, Strauss and Beethoven.

This genteel, refined woman easily became a role model. Always elegantly dressed in classic type outfits, her small sturdy hands usually exhibited a fresh manicure on her short nails. She made it clear that long fingernails were not conducive to skilled piano technique. I remember her short dark hair and olive complexion and her gold-rimmed glasses.

She was an accomplished pianist. Her idol was Ignacy Paderewski, the Polish pianist, composer, and later a diplomat. She recalled his flawless technique—fingers moving across the keys like hammers, with the resulting sounds like raindrops, each note clear, distinctive, and separate.

Lessons always included an assignment from Kohler or Czerny piano exercises and sheet music. The books for the exercises were sold only in a downtown Detroit music store, Grinell's, on Woodward Avenue. I was allowed to travel by streetcar to purchase these items, which cost about 75 cents or $1. There was a bonus to be gained during these trips. Grinell's sold records, too. I could sample the most popular music of the day in small booths before deciding to purchase any. These booths were on the second floor of the shop and were very popular with teenagers who had little cash but a lot of interest in the latest hits. I believe there was a time limit as to how long a person could use a booth. I did get to use this method of hearing some favorite musical numbers that I could not afford to buy.

I practiced piano after school, usually when my parents could hear me. My dad listened carefully and commented that I made mistakes that he heard even with his untrained ear. After about five years of lessons, my father walked to a lesson with me to ascertain my potential as a musician. Clearly, I was not concert material. I don't know exactly what their conversation disclosed, but I did ask for the opportunity to study modern music, the Hit Parade type songs that we all were singing.

We found another piano teacher. She came to the house and introduced me to current tunes like *Elmer's Tune, Besame Mucho, I'm Dreaming of a White Christmas*, among others. Now I could play for my teenage friends who gathered around the piano to sing along.

I don't remember this teacher's name, but I do remember her appearance. Always a bit flushed and perspiring, with her slip hanging below the hem of her flowered dress, her plump figure rocked to the beat of the popular music that I played. She was beyond middle age so it was not too surprising when she announced that she was retiring after about a year of lessons.

My final lessons were with a male teacher. My father located him somewhere in the city, probably in one of the numerous corner bars in our neighborhood. This man was a defrocked priest, still wearing black suits. To make a living now he was a choir director in the local Polish National Church and also earned extra money teaching piano. Three fingers were missing from his left hand, the result, no doubt, of his attempt to work a job for which he had no training. I was a robust 16-year-old by this time. During the second or third lesson, as he sat next to me on the piano bench, his arms encircled me in a hug and he planted a kiss on my cheek in full view of my father who was sitting in the next room.

After this session, I was strongly reprimanded for allowing such liberties to be taken! I was relieved that no more lessons took place after that.

Learning to play piano had many long-term benefits. I learned to read music, grew to appreciate classical music and became familiar with tunes from operas and operettas that were popular at that time. When I was working at the Polish Aid Society (settlement house), I accompanied the ballet and tap dancing class taught by Miss Betty (Pendracki-Bandyk). This collaboration also led to a lifelong friendship. My playing was often just a bit incorrect, as my right hand struggled to find all the right notes while my left hand never missed the beat, and the rhythm flowed with the movement of the dancers.

Horseradish and Kiełbasa

My father made horseradish to accompany the Christmas and Easter ham. He chose several thick roots sold at Miller's grocery store. They were about as big around as a child's wrist, covered with a brown rind that my father carefully scraped off with a sharp knife. All the crevices and bumps were cleaned leaving a creamy colored woody tuber. My father carried a white enamel pan to the landing, just inside the door to the small upstairs porch. He sat down on one of the steps leading to the attic. The door was pulled open a crack as my father began to use the hand grater inside the pan which he held on his lap. The strong vapors from the freshly grated horseradish permeated the entire stairwell even with the door open to the cold air. All the freshly grated mass was spooned into a glass quart canning jar. Often he filled another half jar. One whiff of this homemade condiment drew tears and cleared the sinuses. It was a very satisfactory ritual I observed for many years at home. At Easter time we used the horseradish when we ate the colored hard-boiled Easter eggs, again wincing as the sharp aroma penetrated our nostrils. Sometimes my mother grated cooked beets to add to some of the horseradish changing its color to a deep red and making it less potent.

Homemade kiełbasa was made indoors, again using the white enamel pan. The meat was pork. A Boston Butt had just enough fat and a minimum of bone. On a wooden cutting board, my father sliced the meat, then cut it into tiny dice, all by hand. He continued to finely mince several cloves of garlic. This he added to the mound of freshly cut up pork. Marjoram, salt and pepper and a generous splash of warm water was added and all the ingredients thoroughly mixed using both hands. A bit of the mixture was tasted and the spices corrected. According to my mother, more salt was needed. The sausage meat then "rested" for a spell while the casings, packed in salt, were soaked in water and examined for tears by blowing air through them. The meat was hand packed through a funnel-like contraption, into the hog casing. A sturdy butcher string held the two ends of the ring of kiełbasa. The aroma of marjoram and garlic filled the house.

Girls Catholic Central High School—1939-1943

(Just One More)

On a muggy, late August day in 1939, my mother, my little brother age 7, and I rode the Woodward streetcar to 60 Parsons Street, near downtown Detroit to enroll me in Girls Catholic Central High School.

We climbed the central staircase leading to the entrance and located the shaded front office of the principal, a nun clothed in the deep blue habit of the order of IHMs (Immaculate Heart of Mary). In a steady calm voice, Sister Juliana informed us that enrollment was closed, the freshman class filled to capacity.

What a disappointment! It was my choice to attend this all girls school, with its reputation of high scholastic standards. The daughter of our former tenant, Eleanor Wesołowski graduated from the school, and now friend and neighbor, Eleanor Jelonek was a sophomore there. My mother sensed my deep dejection and in her broken English pleaded, "Just one more, sister, please."

Here was this plainly dressed mother, clearly foreign born, wanting to fulfill her daughter's dream of attending this tony institution.

The principal relented, agreeing to allow, "just one more" student into the freshman class of 120. The next step was to be fitted for a navy blue uniform at a company located on Woodward Avenue not too far from the school.

My mother and I met another classmate-to-be, Jane Conley, and her mother at the "measuring." Mrs. Conley was well corseted, smartly attired, in dramatic contrast to my mother in her ample, loose fitting, cotton house dress.

The eighth grade graduates of Our Lady Queen of Apostles parochial school went to several local high schools. Most entered Copernicus Junior High, then Hamtramck Senior High School. St. Ladislaus, the local Catholic High School acquired some Q. of A. students. Raymond Skoney enrolled at Boys Catholic Central as a prelude to entering priesthood. My best friend, Jane Ciwinska, was the recipient of the Medal of the American Legion, earning her admission to Cass Technical High School in Detroit. Irene

Skoney, sister of Raymond, Laura Lalewicz and I were the three young women "signed up" for Girls Catholic Central High School.

Just getting to the school by one bus and one streetcar opened up a whole new world for me. Irene Skoney walked the 11 blocks from Sobieski to Trowbridge Streets before we both hiked back one block to the corner of Conant and Caniff Avenues. At the Caniff bus stop, we often met Laura Lalewicz, Eleanor Wietnik, Eleanor Jelonek and Henrietta Wykowski. Laura's father was a successful contractor. Eleanor Wietnik's father owned a casket factory. Eleanor Jelonek's parents ran our neighborhood "beer garden" and Henrietta Wykowski's mother owned the corner beauty salon. Irene Skoney's father was a skilled tool and die designer in his brother-in-law's shop.

So I was glad we wore uniforms to classes and that scholastic achievement was stressed in school. The affluence of many students attending this school was downplayed and we all had to concentrate on "book work." The high school was accredited by the North Central Association and the University of Michigan, attesting to its high standards.

Again, my horizons expanded as I rubbed elbows with young women from many neighborhoods and many parishes in and around the city of Detroit.

I loved everything about the school. The gray stone, ivy-covered building was three stories high. A dozen steps lead to the heavily carved oak doors under a central arched entry way. There were classrooms on each floor and an auditorium with a stage and a balcony. At each end there were stairways leading to the upper floors and to the basement cafeteria. Students' footsteps resounded over the waxed light oak floors and the floor boards creaked in the rush to get from one classroom to the other. Rosalia Mangiapane swung a hand-held, oversized brass school bell indicating it was time to change classes. She stood on the bottom step on the stairway off the central foyer, the sound reaching all the levels. Rosalia held this "job" all four years.

We ate lunch in the cafeteria where a hot dish cost 25 cents, dessert extra. My weekly allowance of $1.25 covered this adequately. I received an additional 14 cents per day for round trip bus fare: 6 cents plus 1 cent for a transfer each way.

Our teachers, all nuns, lived in the convent, a free standing one-story stone structure on the lot west of the school. The "cells" were off limits to all, but a visitor's room was located near the front entrance where a student was permitted to arrange a one-to-one conference with a teacher. I heard that our favorite nun, Sister Marie Aimee loved to receive company and enjoyed being remembered at Christmas time, relishing one gift, a bottle of wine, that she vowed would be shared. The nuns wore habits of a medium blue serge, floor length with black veils, and narrow starched white bands covering their foreheads and necks. They were strict teachers, but did not use corporal punishment in any form. It was a change I welcomed, feeling I reached a certain level of maturity now.

Most of the students arrived each morning on school buses. Some parishes had a sizeable number of young women attending this centrally located institution, warranting their own transportation. Others, from the east, north, and northeast areas of Detroit used the public buses and streetcars along with other students attending schools along the route. I hoped to catch the bus with "the green hornet"—a Boys Catholic Central High student wearing the school's green jacket with a sport letter on the sleeve. Standing in the aisle I "took in" his rosy cheeks and handsome face without his being aware of my interest in him.

I learned of the existence of many other Catholic churches: St. Cecilia, St. Dominic, Visitation, Gesu, St. Benedict, Precious blood. All had large congregations funneling students to this centrally located school. And students had given first names that began with letters near the end of the alphabet: Rosalia, Suzanne, Shirley, Vivian, Yvonne, Wanda, Zelda.

As in elementary school, Religion was a required class. Sister Norine, early in the first semester asked who could recite the Credo. I raised my hand qualifying my ability: I could, knew it in Polish. She listened to it apparently satisfied. At the end of the first card marking, Sister Norine asked if anyone was dissatisfied with the grade they received. I stood up, believing my knowledge of the subject matter and class participation deserved an A. I became an honor roll student, and remained on the honor roll all four years of high school.

Girls Catholic Central High School stressed college preparatory courses. Latin was basic to this curriculum and gave us an introduction to the classics. I know it gave me a deeper appreciation of the English language, finding many of the roots of English words coming from this ancient language. I also discovered the rhythms in poems we read in English classes. Much to my surprise, the most relevant and useful class for me was physics, as it dealt with matter familiar to me in every day life: water, air, electricity, etc.

The high school had no gym or physical education requirement, but a class in fencing was offered after school hours. I was in awe of this skill, but the family budget would not allow this "frill."

Attending an all-school winter tobogganing trip to River Rouge Park was not a frill, but did require the purchase of the proper gear. My father and I traveled to a downtown Detroit department store where I chose a burgundy wool "snow suit." It consisted of a zippered reversible sheepskin jacket and heavy flannel lined pants with knit cuffs. I don't remember much of the excursion, but the snowsuit had a second life when the pants were cut down into knicker length, very fashionable for cross country skiing. The jacket was sent to a cousin in Poland who had a teen-aged daughter.

There were other enticements that attracted us and were within walking distance of the school. Just south of Vernor Street we located a Sanders Bakery and Ice Cream Parlor. Their hot fudge sundaes were legendary and worth the distance.

The Copper Kettle Restaurant was housed in the tall red brick League of Catholic Women building at the corner of Parsons Street and Cass Avenue. Their specialty was Chicken Pot Pie. The upperclass students of the high school frequently sneaked out to buy their lunch there instead of in the basement cafeteria. It was a luxury, not affordable, given my allowance. After I was gainfully employed, I made occasional trips to the League and found the Chicken Pot Pie still a tasty menu item.

Socially, I still kept in touch with my best friend from grade school, Jane Ciwinska, and was active in the parish youth group with Hedy, Eleanor, Dolores, and Irene and Ray Skoney. But gradually, my circle of friends encompassed classmates who attended the high school and lived in other sections of Detroit.

Our large freshman class had many "clusters" of students who traveled together daily from their own neighborhoods and understandably sought out each other during school hours, e.g., at lunch time and study hour in the first floor library. Those on the "fringe," coming in smaller numbers, commuting on the D.S.R. (Detroit Street Railways), formed their own clusters before the second semester ended. The faculty discouraged sorority membership but they existed.

Sorority pins and fraternity pins were worn by those young women who somehow "belonged" or were "pinned," i.e., were "going steady" with a young man who was a "Frat." I became part of a group of classmates, all honor students, who formed their own "sorority." We chose a Latin name, "Aequo auns" (equal in mind) and designed a pin. I remember it was encircled with seed pearls, the initials on an enamel background. The name was a contraction of Aequo Animo.

Recruitment was done casually. The final count was 12 young women who met once a month on a Sunday afternoon for chatting and light refreshments provided by the mother. Getting to the member's home provided us familiarity with the public transportation system and feeling comfortable locating addresses. The twelve were: cousins, Geraldine Bieszki, Margaret Ellen Bieszke, Alice Christine Cieszynski; Rita Engler, Marie Therese Gutman, Laura Lalewicz, Mary Lucas, Betty Perry, Anne Tomas, Helen Wawrzynkiewicz, Loretta Wolf, and Lottie Kasperowicz. Eight of the above attended the 50th class reunion at the Whitney Restaurant on Woodward Avenue in 1993.

Classes without the distraction of the opposite sex did not diminish our desire to socialize with them. Our high school sponsored roller skating parties at the Arena Roller Rink on Woodward Avenue. Invitations went out to all the boys' high schools. We could count on Boys Catholic Central, De La Salle, and the U. of D. high school to be well represented at this event.

The Arena Gardens had a wooden floor lighted from above with spot lights located in a black ceiling. The music was played on a mighty Wurlitzer organ placed on a balcony just above the moving skaters. We all wore rented shoe skates with wooden wheels.

What a thrill to glide rhythmically across that large expanse in time to the beat reverberating from the booming organ. Girls wore flared skirts and colorful blouses, the boys in school sweaters, some with sport letters on the sleeve. The Skoney brothers, Raymond and Dan, could be depended on to ask their sister's friends for a "skate." The skaters moved counterclockwise for half the evening, changing to a clockwise direction after the refreshment break. Mr. Stanley Skoney drove us home assuring us a safe trip after 11 p.m. His car and its four tires lasted through the war years, providing us with a comfortable and reliable transport on numerous occasions.

The Arena Gardens was the site of my first date. Eugene Wykowski, age 16, was the cousin of my schoolmate Henrietta Wykowski. He was attending De LaSalle High School, had a driver's license and the use of his father's coupe. I was also 16, delighted to be going to a Sunday matinee roller skating session with a date. Before we returned to my address, he picked up Henrietta's younger brother, age 12, for a cruise around Belle Isle Park. Now I sat in the middle of the front seat, closer to Gene, who was behind the steering wheel as the three of us circled the island. It was almost dark when I came home to tell about the afternoon. My mother's response upset me, deeply. She considered driving around in a car with two males, highly reckless, irregular, and questionable. I knew that I could not convince her of the total innocence of my adventure. I did not have any more dates with Eugene. He was a WW II casualty while serving in the Navy. I remember his missing front tooth, replaced with a removable one that he flipped in and out at will during that drive through Belle Isle Park on my first date.

The junior year began with our enrollment cut in half due to the opening of Immaculata High School on West Six Mile Road west of Wyoming Avenue in back of Marygrove College. And the Archdiocese decreed the residents at St. Vincent's Orphanage were to attend community schools instead of having "in house" classes. So we had an influx of classmates, new to us and new to the school who, at the end of the day, returned to their turn of the century edifice on Jefferson Avenue, operated by the Sisters of Charity. Very few were total orphans. Most had one parent unable to provide adequate care. In class, they were sullen, moody, defiant, testing all the rules, regulations and expectations. But the country was now at war, so the disruptions in class were diffused with a greater concern: keeping up the morale of our troops, supporting the war effort, and preparing for the school stage production.

"The Nifty Shop" a one-act, one-scene play set in the reception room of Madame Lazare's exclusive shop for women, called for modeling clothes. Russeks, a downtown Detroit lady's shop supplied the outfits modeled by slim tall young ladies in the junior class.

The second stage presentation was a play titled, "My cousin from Sweden." It also had one act, one scene: the living room in the home of the Mills family. The lead was to speak with a Swedish accent. During auditions for this part, Rosalia Mangiapane and I were finalists. After the second reading I got the part.

Deciding on the proper outfit to wear on the stage was an internal struggle. I bought a pale lavender plaid suit, which de-emphasized the curves of my bust and hips. Then I located a very flattering light wool dress, also lavender, more clinging to the body's outline, but in which I felt very self-conscious. Joe Filip planned to attend the play. I struggled with the decision until the evening of the performance, February 15, 1942. I wore the suit for my stage debut. Both plays were a success. My mother and father did not attend.

Joe Filip was a senior at St. Ladislaus High School, wearing his class ring, confirming his graduation in June 1942. He singled me out at meetings of the Youth Group at our church and at dances at the church hall. He was of short stature, as were his siblings and parents. Dark haired and brown eyed, he had an intensity characteristic of athletes. He was active in organized sports offered by the Catholic Youth Organization. I recall a car ride, probably in his older brother's car, just after he obtained a driver's license. Not a real date, just a "group" activity, called together on short notice. I don't recall the other two males. Joe drove and I sat next to him. Dolores and Eleanor were crunched in the back seat with their "dates." We probably drove to the Detroit City Airport, to be spectators—watching planes land and take off, a popular pastime for couples parked outside the cyclone fence in what was called, "Lover's Lane."

While some "cuddling" went on in the rear, I wheedled Joe's class ring from him. He was agreeable to my wearing it. I did return it to him after a couple of weeks when I realized that it represented a commitment I was not ready for.

THE PLAIN DEALER—A PREFERRED NEW

Pvt. Filip Assists at Mass, Meets Death on Battlefield

How Pvt. Joseph L. Filip, 20-year-old son of Mrs. Mary Filip, of 3893 Harold, was killed in action in the battle of France a few hours after writing his mother what turned out to be his final letter, was related this week by Mrs. Filip.

The letter was dated Sunday, July 9, and in it Joseph told of assisting at Holy Mass and Holy Communion, a chore he frequently performed in his home church, Our Lady Queen of Apostles, in Hamtramck.

Not quite three weeks later, on July 27, his mother received that brief but heart-rending message from the War department . . . "regret to inform you that your son . . . killed in action . . . somewhere in France . . . on July 9."

Pvt. Filip

On August 2, a solemn Memorial Mass of Requiem was sung in Joseph's beloved church by his own brother, Father Michael S. Filip. Assisting at mass were Father W. J. Wolschan, deacon, and Father Jerome A. Herman, subdeacon.

Pvt. Filip frequently served at Mass with his three brothers and was active in the basketball and softball teams of the parish units of the CYO and the YMO. He was also a team member of the Hamtramck Boys' Club in the City League and in the Detroit Baseball Federation for the Falcons' ball club.

Joseph entered the army on Feb. 16, 1943 and trained at Fort Custer, Camp Maxey and Camp Barkeley, both in Texas.

On August 2, 1943, he left for overseas duty with a medical detachment and subsequently took part in the invasion of France on June 6.

Joseph came to Detroit in 1928 from Pennsylvania where he was born in 1923 and attended the Queen of Apostles parish school. He was graduated from St. Ladislaus high school, and was active in Alumni Association activities. He would have been 21 years old on Sept. 9.

Besides his mother and brother, Rev. Filip, Pvt. Filip leaves three other brothers, Pfc. John Filip, also in France, Pvt. Mitchell, a Marine at Camp Pendleton, and Stanley, Jr., at home, and one sister, Honorata.

Joseph met his brother, John, in England where both served prior to the invasion of France.

JOSEPH FILIP AND ARTICLE

In the fall of 1942, I was elected Treasurer of the senior class. The most important task was planning and financing the Senior Prom: choosing the orchestra and the dance hall. Finding a date for the prom was another formidable assignment for every senior. Young men still available were finishing high school, and others were deferred from service, with the title 4F. Hank Koczkodan had a 4F deferment, allegedly because of either a punctured ear drum or a damaged knee. He accepted my invitation, would get his father's car for the occasion. He called for me wearing a dark suit, smiling a wide grin and holding a florist's box with a single purple orchid. My gown was pink lace. The prom site was the Collonade Room of the Masonic Temple. Lowry Clark's orchestra provided the dance music.

We ended the evening by driving north on Woodward Avenue and Eleven Mile Road, to The Wigwam, a popular eatery, known for its Hamburgers and French Fries.

Our 1943 yearbook was modest due to the war. Restrictions, shortages, and rationing affected many aspects of daily life. However, the yearbook included reminiscences, a list of War Time Activities and a Prophecy. I was named a "speeding columnist" at an international daily.

There were graduates in white cap and gown filing down the main isle of the Chapel of the Little Flower on June 6, 1943. The pastor, Rev. Walter Hardy, who distributed our report cards each quarter, now handed out the diplomas.

The Chapel of the Little Flower was part of St. Patrick's Parish, served by four priests assigned to the main church located on John R. Street. There was a daily Mass offered at the Chapel, attended by a couple dozen students. The Chapel stood next and just east of the school building behind Orchestra Hall. The chapel got a lot of use during the school months: the First Friday observance, the annual Retreat, the May Day Crowning, and Senior Dedication.

The dim, cool interior of this house of worship was very conducive to prayer and contemplation. Romanesque arches graced the length of the nave. The main altar had a high back, flanked on each side by two carved stone pillars. A statue of the patroness, St. Therese of Lisieux holding a bouquet of roses, stood on a small platform between the pillars. Above the altar, outdoor light filtered through three long stained glass windows arched at the top. Worshipers knelt in dark oak pews and faced the sanctuary and the low wrought iron communion railing.

The Commencement exercises ended and 67 graduates left, remembering the golden days of youth spent learning and expanding our horizons. Of the 67, 12 were going on to college, two to the University of Detroit, and the other ten to Marygrove College. The I.H.M. nuns also taught at Marygrove. I was accepted into the freshman class of 1947. This was plan B. My earlier ambition of becoming a nurse thwarted, since, in 1943, nursing schools expected students to live on the premises. I believed my responsibility was to help out at home. My brother was 11 years old, my father working full time, my mother's hospital stay indefinite. My perception of the "surrogate mother" role was that it came with responsibilities and duties and I felt it restricted me for many years.

A favorite prayer tucked into the right corner of the mirror above the dresser in my bedroom on Trowbridge Street and recited nightly.

Good Night My Jesus

Jesus dear, the day is over
Now I leave my labor light
And before I seek my slumber
Come to say a sweet Good Night.

Would that I might tarry near
Rest before thy lonely shrine
Thou wouldst whisper loving secrets,
And I'd tell thee all of mine.

But I cannot linger, Jesus
I must leave for a while
Now bestow on me a blessing
And a fond approving smile.

I will leave my heart beside thee
It will rest securest there,
And within thy fond embraces,
It will grow to thee more dear.

So good night once more my Jesus,
Grant no matter where I be
All my day thoughts and night dreams,
Be of thee and only thee.

Miller's Grocery Store

Before we acquired an ice box, some member of my family made a daily trip to the corner grocery, Miller's, which sat on the corner of Conant and Caniff Streets. This two-story, light yellow brick structure extended a half block each way.

Every member of the Miller family had a responsibility in this hub establishment in our neighborhood. Robust, ruddy-faced Mr. Miller was the owner and butcher. His short plump, genial wife, Camilla, was usually in the cashier's booth. Mrs. Miller's three adult children, Jerry, Jadzia, and Mac, took turns at all the counters and the cash register. The family lived in an apartment above the store.

Miller's grocery was large by the standards of the 1930s. The local C.F. Smith and Kroger, both chain groceries in Hamtramck, were less than half the size of the Miller store. Miller's fresh meat counter extended almost the entire length of the north wall. Fresh produce, fruits, and vegetables filled bins under the large plate glass corner windows and were visible to passers by. Along the south wall stood a cheese and butter cooler and display case. On the ledge behind this showcase stood a scale and a mechanical slicer. The rest of the south end of the store had shelves stacked with canned and packaged goods from the floor to the ceiling. The shelves along the back or west wall held boxed soap powders and cleaners.

Mrs. Miller's brother, Mr. Z. worked as a butcher. He and his family also lived in an apartment above the store. Besides the family members, several other men were employed at the grocery store. There was another butcher, Leo, who was a short, taciturn, bleary-eyed middle-aged man who took meat orders in both English and Polish. Mr. Stanley Gac also worked behind the butcher's counter. He was handsome, tall, and middle-aged with wavy brown hair and a gold front tooth. A recent émigré, he had left a wife and family in Poland to seek fortune in America. And there was Johnny, a happy-go-lucky single man with the deep blue pop eyes. He scampered back and forth behind the counter, joking and teasing with the women customers.

The men's responsibilities were not limited to the meat counter. All the store clerks used a long-handled retriever to remove food items from high shelves. Johnny was especially adept at this. The shoppers stood on one side of the low counter reading off their lists while the clerks placed everything into a brown paper bag, added the total price and wrote it on the bag. Eventually an adding machine appeared on the counter, simplifying and expediting the process of totaling the sacks' contents.

Weekend specials appeared each week on the plate glass windows, painted on the surface with water soluble paints. Johnny was also especially adept at this artistic skill. It amazed me. His lettering was even and neat. He used several pastel colors to further attract shoppers. When the time arrived for the following group of specials, he washed away his art, making room for the next message.

The store was closed on Sundays. But since we knew the owners lived above the store, ringing the side door bell always brought somebody downstairs. I remember having to embark on this unpopular mission when I was 13 years old and in the 8th grade. Mrs. Z., a toothy, tall middle-aged woman opened the door. She called for her husband to go with me into the dark grocery store, and then she disappeared into their flat. Mr. Z., also middle-aged with gray thinning hair and a receding hair line, willingly sliced the quarter pound of ham that I was sent to purchase. When he finished, we both moved through the dim aisles toward the exit. As he handed me the meat, wrapped neatly in white butcher paper, he reached his free arm around my shoulders and pulled me toward his side in a hearty hug. Startled at this unsolicited expression of affection, I rushed out of the building without another word. Of course, I never mentioned the incident to my mother, and I never shopped on Sunday at Miller's Grocery again!

My first job was clerking at Miller's. In the summer of 1942 just before I turned 17. Mrs. Miller agreed to employ me on Friday evenings and Saturdays. We did not, however, agree to my wage. I quickly learned that I should have discussed this important aspect of employment before starting the job. My hours were 5 to 9 p.m. on Friday evenings and from 9 a.m. to 9 p.m. on Saturdays. When I walked up to the cashier's cage at closing time, Mrs. Miller pushed the lever sending the money drawer of the cash register toward her ample bosom. She reached in for a single five dollar bill. I was crestfallen and disappointed, figuring my rate of pay at 37 cents per hour. I quit after the third weekend, determined to seek another opportunity to earn money.

Because money and jobs were scarce in the 1930's, Miller's grocery allowed "on the cuff" or "na kartke" purchases. The buyer's last name was recorded on a page of a small tablet and stored near the cash register. When the customer cashed his paycheck, he paid the debt.

By this time I did most of the grocery shopping and had to approach my father for money when it was time to settle the bill. One time he was especially diligent about the total amount that the grocery store presented. He suspected that the Millers had padded the bill, but he could not substantiate this as we did not keep receipts.

The Miller family members were part of my social life for years. I learned from local gossip that, after Camilla had divorced her first husband, her three children from that marriage took Mr. Miller's name.

Following World War II, Jadzia (Hedwig) Miller met and married Joseph Stark after he was discharged from the Navy. She continued to help in the grocery until she and her husband purchased a bar on Mt. Elliott Street across from the Dodge factory. They later sold the bar and Joseph returned to his first occupation, a pharmacist. Jadzia died in 1993.

Jerry Miller, Johnny, Mac and Stanley Gac were all drafted into military service during WWII. Jerry Miller married the oldest Pawlowski daughter and raised four sons. After he succumbed to a heart attack in the 1950s, his wife and her sister Henia operated the grocery store, eventually converting it into a small supermarket. The elder Mr. Miller also died of a heart attack several years earlier. Camilla Miller surprised the community by marrying Mr. Gac, which raised a lot of eyebrows since he was several years younger than she. Johnny became a bartender at Jax Bar, which was operated by Mrs. Miller's brother.

Mr. Miller's grocery and the Miller family were an important part of my life in Hamtramck.

"Rats"

My early memory of my mother's hair was that it was chestnut colored, and reached halfway to her waist when it was not coiled into a bun at the back of her neck. Tortoise shell pins held the twist of hair in place. She parted it in the middle, and to full out the tresses she made a "rat." This was a small powder-puff sized pad of loose hair strands that she formed and then placed on each side of her head under the straight hair to give it the appearance of fullness. This was before teasing and back combing and before permanents transformed and augmented a head of hair.

My mother taught me to braid hair when I was about 6 years old. She sat while I plaited her long strands, and she invariably started to doze off. In the late 1930s she made one trip to the nearby beauty parlor to get her hair cut for a permanent. She saved the long switch of hair by wrapping it in a silk handkerchief that was stored in the big black metal trunk in the attic.

When the permanent grew out, she left her hair straight, pinning it back behind her ears, but it never had the look or the neatness of the coil pinned with tortoise shell pins at the back of her neck.

After her hair turned gray and she lived in a retirement home, I arranged periodic visits to the hair dresser for permanents to assure a curly top and a wash and wear style that suited her well during her later years.

She always enjoyed the pampering and the results, teasing that she was now ready to look for a boyfriend with her new look.

"Callings"

As a child and preteen I heard repeated references to the hardships and losses my mother endured as a wife. She lost her first two full-term babies at birth, she was thwarted in her wish to return to her homeland, then struggled through the Great Depression, bankruptcy, a disastrous fire and my father's kidney operations. Her fragile psyche connected all these happenings to her marital state. These connections were transmitted to me and she admonished me to avoid getting married. I began to repeat what I was told. "I'm never going to get married," I announced to the two roomer bachelors, Mr. Stanley Oktaba and Mr. Stanley Trochomowicz, whenever they teased me about this.

Interestingly, the message from the parish priest who conducted the high school youth group, was—there were essentially two "callings"—the marital state and religious life. The single life in the world was a "minor" life style. A person made a choice. The eighth grade home room teacher asked me that year if I might consider becoming a nun. But already in the seventh grade I was drawn to the best looking boy in our class: Adolph Staszewski. He was aloof and did not show any overt interest in any of the females in the seventh grade. I was also "ga-ga" over the heart throbs of the silver screen: Nelson Eddy, Robert Stack, Tyrone Power, Charles Boyer, Gregory Peck, and Robert Taylor. My pulse quickened, my imagination soared in the darkened movie theatre whenever these leading men appeared. So, not surprisingly, my reply to the sister was a definite, "No, I'm not interested in religious life."

But I did bring up the topic individually to our two assistant priests. Father Wolschon recommended the religious life. (His sister was divorced from an alcoholic and was working to support herself.) Father Behrendt's assessment: marriage. He was standing behind me. I was seated, counting the Sunday collection in the rectory basement. He placed his two hands on each side of my face, turned my head back and gave me a quick kiss. The entire scene and exchange left me just as puzzled as ever.

The Rooming House

There was one distinctive two-story white frame dwelling just a half block from the Baker Street Car line. It was on the north side of Trowbridge Street, and I walked by it every time I had an errand that took me to the Hamtramck shopping center on Joseph Campau Street. The building was designed to provide sleeping rooms for single men and women.

The structure filled the entire lot right up to the sidewalk. A staircase on the east side of the building led to the landlady's first floor living quarters. Another, on the opposite side of the building, led to the long staircases inside the door to the second floor where the residents' rooms were located. I seldom saw the landlady, except occasionally when she peered through the potted begonias and mother-in-law tongues and ferns pressed against the small window panes of the glassed-in front porch. She seemed to operate this hostel alone. Throughout the 30 years of my living in Hamtramck, this building did not change in appearance except to acquire a run-down look from neglect.

My godmother, from confirmation, lived in this rooming house after she moved out of our house. She had rented one of our spare bedrooms, and we considered her part of the family when I was starting elementary school. Her name was Lottie Stelmaszczuk. Everyone called her Władzia, which was also my name. She was also an immigrant from the same area of Poland as my parents. She spoke with a Russian slur to her pronunciation. Of course in our home the spoken language was Polish. English was used rarely. Lottie was past being a young woman, probably in her late 30s. Short and sturdy, she had pitch-black hair that sometimes revealed gray roots. Her full round face was usually powdered faintly, and her cheeks had small round circles of rouge. She wore lipstick on her full lips. I remember her smile that showed strong white teeth, unusual in my family. But what I remember the most were her earrings. Each evening after she returned from her factory job, she pulled them off her earlobes, first one then the other. They were grape-sized coral with gold prongs that held the stone and were fashioned for pierced ears. When she removed them, her hands and fingers reflected the tedious work she had been doing in the shop. Her fingernails were worn down and the skin on her fingertips was stained with dark oil. She never complained about her tiring occupation, nor did she ever discuss the place where she earned her livelihood.

I chose Lottie to be my sponsor when I was to be confirmed in the fourth grade and chose my grandmother's name, Ann, to be my confirmation or middle name. The event went without a hitch, but there was some kind of misunderstanding involving my mother and Lottie, resulting in her moving to the rooming house. My mother perceived a developing attraction between my father and Lottie and wanted her out of the house.

Lottie invited me to visit her and I did. When I reached the second story, I found myself in a long hallway that stretched the length of the building. A narrow dark striped runner muffled my steps as I walked to the door of Lottie's room. It was essentially a sleeping room crowded with other personal items and small furniture. Near the window a narrow stand held an electric plate with a tea kettle. Below, on a shelf, a small pot and pan attested that Lottie had some of her meals indoors. It was quiet, as the other tenants were either at work or inside their rooms. I found the environment quite bleak.

Several years later I learned that Lottie married a much older man. We lost contact with each other before I found out that she had died of cancer. I guess I was comforted to know that she did eventually acquire a husband and a home and her modest circumstances at the rooming house had ended.

Forty years later, in 1975, while shopping for coral jewelry in Italy, I sought to replicate those prong-held earrings to no avail. I chose a pair somewhat similar as a reminder.

1st COMMUNION OF LEONARD [brother])

Avocations and Sports

When I was in elementary school in the 1930s I played many games with my classmates during our daily "Pauza" or recess, the midmorning play period outdoors on the playground adjacent to the school building. Skipping rope, London Bridge, Statues, and Hop Scotch were favorites. They all required little or no equipment and cost nothing.

Cost was of utmost importance. Walking cost nothing. Swimming was in the chilly Detroit River, so we waited for the hot days of midsummer before making that trip. For 10 cents the Belle Isle bath house furnished a towel, a locker with a key and a cotton tank type bathing suit if a person needed one.

My first tennis racket cost a hefty $1.25. There were free municipal tennis courts in Hamtramck and nearby Detroit within walking distance of my home. The teenage crowd I was part of was all willing to play tennis for the same reasons—it was inexpensive, got us outdoors, and was good exercise. None of us became good or expert at this game, except Eleanor (Jasinski) Woźniak who qualified for one of the Detroit City Finals.

As soon as I was in high school, dad bought me a blue and white Flyer bicycle. It expanded my horizons tremendously. Now Jane Ciwinska and I had transportation to parks and places of interest. Of course this gave my mother another concern regarding my safety. She was always very relieved when I returned from a trip, claiming that she was worried the entire time that something could be happening, a traffic accident, or something!

As a teenager and as an adult I "took up" ping pong, archery, badminton, snow skiing, and dancing.

The Skoney family owned a ping pong table that stood in their basement. It became a favorite place for us. The Jayne Field tennis courts were a short distance from Sobieski Street where Irene Skoney and her three brothers lived with their accommodating parents. A snack of ground baloney sandwiches and toll house cookies was a standard offering after we played tennis or "recreated" in the basement.

Canoeing on the lagoons at Belle Isle was leisurely and diversional, rather than strenuous. Privately owned canoes in the 1930s sported red velvet "fittings" and linings, a record player with a "trumpet" speaker, and a lot of satin-covered pillows for reclining.

The rented canoes from the Livery were painted an olive green, and usually leaked just enough to get your shoes wet.

The first time I had a ride in one of those canoes was during a grade school excursion. Jane Ciwinska and I along with her older sister Josephine were in one canoe. We knew nothing about steering or paddling so our canoe veered into the banks and had a number of collisions with other canoes. But we enjoyed every moment gliding along that deep green and very calm lagoon surface.

Ice skating was another inexpensive sport to enjoy in and around Detroit. The best ice skating was outdoors at Belle Isle after the lagoons froze and the ice-skating pavilion opened for warmth, shelter and snacks. All ages skated there. Hockey players practiced in one area, mostly burly teenagers wearing hockey skates and holding hockey sticks. Toddlers on sleds were pulled by fathers or mothers near the shore. An occasional "figure" skater practiced twirls and figure eights. These were usually young women wearing leotards and short-flared skirts.

Inside the gray shingled pavilion, the air was steamy as skaters were either putting on skates or pulling them off while sitting on straight wooden benches circling the pot bellied wood burning stove that heated the interior. Hot cocoa and a hot dog was a welcome snack. The trip home was by street car with the ice skates tied together by the laces and flung over one shoulder.

Roller skating at the Arena Gardens on Woodward near Forest in Detroit was very popular while I was in high school. We "sponsored" roller skating parties to which we invited the area boys' high schools: De Lasalle, U.of D. High School and especially our counterpart, Boys Catholic Central. Moving around that drafty interior, with the slick wooden floor and the Wurlitzer Organ playing all the popular tunes in greater than life volume was the zenith of excitement. The dress had to be a circular skirt that would sway with the movement and rhythm of the music. Our male partners often wore school sweaters with their sports letters and school insignia. Others sported plaid shirts and cardigans.

Once I began working after graduating from College, I could afford to join the Church Ladies Bowling League. I liked the game but did poorly. In fact, I usually received the "booby" prize ($.50) for the lowest score on my team. However it was a plus to know the rules of the game when I began to date. Bowling Lanes were located on Joseph Campau and were within easy walking distance from our home.

My experience with golf was quite brief and limited. The first person I knew that played golf was Irene Skoney's father. Then Irene's brother Raymond and his buddy Eugene Arjeski worked as caddies. Because of the expense involved, I borrowed three clubs and a golf bag from my boss at the time, Irene Mayes. Eleonor (Jasinski) Woźniak and I played golf at the low cost municipal courses at Belle Isle, Palmer Park, and Chandler Park. Eleonor is still playing the game, and so is her whole family—husband and three sons. My pursuits were with activities that suited my skills better, could be practiced year round and were less competitive than golf.

Dancing. It has a carryover feature, can be enjoyed at all ages without special equipment, outside of music. About age ten I began taking Polish Folk Dancing. At 10 cents a lesson, an older male teacher taught us the rudiments of a Krakowiak, Mazur and the Russian Kołomyjka. The lessons took place at the Polish Falcons Hall on the corner of Caniff and Gallagher. Our dance recital was at a Memorial Day Parade that marched north on Joseph Campau Street. I wore a borrowed costume of a Krakowiak. Since we had too few males in our class, I had to take the part of the "boy" which meant I wore black boots, striped red and white knickers and a white blouse. The girls got to wear the red velvet boleros with the embroidery and the wreath on their head with all the satin ribbons in a rainbow of colors cascading down their back. Needless to say, I envied their costumes.

To learn Latin American dancing in the 1940s meant a trip to the downtown Detroit YMCA. I liked the music and the rhythm of the Cha Cha, Rumba, Tango, Samba, and Meringue. Lessons were reasonably priced, and the teachers accompanied us to the area "lounges" or night clubs that had live music. Don Pablo and his orchestra played in one of the establishments on Washington Boulevard in downtown Detroit. Right after our class ended about 9 p.m., we got to practice what we learned on a real dance floor to live music.

In the 1960s, husband Ed and I joined a Western Square Dance class offered at the Southfield City Hall. The Cross Trailers Square Dance Club opened up a whole new world of enjoyment for us. We attended regular sessions at The Barn in Livonia for several years. Chuck Dillinbeck, a fireman by day, was our favorite caller. It was healthful and no alcoholic beverages were allowed in the dance hall. A wooden floor was the best for dancing, and appropriate "western" attire was encouraged. Men wore long sleeved shirts so the ladies did not have to grasp a hairy, sweaty arm. The women's dresses had wide skirts trimmed with rick rack, ribbons, intricate stitching, and, always, a voluminous frilly layered petticoat and lacy pettipants. Statewide and countrywide "conventions" of square dancers brought together many nationally recognized callers and dancers.

One weekend, I remember attending a dance at the Greenbush Inn, a Michigan resort on the banks of Lake Huron, north of Oscoda. Some of the sessions took place in a two-story outdoor dance pavilion overlooking the water. The Greenbush Inn, built in the early 1900's, catered to a downstate crowd who traveled north by train for winter and summer sports. An old brochure pictured golf players wearing knickers and ladies in parkas sitting on toboggans.

I "sampled" art in adult education classes after graduating from college. Oil painting was my favorite medium. Two examples of my attempts exist somewhere: a still life and a head of a woman.

As a preteen, I learned to embroider from a local woman who took on this task with a small group that came to her house on Conant about five blocks away from Trowbridge. I learned to cross stitch, using it to embellish a linen runner with several shades of blue floss. I used it as a Mother's Day gift for my mother.

I thank the Tau Beta Community house on Hanley Street in Hamtramck for lessons in cooking, knitting, and sewing, offered for a low fee to school-age children. I eagerly walked the ten blocks to join other girls my age who wanted to learn skills that were different from what their mothers taught them.

The sewing teacher stressed attention to details such as even basting stitches and exact measured hems. My first project was a petticoat with built up shoulder straps. Many years later I sewed this type of slip for my mother when she lived in a home for the aged and then in a nursing home. I always added a strip of lace to the hem to accommodate her wish for a feminine touch.

In knitting class we used a plain knit stitch to fashion a small clutch purse. I remember attaching a lining and a zipper to complete this first effort.

While in high school, I signed up for free sewing lessons given by the Singer Sewing Machine Company Store of Caniff Street. It involved choosing a dress pattern with button holes, sleeves, cuffs, two double pleats in front, and a belt. I completed everything satisfactorily, but wore the dress infrequently as the moss green color was dull, not very flattering and the fabric difficult to iron.

Knowledge of basics in sewing made it easy to "whip" up draperies for the dining room windows of the house on Trowbridge Street. I remember purchasing yards of off white nubby cotton at Sears for the ceiling to floor draperies that covered the entire wall for a very dramatic effect. When the house was sold, I cut the panels to fit the windows in the two bedrooms of our house in Southfield.

Our RCA Victor radio stood in the dining room, the wrought iron bench with a velour-covered seat nearby. I draped myself across this seat, with my head close to the speaker to listen to my favorite afternoon programs. Starting at 4 p.m. daily, my imagination reveled in the adventures of Little Orphan Annie, Jack Armstrong, Renfro of the Mounted, and the Green Hornet.

The makers of Ovaltine sponsored Little Orphan Annie. Once

a person used that product, a chocolate-malted drink made using their boxed powder and milk, "premiums" could be obtained through the mail. I remember sending for a Bakelite shaker for blending the milk and powder. But the best prize was the DECODER RING. At the end of an episode on the radio, I copied the numbers, given, then changed them into letters by turning the movable dial on the front of the ring. The letters formed words that gave the clue to the next day's story line.

But the suspense, horror, mystery program was "The Inner Sanctum" airing at 10 p.m. on Sunday night. I was invited to the Jelonek household for this event. Eleanor and her brothers, Philip and Edward, and neighbors Lillian and her brother and I gathered in the living room above the beer garden. Each of us received a bag of potato chips, courtesy of the business below, and found a comfortable spot to sit listening for the opening—the unmistakable sound of a creaking door swinging ajar on rusty hinges. All the lamps in the room were turned off. The only light came from the street lamppost. We trembled in delight during the program, our imagination stimulated by the verbal narration. For me it was a sleep over opportunity so I would not have to go home in the dark. It's a happy memory from my grade school years.

When I think of lace tatting, I picture Virginia Laskowski sitting on her front porch across from the Queen of Apostles church, on Prescott St., deftly fingering the fine thread and metal shuttle, forming delicate edgings for ladies' linen handkerchiefs. Her figure was equally delicate. Small boned, with high cheek bones, corn silk blonde hair, clear blue eyes, her quick smile showed a perfect set of teeth. At the time I observed what looked like "the hand was quicker than the eye" maneuvers followed by the resulting fine rings and even finer loops of tatted lace.

After I retired for the first time in 1985, I used the leisure time to learn lace tatting and later needlepoint. Both skills give much satisfaction and fulfillment.

My mother made references to hand weaving, spinning, growing flax and preparing it for use as linen. The women in her family were involved in all aspects of producing cloth for daily uses. She told how the coarse thread showed up in work clothing and bed linens. They used finer yarn for tea towels and tablecloths. Spinning went on during the winter months. By the time Lent started, serious weaving got under way in her household.

In 1959, my cousins in Poland bequeathed two hand-woven coverlets as mementoes of my visit. Inspired, I enrolled in a course of weaving and textile design at Wayne State University. The teacher was Ruth Ingvarson, who learned weaving in her native Sweden. This "hobby" has been a source of much satisfaction throughout my adult life. My first floor loom was a used Leclerc, 36-inch width, purchased from the Ford Hospital occupational therapy department. I sold it thirty years later to a community college in northern Michigan. However, two newer looms moved to Florida when we relocated in 1993. The Norwood, 40-inch wide, has eight harnesses, the Dorset is 20 inches wide, with four harnesses. The smaller loom folds up for easy transport to workshops and conferences.

YOGA. This method of stretching and flexing the spine and the whole body became a Godsend when I developed back aches from sitting in a fixed position while interviewing and driving long distances. About 1968 I located Yoga classes held at Duns Scotus College in Southfield, Michigan. The benefits were noteworthy. On the day Yoga class took place, my evening meal was consumed earlier and was smaller in size. Relaxed and "stretched" after a session, I always slept better and woke up the next morning refreshed and energized. The only equipment needed is a padded mat.

Downhill skiing: watching movies with Sonja Henie skillfully maneuvering snow-covered Colorado mountains sure gave me an appetite for that sport. The American Youth Hostel association offered the lowest cost trips by train to St.Jovite, north of Montreal, in the Laurentian mountains. At age 29, I finally gathered up the proper equipment for a week at Gray Rocks Inn with this group. My good friends from the Polish Aid Society accompanied me as far as the Michigan Central Railroad Station in Detroit, wishing me well with this new venture. I was the first in the group to attempt skiing. The following year I traveled solo to the same area and was accompanied by Eleanor another time. There were a number of skiing trips to Northern Michigan ski areas every winter with our friends who got into this popular winter sport.

In 1971, I switched to cross country skiing. As it became more popular, golf courses and state parks offered trails within driving distances of our home in Southfield. In fact, the Inglenook Park was within walking distance from our Ranchwood Road address. Again, no cost was involved, once a person purchased the equipment. And, winter, with enough snow on the ground, was welcomed and enjoyed. I remember striking out on a Sunday afternoon, skiing across Ranchwood, finding the path through the vacant lot that led to the Inglenook park. Sometimes I followed a trail already formed by an earlier skier, then added another loop here and there. Another cross country skiing area is at the Harrisville second home of the Utechts, featuring back roads with almost no traffic, human or vehicular.

While in high school, the main spectator sport was football. Often our "gang" attended the games between Boys Catholic Central and other teams in their league. Also, I remember going to Keyworth Stadium in Hamtramck to watch the Hamtramck High School football team play rivals from the area. Of course, the football players had a high ranking in our minds as desirable date material. But it never happened! We would note the girls wearing huge chrysanthemums indicating they had a date. Jane Rzepka, freckled faced, had all the luck. She attracted the captain of the Hamtramck High School football team, and was the envy of all that knew her from grade school days.

I tried to follow the baseball games when they were broadcast on the radio. As an adult, I sometimes joined a group for a live game of baseball at Briggs Stadium, later called Tiger Stadium. The Detroit Red Wings Hockey team played at the Olympia Stadium on Grand River. I sat high up watching some of their games in the past, too.

A special spectator sport was a tennis game I attended at the Detroit Tennis Club. Pancho Gonzales played on their red clay court, demonstrating his powerful backhand. He held the tennis racket with both hands to deliver his signature stroke. I still like to follow tennis finals on TV.

Since "retiring," fitness of body and mind is of paramount importance to me. I begin many mornings at 6:30 a.m. following "The Body Electric" TV exercise program on PBS. Then, from 9:00 a.m. to 10:00 a.m., I take part in Water Aerobics at least twice each week. Usually on Saturday, Ed and I walk on the beach at Henderson State Park. We volunteer to do "maintenance," picking up debris: flotsam and jetsam found on the shore.

Our latest volunteer activity is at Resurrection Church where we usher at the 8:00 a.m. Sunday Mass. It's our personal contribution to the needs of the congregation.

Wars and Their Influence in My Life

When Hitler marched into Poland in 1939, my mother reacted with alarm and fear. She relived all the hardships of the war in 1914 and empathized with relatives who would be going through all those horrors once more. But the full impact of our country at war began with Pearl Harbor, December 7, 1941. I was a junior in high school and 16 years old. I had just had my first date with a boy named Eugene Wykowski.

Suddenly, it seemed the entire production of daily necessities became a luxury, and the factories were converted to turning out defense items. The auto assembly lines began producing airplanes, tanks, jeeps, and munitions. The Willow Run plant attracted hundreds of workers that streamed north to Michigan from the Appalachians and from the Bible Belt states. All sorts of small shops popped up, filling government orders for parts needed by the larger assembly plants. It was during this time that I became surrogate mother and housekeeper due to my mother's hospitalization.

When the U.S. entered the war, my classmates from elementary school, their brothers, neighbors, relatives and friends were either drafted or enlisted in the various branches of service. We noticed very quickly fewer and fewer eligible young men in the neighborhood. There were some very visible 4Fs. Rumor had it that Hank Koczkodan had a punctured ear drum or water on the knee. He was my date to the high school senior prom. Another local deferred male was a Bible wielding seminarian who never completed his studies in the seminary. During the war years, he wore only black suits and a somber, pious look on his face.

At home we received rationing coupons for sugar, butter and meat. They were a bit of a nuisance but not so restrictive to affect our nutrition. Oleo margarine was discovered. It took some elbow grease to knead in the color capsule that made the white blob of fat look like butter. We never felt deprived with the prescribed number of ounces of meat per person per week.

Switching to rayon hosiery after just discovering silk stockings meant dealing with sagging and stretching around the ankles and calves. Defense workers and women, started to wear slacks to their factory jobs and probably did not have to bother with garter belts anymore.

In high school, we studied aeronautics under the guidance of Sister Marie Aimee, a 4-foot, 8-inch nun whom I suspect was an Amelia Earhart admirer.

With navy blue yarn and directions, we knitted sweaters for the Navy. We also volunteered for work with the Red Cross Blood Bank and learned Home Nursing techniques. I still turn under bed sheets in the manner learned back then. In addition, entertaining servicemen at home, at church, and in community centers became popular.

Families were encouraged to invite servicemen for holidays and special dinners through the local U.S.O. Young women, as a group, could entertain by arranging dances. This was very enriching and gratifying, expanding our horizons as it attracted servicemen from various countries that were passing through our city. Some torrid romances resulted and at least one marriage was attributed to one of these dances. Mary Lucas met Ray Colie, her husband-to-be, during this time. Hedy Jurewicz was smitten by a dashing second lieutenant, but this pairing was snafued by Hedy's mother who would not accept this as a serious courtship since he was not Catholic. Charlie O'Shields, a PFC from Miami with a dripping drawl and a chipped front tooth, paid attention and escorted me on a few dates. I did not encourage him, so his last letter from England contained photos of his wedding to an English girl. Our high school sorority, the Aequs Auns used a room in the International Institute on East Grand Boulevard, near Joseph Campau for these Saturday night U.S.O. type entertainments.

My family rented the two spare bedrooms to roomers. Two brothers and their friend, recent émigrés from Poland, were drafted and replaced by three women defense workers. Two were friends from a town in Pennsylvania and the third, Lillian Patrzalek, was from Logan, West Virginia. Lillian eventually brought her entire family to Detroit. Her two younger brothers slept in our living room, which was converted into a quickie bedroom with the French doors curtained for privacy. These two were also drafted into the Navy.

The greatest influence in my life during this time was experiencing my initiation into love. Those first stirrings of desires, emotions, attraction, and attention by a male whose toes trod the same mud as mine. This first love was Bernie Zacharias, a pen pal and serviceman studying meteorology at Brown University in 1943.

The Roomers

Our family life on Norwalk Street in 1928-1929 was disrupted periodically, when my father rented the front room (living room) to a roomer. Immigrants from Poland, usually male, willingly paid $5.00 per week for a furnished sleeping room. I recall a narrow bed with a headboard of metal, painted dark brown, tucked under the sloping ceiling along one wall of what was our parlor. Two roomers come to mind. The first one was a man who, I observed as a 3-year-old, daubing black dye on his mustache and hair. He came back from a Saturday night brawl with a bloody wound on his forehead, asking my mother for a bandage. He moved out shortly after. Then, a man and his toddler daughter sought refuge from some domestic breakup. I felt neglected as my mother fed, bathed, clothed, and watched this child who was crying a lot in unfamiliar surroundings. But their stay was very short as this man was not able to pay the rent. Instead, when he left with his child, his payment "in kind" was a set of tableware, two tall heavy square pressed glass vases and a bottle-green glass fruit bowl on its own silver plated stand, with a filigree handle. These decorative accessories moved with us to Trowbridge Street where the next paying lodgers came with the house.

Stanley Oktaba and Stanley Trochomowicz stayed on after the Borucki family, with two of their sons returned to Poland after selling the house to my parents. The oldest son, also Stanley, was studying for the priesthood at Orchard Lake Seminary. The income from the two roomers and the downstairs flat would help make the house payment. Stanley would collect the house payment which would finance his education. He made visits to our flat, probably to collect the payment and to visit with Stanley Oktaba who took a keen interest in his studies. I remember once he engaged in a friendly show of strength when he stood behind me and lifted me straight up by cupping his hands over my elbows as I held them firmly against my sides.

Both Mr. Oktaba and Mr. Trochomowicz were teetotalers and both were gainfully employed. They were about my parent's age, coming to the U.S. in the 1920s as single men. Mr. Oktaba gave up alcohol and became very religious after losing three fingers of his right hand in an industrial accident. Mr. Trochomowicz often spoke of Zamość, the town near Lublin, Poland, his birthplace. My mother's responsibility was to clean their room and change the bed linens weekly. They ate their meals out and carried their personal laundry to the commercial laundry on Caniff Street. Mr. Oktaba liked to snack on fruit and pumpernickel bread which he brought with him after his supper. I watched wide eyed as he deftly peeled a Delicious apple using his pocket knife blade. One long red spiral hung down and swung back and forth as he turned the fruit in his hand. Mr. Trochomowicz and my father had frequent heated discussions about European politics after they read the *Polish Daily News* and listened to the radio news reports on WJLB, the station with a program in the Polish language. I never heard Mr. Trochomowicz use strong language, but when exasperated, he burst out, "Son of a sixty-seven and a half!" They were like a couple of benign uncles easily integrating into our family routine. When my brother was born in March 1932, Mr. Trochomowicz entertained him by pushing and pulling the buggy when he was in it. He sat at the table, fastened his belt to the handle on the front of the buggy, then holding the end of the belt, sent the buggy forward and drew it back with the belt.

Mr. Oktaba moved out following the fire in 1933, but stayed in the neighborhood. We saw him every time we attended our parish church where he became the sacristan. Whenever he scurried about inside the church, from one altar to another, his right hand with the missing fingers always rested over his heart.

Lottie Stelmaszczuk, a personable and friendly middle-aged lady, rented the bedroom vacated by Mr. Oktaba. I quickly responded to her open personality. Each evening I looked on as she removed the round coral earrings from her pierced ears. Each stone, the size of a grape, was held in place by four gold prongs.

Lottie pulled on her ear lobe with her fingers, stained with dark machine oil used in her factory job. In 1934 I chose Lottie to be my sponsor for Confirmation.

The following year, Lottie moved out and Alex rented the room. I don't remember his last name, but do remember his body building exercises with a hand held stretching band. In the summer months he acquired a deep tan which seemed to highlight his physical fitness: bulging biceps and deep pectorals. He was quiet and low key, keeping to himself most of the time.

The mid 1930s and beyond, brought more employment, and a new wave of younger immigrants on the scene. All of Europe sensed turmoil, unrest, stirrings, and the threat of compulsory, military service.

About this time Alex and Lottie moved out. Three younger males moved in: brothers Norbert and Stanley Basak and their friend, Alfred Ullman. All were employed and spent their free time away from the house. It was possible to hear bits of conversation among them confirming an active social life. They were learning English, getting acculturated to life in the U.S.A. As soon as the U.S.A. started drafting males into the services, all three were drafted into the Army. Norbert became a pen pal, keeping in touch, sending photos of himself in uniform holding a rifle.

I was in high school, committed to keeping up morale of our fighting servicemen.

I was busy with teen age activities so hardly noticed when a Mr. Czaplicki and a Mr. Halasz came to occupy those two spare bedrooms. Mr. Czaplicki was a mousy older man, keeping his own schedule, noncommital and not involved in any of our family life. Mr. Halasz, on the other hand, could not be ignored. His was a bulky figure, a wide girth to match, penetrating steel blue eyes and rosacea-tinged cheeks. Probably in his fifties, he was not going to be drafted. I bristled when he sat at the dining room table, intently watching me doing home work. Finishing assignments quickly and getting away became a priority. My mother, under pressure, agreed to serve him dinner every day. It had to be according to his specifications, causing her unnecessary aggravation.

In May 1942, my mother suffered a mental breakdown requiring hospitalization. Mr. Halasz left, but was a delusional element in my mother's psyche for the rest of her life.

His room was rented out to two young women from Pennsylvania who were in their late twenties. I became aware of their Saturday night "on the town" escapades. The transformation from defense factory workers to femme fatales necessitated a heavy application of mascara and a dousing with Tabu cologne. The cloying fragrance permeated the air as they prepared to leave the house dressed in glittery dresses heading for their trysts. Many months passed by with their free time spent away from their room. Then, one day, the older and plainer one, announced she was returning to her family, giving no other reason. But as she hastened to leave, her coat, unbuttoned, revealed a very full and expanded waistline. I don't remember the fate of the younger, sultry one, but she was soon gone as well.

Logan, West Virginia, was the hometown of Lillian Patrzalek who replaced the two "free spirits." The oldest in the family, Lillian ventured north leaving her parents, two brothers, and a younger sister. She plunged into a defense job, working diligently. Soon a younger brother came to Michigan. My father converted the living room for his use.

Lillian used her free time to take care of her personal needs: meals, laundry, and keeping in touch with her family. I felt like a younger sister when we engaged in "girl talk." A foreman at the factory was pressuring her for a "date" which she repeatedly refused knowing that he was married. Some health problems resolved when she improved her eating habits. She became a member of our parish church and joined the Young Ladies Sodality. Her brother was drafted into the Navy and we reclaimed the living room. The younger sister married at age sixteen. Another brother, Carl, was drafted into the U.S. Cavalry and became my pen pal during his time in the service. Finally, the elderly parents moved to Michigan when Lillian used her savings as down payment on a small frame house on Fredro Street. She left to be with them.

A Mrs. Stempien was the next occupant of the room vacated by Lillian. She was a past-middle-age-matron, with clicking false teeth and cropped hair, dyed black. She preferred to eat in, hustling around the kitchen with her own pots and pans. Her personal laundry was usually drying on a hook in the bathroom. I was immersed in college studies, months passed, then this woman announced she was leaving. She called me aside and confided that she was very disturbed because my father attempted to "get familiar" with her. This was carnal knowledge, I felt I was too young and definitely too immature to process.

My brother now moved into this spare room. As a teenager he needed his own space. So only one roomer remained. A retiree who came and went unobtrusively. I had just graduated from college, it was 1947, and I entered the work world. I suggested to my father that moving downstairs, the three-bedroom flat would serve us better. The upstairs flat could be rented out. He agreed. My upright piano had to be swung over the upper front porch railing before it was transferred to the downstairs vestibule. Our address changed from 3291 to 3293 Trowbridge. I was happy to be freed of roomers at last.

After we moved downstairs, my father never mentioned needing extra income from roomers. From 1930 to 1947, he used this practical method to increase the family income. His was an unskilled laborer job with no hope of advancement. Until my father married in 1921, at age 31, he, too, lived with a family in a rented furnished room on a street in what is now called Poletown.

There were always "restrictions" as a result of having a non-family member part of the household. As a growing female, I could never walk through the house in a slip or pajamas, while a roomer was present. Also having a girl friend come for a sleep over was awkward until our family moved downstairs. I often stayed overnight at the Jelonek flat above their beer garden, with Lillian Baranowski in the living quarters in back of the confectionery, and with Dolores Wójcik after she moved to Fairport Street. I envied my friends who had more freedom inside their house than I did, and was relieved when I was successful in bringing it all to an end.

It was different with some of the renters on Norwalk and on Trowbridge Streets. Nick Mistinetz, whose dog Jackie became our pet, visited our family from time to time. During WW II, I was a teenager, opened the door to an FBI agent, who was doing a "Character Check" on Mr. Mistinetz. I was surprised that he was satisfied with my positive assessment of Nick's integrity. His job probably required a background check as a condition of employment.

Eleonor Wesołowski, daughter of the Dry Goods Store Wesołowski, who lived downstairs around the time of the great fire, became an accomplished vocalist, often featured as a soloist at the Band Shell concerts at Belle Isle Park. My mother and I made special trips to hear her for a number of years after the family moved away and Eleanor married John Hirt.

The roomers and the renters were part of my life on Norwalk and on Trowbridge Street.

Precipitating Factors

Mr. Halash, a portly middle-aged man with piercing blue eyes, thinning black hair and rosacea patches on each cheek, rented one of the bedrooms on Trowbridge in early 1942. He asked my mother to prepare his evening meal. She was not expected to do this for the other roomer, but she finally agreed at my father's insistence. It meant additional income. But Mr. Halash was critical of the menu. He requested food that we usually only ate on Sundays, like roast chicken, baked pork chops, fresh fruit and vegetables. My mother tried to accommodate his culinary cravings, although she complained privately about having to cook two different evening meals. Mr. Halash was employed in defense work in the area. We didn't know much else about him. He was an emigre from Poland, having left his home for the United States to escape Poland's escalating conflicts. I found this man's presence irritating and annoying, especially when he sat at the dining room table across from where I was doing my homework, watching me intently. I rushed to finish my assignment so I could leave the room.

He was watching my mother intently, too. One day they were alone in the house. He made a pretense of needing something in his room. When she entered, he began to grope and fondle her in a brusque and crude manner. The shock, fright, and surprise of his action became a traumatic episode that she recalled time and time again. Although I read about the incident in the hospital admission record that described the precipitating factors of my mother's depression and mental breakdown, my mother did not talk to me about it until many years after I was married. My mother had a rigid and severe code of behavior expected of married women. She was appalled to learn that I danced with men other than my husband at social events. I never even saw my mother give a hello or goodbye hug to any close relative, like her brother-in-law Frank, or his grown sons, who were her nephews.

She was scarred by the vivid memory of a near rape and its subsequent sense of shame and overwhelming guilt. She relived the incident in frequent flashbacks and conveyed the details to me many times after I was married. Another, even more disturbing event, happened when she was a mere child. This too, she revealed only after my marriage.

In 1902, my grandparents, Anna and Alexander Wróblewski, moved from the town of Białystok to the village of Gibulicze, which was about five kilometers west of Grodno, a large city in eastern Poland. My mother was 5 years old. While playing outdoors, a hired hand spotted her romping through the adjacent yard. He sought an accomplice, a young boy from the neighborhood. The two men grabbed her and tossed her to the ground. The young boy squelched her cries and struggles by sitting on her face. The hired hand raped her, leaving her unconscious. My grandmother eventually missed her, went looking for her, and found her bruised and bleeding. They took a horse-drawn wagon to see a doctor in Grodno who provided instructions for caring for the blisters that were left on her private parts by the rapist.

I asked my mother what happened to the perpetrator of this horrendous deed. She told me that he "was sent from the village," with no further punishment. My mother's recollection of the event included a witness, a neighbor who my mother thought may have observed the attack through a window of her hut across the dirt road. The validity of this portion of my mother's recollection is impossible to verify. My mother placed blame on the woman, who was unpopular in the neighborhood.

Surrogate Mother

The first event that dramatically changed my life was the move to Trowbridge Street in 1930. The second event, 12 years later, brought even more profound changes in my daily activities and left the most lasting effect.

In May 1942, my junior year in high school was coming to an end. I was 16 years old and my brother Leonard was 10. The U.S. was at war after the attack on Pearl Harbor. Since Hitler had invaded Poland in 1939, my mother had been concerned about her brother John and sister Eva who were still there living under foreign rule. She began to relive her own painful memories of WW I. When the letters from her family in the old country stopped, her fears and apprehension escalated. Our three young male roomers were drafted and replaced with two older men who had jobs in the defense factories around Hamtramck. Life as we knew it was changing daily.

And my mother was also going through changes. That May morning, she did not come out of her bedroom, get dressed or attend to any of the household chores. My brother, father, and I found her in bed, sobbing and wailing, oblivious to us.

I contacted the assistant pastor, Rev. Edmund Behrendt, and asked him to visit and administer the sacraments. I was confident that the Sacrament of Penance and Holy Eucharist, and perhaps the Last Rites, would restore her to her former self. The Catholic Church may have the words of eternal-life but it does not have miracle cures for temporal illness. My father prevailed on her to get dressed and walked with her to St. Francis Hospital, three blocks away. She continued to cry, wring her hands and pace the hallways. I heard her mutter to herself and berate herself for something that she did not share with us.

My father had summoned Dr. Kłosowski, our local general practitioner, who diagnosed her with involutional melancholia, menopausal. He recommended further treatment, which was available at the Wayne County General in Eloise, Michigan, which is now Wayne, Michigan. She was treated for her depression with electroshock therapy, but it brought only brief improvement. Years later my mother remembered the day in May 1942, when she was transferred to the county hospital. She had called it kidnapping.

Our life at home was devastated. Returning from work, my father sat down on his stool next to the stove in the kitchen, his hands covering his face as he sobbed over his loss. I started to attend daily mass at our parish church during the summer months, dejected, praying for my mother's return to health and family. Overnight I had become a surrogate mother to my brother and a housekeeper to my grieving father. My carefree teen years took on a level of responsibility beyond getting good grades and finding a date to the senior prom. I was determined to keep up my high school honor roll standing, attend social activities with my friends and prepare for college. Dreams of dating and marriage were also in the back of my mind. A strong sense of duty and obligation plunged me into my new role.

Juggling time, energy, housekeeping, cooking and managing my younger brother absorbed all my waking hours after a school day. Any disciplining of Leonard met with failure as my father never supported or reinforced it. My cooking skills needed a crash course. Pastor Szok's cook shared a recipe for borscht with me. A cookbook that I bought offered recipes and sample menus. Throughout all this I hoped for my mother's return to health. The void that she left could not be filled.

Visiting my mother in the hospital meant walking seven blocks to catch the Baker Street Car that ran from Joseph Campau Street to downtown Detroit. An interurban bus started from Cadillac Square, rode west on Michigan Avenue to Eloise. County General's D Building was just inside an arch, an iron gateway with E L O I S E across its top. Admissions, information, and doctors' offices were located in the D Building, a red brick structure and the facility's newest. All the other buildings, which were also assigned letters, were older. They were spaced around many acres of what was essentially a rural area. Besides the general medical hospital, mentally ill patients were housed initially in the D Building. There was a special building, commonly known as the "poor farm," for the indigent. Homeless men without any means of support were sent to the "poor farm" for bed and board.

My first visit to D Building was traumatic. Children under 14 were not permitted to visit, so I traveled alone that Sunday afternoon. I was led through doors that opened with a key. My mother was sitting on a chair, rocking back and forth, her face pulled into a worried, distraught frown. I could not see her arms. They were drawn into a straight jacket, its sleeves pulled across her front and tied in back. She started to cry and called me by name. She told me how unlucky she was to find herself in these circumstances. I don't remember much else from that first visit except that I, too, felt very unlucky to find myself part of the stigma and shame attached to having a family member dispatched to Eloise.

My father visited my mother about once a month, but he quickly lost patience. Conversation was not possible because of her delusional thinking. She could recognize us, but the delusions left us frustrated and hopeless. She always had crying spells and was despondent and despairing. When I was in graduate school, I read her admission history which gave the precipitating factors of her mental breakdown.

Not long after my mother's transfer to County Hospital, a hospital social worker paid us a visit. She came during the day when my father was at work, so she interviewed me. A middle-aged woman, tall and ample-figured, she was perspiring after climbing the stairs to the second floor. I noted her loose-fitting flowered dress. She asked how we were managing, and my response must have satisfied her. As she was ready to leave, I asked, "Is my mother's sickness contagious?" I don't recall her answer, but it was not convincing. She never came back. A gnawing apprehension permeated my psyche for a long time. Many years later I worked with psychiatric patients at a mental health clinic. I learned to be comfortable with this segment of our population and came to terms with mental illness. My heart goes out to families whose lives are permanently affected when a member is diagnosed with a major psychosis.

Alice Brady was another social worker who was assigned to our case. She had just graduated from the Catholic University in Washington, DC, and had a sister who taught history at Marygrove College. The sister was an Immaculate Heart of Mary nun. Alice's father worked at the Aluminum Company of America. Alice Brady became a role model. She became a social worker at the Youth Services Department of Catholic Charities where I did a practicum between my junior and senior years of college. She recommended me for a summer job in 1944 at her father's place of employment. The Alcoa offices where I worked were located in the New Center Building on Second Avenue near the Fisher Building. Mr. Brady was the head of the department where I became a member of the typing pool.

Alice married John Ainsworth and moved to Port Huron, Michigan. They had a daughter. Years later, at a social work function, she recalled how well I managed our home during my mother's absence. I knew that I had taken extra steps to make sure that everything was spic and span for her first visit to our home.

After my mother became ill, my father cooked some meals on weekends and prepared his own lunches daily. I arranged for Leonard to eat lunch at the Skoney's. Ronald, the youngest in the Skoney family, also attended Our Lady Queen of the Apostles School. Mrs. Skoney graciously agreed to serve lunch to both boys during the school year. Ronnie would sit on the handle bars of my brother's bicycle as they rode to the Skoney house on Sobieski Street. Irene and I attended the same high school, and we ate cafeteria style lunches together in the basement of the school building.

Our living room became a bedroom as my father recruited more war industry workers to rent space in our seven-room flat. What a treadmill of activity, with no privacy for any of us! Three rooms were rented. The converted living room, with French doors, was curtained for what little privacy we had.

The discovery of major tranquilizers and other psychotropic drugs finally made an impact on my mother's condition. The voices that she heard, which she attributed to a "magic aerial," bothered her less and less. She was finally discharged. After 15 years as an inpatient, she returned to Trowbridge in 1957 shortly after my father's death.

She needed us more than ever. My brother was responsible for providing her with shelter, and I transported her to medical appointments and follow-up visits to a psychiatrist. Stressful situations and missed doses of her medication resulted in many re-admissions to the psychiatric unit of the county hospital.

Her follow-up care continued into her 80s. It was the most successful means of monitoring her medications and her response to them. I could usually redirect her to reality, and she could function and attend to her daily living, grateful for the help she received from us.

CHAPTER II

A Not So Brief Encounter

"Of all the throbbing teenage hearts in all the flats and bungalows on all the streets of Hamtramck, HE found, invaded and captured mine."

It was 1943. I had a high school diploma and a summer job as a typist at the Chrysler Lynch Road plant. WWII was raging in many countries around the globe.

The *Hamtramck Citizen*, our city's newspaper, listed names and addresses of local servicemen who were asking for letters from "home" as morale boosters. Pfc Bernard J. Zacharias was at Brown University, Rhode Island. I initiated the correspondence as I had with other GI's in this country and abroad. Letters led to photos being exchanged and a meeting date promised when his next furlough came up. The small snapshot was of a soldier in a khaki shirt and trousers wearing a rimmed hat with the insignia of the Army Air Force. One leg was up on a step leading to a campus building. A slight smile was on his otherwise serious face. I sent a high school graduation photo in which I wore a black cap and gown.

The circumstances of our first meeting are blurred. We probably exchanged short biographical information. I was enrolled in the freshman class at Marygrove College, living at home, had a job as a typist and was enjoying the summer vacation weekends before the fall semester began. His family lived on Casmere Street, west of Joseph Campau, less than a mile from my house on Trowbridge Street. One of twelve children, he had an older sister, Leona, and a brand new baby sister, Bernadette. Bernie was one year older than

me, graduated from Hamtramck High School in 1942. The Army
Air Force sent him to study meteorology at Brown. He was dark
haired, brown eyed, slim, trim, and with a calm, but intense
demeanor I found very appealing.

My introverted heart skipped a beat when Bernie asked if I
was free to meet again. One segment of that encounter was seared
into my inner core.

We stood in the late afternoon shade, next to the building on
the corner of Woodward and Calvert, waiting for the Caniff bus to
carry us back to Hamtramck. It was a golden August day.

Out of his khaki trouser back pocket, Bernie pulled out a stick
of Double Mint gum. As I looked on with interest, he creased it in
the middle, then broke the piece in two. He leaned toward me to
hand me a half stick, confiding, "I've quit smoking. This is my
substitute." I was speechless. This was an unexpected sharing
gesture. I fixed my eyes on that half stick of gum, reached for it,
unwrapped it and placed it into my mouth. My cheeks flushed
hot and a tingling warmth washed over my body. His words were
sincere. His penetrating gaze melted my knees to soft butter. It
was the first time anyone acted on a dislike I expressed.

During our initial meeting, Bernie asked if I minded if he
smoked, as he held a pack of cigarettes, removing one to light it.
My truthful negative response resulted in his decision to quit.

The initial appeal I felt, was developing into an attraction for
this lean, brown-haired soldier with those smoldering deep brown
eyes. Bernie was my first real BEAU! He continued to make plans
for the two of us. My August birthday was coming up. We traveled
by streetcar to celebrate the occasion at Hund's Candlelight Room,
a popular restaurant in downtown Detroit. Bernie suggested a mild
cocktail—my first—a Pink Lady.

Bernie's furlough ended. "Morale Booster" letters resumed,
now ending in "As ever" instead of "Yours truly." In early September,
I began freshman classes at Marygrove College. I was reliving those
special times with my soldier beau, basking in the memories of his
attentiveness when we were together. Adjusting to college life was
overwhelming, especially when compounded by a rush of emotions

that had nothing to do with the curriculum. I was LOVE STRUCK! So much so, that my reveries escalated to an early commitment, an engagement! I even borrowed a diamond ring, wearing it on the third finger of my left hand! After a week, I returned it as reality kicked in and I began to feel foolish over this ridiculous deception. There were strong demands of an 18-hour semester and managing the motherless household on Trowbridge.

Bernie was home briefly at Christmas. We exchanged gifts during a short visit he made to my house. We were in the living room, the afternoon sun streaming in the windows. He did not sit down nor remove his heavy overcoat. His parents expected him to be at their family Christmas dinner and he was complying with their wishes.

I received a pink gold heart-shaped locket with silver Air Corps wings on the front. My gift to him was an unimaginative box of white handkerchiefs. The locket opened to hold two pictures, one on each side. I found a snapshot of Bernie, cut out the face to fit inside. He was a composite of Gregory Peck and Charles Boyer in his looks and demeanor.

At semester break in January, Bernie had another furlough. We shared a memorable meal at the Russian Bear Restaurant on Elizabeth Street and Woodward Avenue, near the Fox Theatre, downtown. It was almost dark as we hurried down a short flight of stairs to enter this below ground-level eatery. The Balalaika orchestra, men dressed in bright shiny satin shirts with sashes, played "Dark Eyes" as we savored beef stroganoff served over fine shoestring potatoes.

We were in a high backed, dark wood booth, sitting across from each other, secluded and oblivious to the other patrons. The tabletop had a shaded lamp whose low-watt lamp bulb was further dimmed by a square flowered silk kerchief draped over, the corners hanging below the round edge of the shade.

The unique sounds from the Balalaika orchestra continued: "Two Guitars," then, "At the Balalaika." For dessert we ordered delicate blintzes with a dusting of powdered sugar. I felt exhilarated and aglow in the warm rose tinted light, surrounded by romantic tunes, and the center of attention of this conversational, serious, captivating man in uniform.

It was time to leave this atmosphere filled enclosure. We shivered as we stepped out into the dark, small entryway. Before proceeding, Bernie sealed this evening by carving our initials inside a heart shape on the rough heavy beams: BZ + LK. He had to blow on his bare hands to keep them warmed while whittling on the surface. A gentle snowfall muffled our travel back to Hamtramck via streetcar and bus.

The first love brought a number of "firsts" into my love parched life. Besides drinking my first cocktail with Bernie, I experienced my first roller coaster ride with him at the Jefferson Beach Amusement Park the following spring. As we tumbled rickety-split with the wind rushing at our faces and through our hair, his arms reached around my shoulders, my head and side pressed against his firm chest. We were still clinging together as the wheels rumbled to a stop. When the short ride ended, I was eager to repeat it. But we headed to the dance pavilion where a big band was playing, to finish off the evening dancing. We were both filled with the ardor and glow of youthful love.

The zenith of all our "encounters" was a surprise visit that sent my heart reeling. It was the middle of 1944.

I was in the company of three girlfriends this one July Saturday night. In our party dresses we walked to the Knights of Columbus Hall at the corner of Conant and Evaline in Hamtramck. A summer wedding reception, of one of our parish young women, was in full swing. The wooden floor had a fresh coat of powdered wax and was buffed into a slick finish by shoes sliding and stomping to the peppy "Beer Barrel Polka." A perspiring band beat out the rhythm. The lights in the ceiling were dimmed, the enthusiasm of the dancers notable. Our quartet paired off to dance. When the music stopped, the handful of past middle-age males on the dance floor pulled out kerchiefs to mop their brows. The women retreated to the sidelines, plopping down on benches along the wall, fanning their faces with open palms. Through the open door leading to the basement rose the aroma of baking chicken and brewing coffee.

At the front entry way, the double doors opened. The corner street light silhouetted a figure in the narrow vestibule. A trim uniformed soldier, in a neatly pressed light khaki shirt and trousers, was holding a folded garrison cap. The sleeve of his upper arm had a single stripe and the Army Corps wings. He stopped at the edge of the dance floor, his gaze searching the seated guests. "He's asking for you," I was told. I recognized Bernie and stood up. "How did he find me here?" I wondered. We began to walk toward each other across the uncrowded floor. It was then I noticed, "Oh, how tanned," swallowing hard to check the rising flood of feeling. Both of his arms reached out to mine. Our fingertips connected, sending a swift current through my limbs and cascading down my spine, to the bottom of my feet. A closer look at his face, cleanly shaven, revealed highlights of gold in the rich brown hair, accentuating each temple, outlining his eyebrows, and defining the hairline above the forehead.

Now both of my hands were in his. In a low voice he explained, "I'm on a weekend pass, hitched a ride from Myrtle Beach. Tomorrow I'll be with my family. Tonight I wanted to be with you." His soulful serious deep brown eyes fixed a penetrating gaze on my upturned face—oh, what is that surging wave crashing inside?

He continued to tell me that he arrived at my house this evening, where he learned from my father where to find me.

The musicians on the stage shuffled sheet music, poised to play the next dance selection. Bernie drew me toward him, one arm encircling my back at the waist. I lifted my left arm onto his shoulder, firm and hard after months of basic training. His deeply tanned cheek pressed against my flushed forehead, brushing aside strands of my blond hair. We began to bend and sway to the first bars of music. The impact of Bernie's surprise appearance began to sink in as I heard and recognized the music being played. It was from the season's hit musical, "Oklahoma."

"DON'T THROW BOUQUETS AT ME, DON'T SIGH
AND GAZE AT ME, DON'T KEEP YOUR HAND IN
MINE, YOUR HAND FEELS SO GRAND IN MINE,

DON'T DANCE ALL NIGHT WITH ME, THEY'RE
SUSPECTING THINGS, *PEOPLE WILL SAY WE'RE IN
LOVE.*"

But in my insecure mind, I feared, "what will people say?"
seeing such public demonstrations of attraction. When friends asked,
"How did you meet?" Telling the circumstances was like admitting
I pulled his name out of a hat. After all we had not been "formally"
introduced! I was uncomfortable getting so much attention in spite
of the strong feelings I was experiencing. Our first meeting ignited
a flame of romance that was fanned into a blaze with each
subsequent encounter.

Bernie and I left the K. of C. Hall and my three girl friends. It
was a short three blocks to the two-family house on Trowbridge.
Hand in hand, our heads on cloud nine, my Army Air Corps beau
and I strolled leisurely in the warm summer moonlight to the left
front stoop of the white painted frame structure. We soon stood at
the glass paneled door. I handed him the metal skeleton key. He
unlocked the door, opening it with one twist of the round brass
knob. I reached for the right wall, flicked up the switch for the 40-
watt bare bulb at the top of the long wood stairway. We reached
the landing, stopping under the overhead light. We stood on a
narrow gray runner that extended the length of the short hallway.
Ahead, a solid oak door lead to the dining room beyond. Along
the wall, an opened ironing board was stored, the supporting wood
legs too cumbersome to be folded after each use. We were facing
each other, our voices at whisper level. Yes, we'll continue to write,
the next meeting indefinite. "I want you to meet my sister Leona.
She's the head of the Sander's kitchen downtown store," he offered
proudly.

His arms reached around my shoulders, tugging me toward
him. It was a short distance to my upturned face. He planted a
firm kiss on my waiting lips: brief, ardent, decisive. Those velvety
chocolate brown eyes had an unmistaken gleam, were riveting,
penetrating. Did I imagine a hesitation to release me from his
warm embrace?

I blurted, "You know my mother is in the hospital." This was the baggage I carried, the apron strings that tied me down, the web that trapped me in a way I did not fully understand. Duty and responsibility as caretaker at home were paramount.

With quick light steps Bernie descended the bare varnished stairs, walking onto the dark porch, closing the door behind him. It was 10 blocks to his parents' home on Casmere Street, west of Joseph Campau.

I tiptoed into the dark dining room, then into my bedroom on the left. Fluttering butterflies were in the pit of my stomach, my cheeks radiating heat, a lightheadedness and bliss permeating my consciousness. Bernie's earnest attention and low profile virility could not be denied. It consumed me. Lying on my back in the dark, flights of fancy transported me to a consummation. If he was a husband, I would be a willing accepting vessel. Carefully I considered the physical aspects of this act. The bodies would be bare, a contact would follow. Love would triumph!

A short time later, Bernie's sister Leona and I planned an activity that took us to a War Rally at the University of Detroit stadium. There was patriotic singing and a demonstration of the value of blackouts. Even one lighted match was seen in that huge arena.

In August 1944, Bernie and I celebrated my birthday with a meal at the top of the Penobscot Building, the tallest skyscraper in Downtown Detroit. I bought a gray silk, flowered dress with a ruffled U neckline. A purple orchid arrived from the florist, and I set the box inside the ice box. When Bernie came in to get me, he asked, "Did you get my corsage?" "What corsage?" I teased, in a backhanded sense of humor. He looked alarmed, and I relented, assuring him that the delivery was made. Bernie's gift was a small, footed silver jewelry chest with black velvet lining. He told me that his sister Leona enjoyed our meeting. Then he asked about the weekend.

Bernie's furlough was for a week. It was the same week I committed myself to a week with high school friends, Ann Tomas and Rita Engler. I felt bound to keep the commitment. Just staying at home to be "available" was too "obvious" in my naive, immature, inexperienced mind. Bernie reacted with a start, well-controlled, gentleman-like, when I related my decision. At the cottage, we had a portable record player and a long-playing record of "Oklahoma." I was in a heady whirl, day dreaming, reliving my recent date with Bernie.

The "Dear Jane" letter, stunned me like a thunderbolt. Bernie wrote of spending another two-week furlough at home. I read the words, a shudder going through me. Fourteen days in town without any word or contact! Also he told of being transferred out of the meteorology program and considering the paratroopers. Another wave, now of apprehension, such a dangerous and risk-filled prospect! I replied telling of my fearful reaction to the paratrooper idea, but avoided mentioning feeling crushed and devastated at not getting to see him.

There were no more letters. Puzzled and perplexed, my code of behavior precluded any further overt action. An acquaintance agreed to send a letter to Bernie telling him I was hoping to hear from him. It brought no results.

For results, I turned to prayers. "Ask and you shall receive" and "more things are wrought through prayer" I heard throughout my years of religious education. So I undertook the Super Novena: 3 x 9-27 days, the Rosary Novena. It consists of five decades of the rosary, recited each day for 27 days in petition; then immediately, five decades of the rosary, daily for 27 days in thanksgiving, whether or not the request was granted. The pamphlet describes it as a laborious Novena, "You who are sincere will not find it too difficult, if you really wish to obtain your request." Mine was "*to see HIM.*" Fervently and with devotion, I fingered the oval wooden beads following the prescribed formula. Each night it was the last activity before turning out the overhead hanging bulb in my small bedroom. An ardent relationship, my first romance, had come to an unclear, heartbreaking ending. The novena was my introverted, gullible, naive ploy to restore what had been.

It took almost a whole month for the petition part. I tried to be hopeful. The following day, I was walking on Joseph Campau

Street, having just left the Martha Washington Bakery. The red traffic light at the corner of Caniff and Joseph Campau brought me to a halt along with several other pedestrians. Ahead of the person in front of me, a profile of a darkly handsome male came into focus. IT WAS HIM.

I froze to the pavement under my shoes. In disbelief I took in his calm stance, then the forward stride that took him across the busy street and out of my life forever. He continued toward Casmere Street. I turned right to the Bank of Commerce.

The super novena brought results—just as I asked—indeed, I did see HIM again.

I was a Sophomore at Marygrove College, absorbed by a class in Sociology that would lead me to my life's work. I had to squelch the heartbreak and placed a tight lid on the cauldron of bubbling emotions resulting from my not so brief encounter. That memory, was buried deep inside and locked.

A poem from the college newspaper reflected my sentiments at the time. It's dated, April 18, 1945:

To An Absent Lover

Our friends have asked me every day
Since you've been gone, if you are well
And "Aren't you lonely since he went away?"
Or, "Does he write often? Does he tell
You of the ways of his new life?" Oh, my dear,
How can they stand so near me and not hear
Your voice, or see your smile, or sense you there
When sunlight or a breeze recalls a spot where
Maples grew and grass was green and flowers
Bright through all the year, to make the magic hours
More magical? But they are unaware.
What can I do but say
That one so much beloved is never far away.
                                        —A Marygrove Student

PFC B. J. ZAHARIAS—1944

Bits of information about Bernie filtered down to me via my Bank Teller friend, Eleanor Jasinski. A younger brother of Bernie banked at the Bank of Commerce where Eleanor worked and followed the lives of many locals. She learned from him that Bernie married sometime in 1946 and then had two daughters.

I determined to complete college. Three classmates, Helen Jedlinski, Christine Cieszynski, and Victoria Zalenski and I were friends throughout the four years, traveling the same buses to the campus each day.

With the war's end, servicemen, now turned civilians, were enrolling in area colleges and universities and often stood with us at the same bus stops.

Helen's high school classmate showed a serious interest in her. They began to "keep company" while he attended the University of Detroit. Eventually she became Mrs. Chester Hill.

Christine Cieszynski had a childhood sweetheart, Don Keefe, who came home from the Army to claim her hand. We met him when he squired her to the College Junior Prom.

One of my parish church youth group members, Eddie Muszynski, discharged from the Army, spoke of returning to school. He accepted my invitation to be my escort at the prom. After the dance was over, I invited another couple, Victoria Zalenski and her date, Ed Borucki, to join us for refreshments at my house on Trowbridge. When Eddie met Vicky, the chemistry between them was "right," leading to their eventual marriage. I was pleased to have been instrumental in the matchmaking.

Both Helen and Vicky became school teachers in the city of Detroit elementary schools. Chris' major was economics and business. She was hired as a secretary to an executive of a paint company. With my degree in Sociology, I looked to be employed in a social agency.

June 1947 saw all four of us embarking on careers.

Marygrove College—1943-1947

My father encouraged higher education. It would assure me that I would not have to do heavy physical labor as he did. Never mind I was doing household chores: laundry, ironing, shopping, cooking (most meals), and cleaning. I was preparing for the future, to qualify for work that would support me until marriage.

I stayed on the Honor Roll throughout the four years of high school. Because of this, I was excused from taking an entrance exam to be admitted to Marygrove College. The same I.H.M. nuns taught at the College as at Girls Catholic Central.

I considered going to the University of Detroit, briefly. When Sister Aquinata at the high school learned of this, she called me in for a "conference." She had a very expressive face and deep brown searching eyes. After a short discussion, she set me back on my heels, inquiring, "What do you think your mother would have wanted?" I dissolved into tears. She struck a vulnerable spot. I would attend Marygrove!

As in high school, my horizons expanded further. This small woman's college (900 students) had "day students" and "residents." The day students commuted by public transportation, from various areas of Detroit and its suburbs. Patricia Smith, who became senior class president, drove a black Ford to school, from Mt. Clemens after WW II ended. It was the lone car parked next to the Liberal Arts Building for a long time. The residents in the Madame Cadillac dormitory were from cities in Michigan, Ohio, and Indiana. All the freshmen were from the top third of their graduating class in high school. Some bright ones had photographic brain cells, enabling them to recite, verbatim, pages from European history texts, English reading assignments, etc.

Every Monday morning, the entire student body assembled in the Auditorium for "Programs." We sat by classes, alphabetically. To my left was Adele Kasper, continually sketching with charcoal, to my right, Mary Claire Kelly. We listened to world renown celebrities: Dorothy Day, Baroness von Hauck, philosophers and famous authors. We pondered social issues, voluntary poverty, and miscegenation.

The faculty members at the college were mainly members of the religious order of Immaculate Heart of Mary. The others were lay men and women and priests. I steered my classes to the secular faculty whenever possible.

First year German was taught by a tall, athletic blond woman. She taught us a number of German songs as well as trying to make sense of the complicated grammar. Professor Guerster, a portly middle-aged man with droopy eyes, soft white hands, and a craggy complexion, was assigned to the second year German class. His background was the humanities, literature, music and opera. How easily we distracted him from explaining the ponderous German sentence structure to elaborating on the glories of language, literature, music, poetry, and opera! His wife, we learned was an opera singer. They both sought asylum in the United States. We quickly learned how to get the best from this professor!

My ethics teacher was a Capuchin Monk from Dun Scotus Franciscan Monastery in Southfield, Michigan. A tall, large-boned man with a big easy smile, he rushed into the classroom just a minute or two late, his long brown wool habit brushing the bare wooden floor, the white cords of his belt swinging as he moved to sit down behind the desk. He explained his speedy drive south on Northwestern Highway to get to class on time. It was here I learned and accepted Existentialism, because it gave a picture of the world as it is, not as we hope it should be. It was Father Hugh, who floored us with news that men possess the "laying" instinct. He lasted one semester. He made it clear to us that giving exams and grading students was a chore he did reluctantly.

The college campus, on Six Mile Road, west of Livernois in Detroit, had two large Gothic style buildings. The Liberal Arts building held the classrooms and chapel. Madame Cadillac was the dormitory, and had the dining room, cafeteria, gym, and Alumnae Hall ballroom. A separate building, smaller, but in the same architectural style, was the residence of the President. "Our Lady of Marygrove," a white marble figure of the blessed Virgin Mary presided over the campus on a raised pedestal, set on stone in the middle of the spacious foreground. The entire campus was enclosed by a tall, black wrought iron fence with square posts made of gray stone.

In 1943, this woman's college had rules for the females attending—no smoking on campus, no slacks, no bare legs with anklets, no married students. Of course, no alcohol on the grounds. The emphasis was on studies, social action in the community, and preparation for a fruitful, fulfilling life in the world. Religion was a required course whether you were a Roman Catholic or not. I recall one Jewish coed and two Protestants who sat in on the once-a-week class, always conducted by an ordained priest. One of the non-Catholic students, Betty Ann Cole, I learned many years later, was the daughter of a well-known black funeral director. She was very light skinned, passing for white. Many students who lived on campus worshiped at the 7:30 a.m. daily mass in the chapel. Others made frequent visits to chapel during the school day, reciting the rosary or other favorite prayers. Everyone prayed for a successful end to the war. Brothers and sweethearts were away in many branches of the service.

College studies were stressful and challenging for me. I was happy when I found sociology such a rewarding class when I began my sophomore year. The chemistry class I struggled through that year lead me to switch from trying to be a lab technician to the social work field.

The 250 freshmen dwindled to 125 after the end of the sophomore year. Concentrating on a major field of study sharpened one's focus. We looked to "field work" or "practice teaching" at the end of the junior year. We anticipated the senior religion sessions on "marriage," when students listened with eyes lowered, hearing about conjugal privileges, consummation, marital rights. From a priest.

Tuition at Marygrove College in 1943 was $150 per semester. My father could afford this sum as long as I lived at home. He gave me a weekly allowance for bus fare and lunches. The tuition was not raised during my four years at the school. Earnings from summer jobs eased the cost of wardrobe needs and extras, such as books, lab fees, etc.

Socially, I kept in contact with former schoolmates from grade school and high school. Many still lived in the neighborhood. The "sorority" formed in high school lost some members who moved away, and added a couple new ones. We still met in each others' homes. Now our topics were more adult-like. We discussed jobs, hobbies, upcoming marriages, then children, and moves to the suburbs.

When V-J Day ended WW II in August of 1945, I still had two more years of college to complete.

One of the returning servicemen was Stanley Basak. (He, and his brother Norbert, rented a room in our house for over a year while I was a young teenager.) They were both drafted. Norbert was the handsomer of the two, with a flashy smile and blue eyes. Stanley had a raw boned, coarser appearance. Norbert and I exchanged letters while he was in the Army, but it was Stanley who made an unexpected visit after the war ended. He proposed marriage. I turned him down. I never thought of him in a romantic manner and did not feel I could develop any feelings that would lead to marriage. I did not tell my father of this development.

All students were required to earn one college credit in Physical education. It was one of the 18 credits I earned as a Freshman. The uniform we wore to this activity was a culotte of apple green cotton. I had poorly developed athletic skills, I learned, when Miss Scanlon announced a tournament in tennis, ping pong, and archery.

I knew the game of tennis, but not as well as my only opponent, "Tex," whose shoulders were like a football player's, who was at least a head taller than me and about 30 pounds heavier. She may have been from Texas, but her southern drawl earned her the nickname. I got eliminated in the first round.

I suffered the same fate in ping pong and archery. Petite Josephine Nardi won the ping pong tourney and Adele Kasper's steady hand and a keen eye prevailed in archery. They both had a stronger sense of competition along with more practice before coming to Marygrove.

I continued to enjoy all the above sports. For two summers, at a girls camp, I taught archery to campers. It was not important to excel in the sport, either for the campers or the teacher.

"Tex" left the campus in the middle of the first semester. She was expelled for allegedly attempting to kiss another female student while riding in the elevator.

Marygrove's heavily wooded campus had a bridle path in 1943, which was used by some students who owned a horse and could board it nearby. In biology class, when we studied flora, we made several "field" trips to gather leaves and study the variety of trees on the property. Spring was glorious on campus when flowering dogwood, magnolias, forsythia, and bridal wreath spiraea bloomed.

Many pairs of hands dusted, polished, mopped, and swept the marble halls and carved wooden staircases in the Liberal Arts Building and Madame Cadillac Dorm. The nuns housed a number of women with developmental disabilities giving them a safe environment and steady employment.

Attending a Catholic college for women continued to define and underscore all the previous years of religious education I had in high school, in elementary school, and at home.

At Queen of Apostles parochial school I heard a lot about the difference between mortal and venial sin, about the obligation to attend Sunday Mass, about not eating meat on Friday, about making my annual Easter duty, observing the Ten Commandments, the value of visiting the Blessed Sacrament, and about the miracles at Lourdes, Fatima, and Częstochowa. We became familiar with the lives of saints. I especially remember St. Stanislaus Kostka, St. Anthony, St. Francis of Assisi, St. Elizabeth of Hungary, St. Bernadette, St. Theresa of the Child Jesus, and other Old Testament saints such as Daniel in the Lions' den and Joseph with his coat of many colors. In every instance, I heard it was a strong and unflinching faith that led to sainthood. When I asked my mother for a nickel every Friday, it was for the Propagation of Faith missions to baptize Chinese pagan babies. I had a picture in my mind of a nun or a priest rescuing slant eyed female infants before they were discarded. With some water and the sign of the cross, they were converted to Christianity and assured eternal life.

In high school, the all-girl student body deepened their devotion to the Blessed Virgin with daily recitation of the Rosary, especially during October. In May, another month devoted to Mary, we had a crowning ceremony in the chapel. A wreath of flowers was placed on the head of the figure of the Mother of Jesus followed by singing of hymns. I learned many new hymns adding to the familiar ones I heard in the Polish language at the parish church. And we experienced the annual "Retreat." This took place over a three-day period, when we were to observe silence, except to talk to the Retreat master who was an "Order" priest, e.g., Redemptorist, Paulist. A lot of soul searching took place, and a lot of resolutions were made. Complete silence was a lofty goal, difficult to maintain for 3 days.

At Marygrove, the annual retreat usually took place during Lent. The 1944 retreat master was a Maryknoll priest, Rev. James Keller. I think the entire female student body wanted to follow this engaging, handsome, virile man of the cloth. Tall, lean, with a wide grin, wavy dark brown hair, laughing blue eyes, he was successful in getting many a struggling student to pledge a monthly sum of money for the Maryknoll missions all over the world. Of course, again, he spoke of China and the needs there. We were enthralled when he told of skiing with Kate Smith, a popular singing star at the time. I remember feeling very conflicted wanting become a missionary, but still harboring an overwhelming romantic attraction for my pen pal and first beau, Bernie Zacharias, and at the same time, answering the tug of responsibility as a surrogate mother and housekeeper at home. Elinor Doherty, my classmate whose presence next to me in chemistry lab helped me pass with a "C," joined the Maryknoll sisters after graduation. Maybe Father Keller's exhortations took root.

"Competence, compassion, and commitment" became a motto, a guidepost, an expectation, at Marygrove. All the students joined a social action program volunteering on weekends and after classes

during the week. I recall Christine Cieszynski and I deciding on
Providence Hospital. They had a nursery where babies of unwed
mothers remained after birth until adoption or other placement.
On Sunday, from 1:00 p.m. to 4:00 p.m., we bottle fed the infants,
cuddled and rocked them, changed the diapers if needed, and
brought them to the window should a mother or other relative
visit. On one occasion, I was asked by a nurse to get a baby boy
out of the crib and bring him to the window. I recognized his
mother, a young woman from our neighborhood, but did not
acknowledge this fact in any way. It would be confidential
information, never revealed to anyone. I later overheard mention
of how this particular young woman had left town for a while.
Childbirth, out of wedlock, in 1943, was a shameful predicament,
marginally tolerated, ending in adoption.

The first Guardian Angel Home operated by the Felician Sisters
was located on the corner or St. Aubin and Canfield. A gothic-
style structure from the turn of the century, it abounded with
long dark corridors and creaking wooden floors. Girls placed there
were from broken homes and from single parent families. It became
my sophomore year choice for social action. My assignment: help
shampoo the hair of the kindergarten age group on Saturday
evening. The building also had served as a boarding school for
high school age girls, but it was being phased out as newer facilities
sprang up around the area. Affluent Polish families sent their
daughters to this in-town boarding school for many years.

The ultimate social action, in my mind, was helping in what
was essentially a shelter for the homeless. It was managed by Justine
L'Esperance Murphy (Marygrove '40) and her husband Louis. Their
vow of voluntary poverty was admired at Marygrove as "Christlike."
Donations "in kind" sustained them and the inhabitants who came
to this facility, a single family house on Leverette Street, on Detroit's
west side. One of the sociology majors, Betty Hogan, chose this
lifestyle after graduation in 1947. I visited her one evening,
intrigued. She related how day-old baked goods from Sander's
bakery and surplus food from downtown restaurants were gathered
and delivered to this dwelling. It was a hand-to-mouth existence.

Betty eventually left for school social work in the Detroit public schools.

During my junior year, with my advisor's approval, I returned to the Tau Beta Community House to experience group work. I was assisting one of the staff who led a Brownie Girl Scout troop. It was a prelude to my graduate school field work when I was assigned to "take over" an all-black Brownie Girl Scout troop at the St. Peter Claver Community House.

Participating in social action groups as a college student broadened my horizons and was a testing ground for my future work in social work.

TOWER DANCE, 1946—MARYGROVE COLLEGE—
CHARLOTTE, 2nd FROM RIGHT

My Father (Tatuś) Andrew Kasperowicz

In 1954, at age 65, my father's employer gave him the option
of retiring or working. I know he thought about this carefully. His
decision was to continue at his current job. I agreed that it was a
good decision. But his health declined dramatically, just about
this time, so he concluded that "they" know when it is better to
stop gainful employment. The Riley Stoker Company announced
a retirement party for all the workers retiring that year. For the
occasion my father took a big step: he purchased a new dress suit.
It was a banker's gray with a fine black stripe and included a vest.
He wore it proudly when he attended the function, receiving a pin
with a diamond chip in the center for 25 years of service. He
attended my three graduations, but it was this event that warranted
a new suit!

Retirement left my father with a lot of unstructured time. For
several months on Saturday mornings we drove to the Riley Stoker
factory where my father collected scrap wood. He unloaded it into
the garage where he removed the nails from the boards. Eventually
he replaced the fence next to the alley using this lumber. It was the
last task he completed before succumbing to ailments that
weakened him so that he needed help with personal grooming.

I recall the binge drinking and gambling sprees that kept
him away from the home sometimes for days. One phone call
from Jax Bar asked me to come get my father as he was not able
to walk. It was Saturday morning. Seated on the sidewalk,
leaning against the brick siding of the bar, my father looked
like a wilted scarecrow. Unshaven, hair tousled, he agreed to be
led home, about half a block. I wanted to die of humiliation.
He had been deprived of his wife's companionship for fifteen
years and missed her deeply. I feel this void affected his choice
of activity after she was hospitalized.

After his retirement, he was diagnosed with prostate cancer.
Surgery at the Veteran's Hospital was intended to arrest the spread
of cancer. He was devastated by the orchiectomy. He lost weight

and grew weaker as the weeks went on. The doctor attending him at the hospital revealed little to me. My father was sensitive to the teams of doctors that circled his bed, discussing his symptoms. He confessed that he felt like a test animal used in the Parke Davis laboratories which were located across the street from the Riley Stoker Factory.

I purchased an electric shaver to use on my father at home. A sponge bath sufficed to keep him clean. Most of his day was spent on a chaise that was set up in the dining room next to the windows. He watched the traffic, pedestrian and motor, move on Trowbridge and Conant Streets.

In February 1957, I started a new job. My salary was $1,000 a year higher than at the Polish Aid Society, but required a return to working afternoons. It was a hard time to leave my father alone. The teenage daughter of renters upstairs agreed to monitor my father's needs. A month later, March 26th, was my brother's 25th birthday. He was away at St. Joseph's College in Rensellear, Indiana. That morning my father was crestfallen, commenting that Leonard would not be coming home for the occasion. No, it was the middle of the week and my brother did not own a car. Service in the U.S. Navy made him eligible for the G.I. Bill paying off his education with little surplus cash to spare. The next day I returned home after dark to a darkened house. My father was in bed, his pills still on the bedside table. Labored breathing and poor color sent an alarm through me. He was not going to take any more medicine but agreed to let me take him to the Veteran's Hospital for any comfort measures they could provide. Hurriedly I phoned Helen and Irene Mayes asking that they accompany me to Allen Park, about a half hour drive. We all got into my 1950 Plymouth after my father dressed and put on my brother's Navy Pea jacket. The emergency room staff was very accommodating, rushing my father onto a hospital bed with an oxygen tent over his upper body. Helen sought out the Catholic chaplain who refused to give the last sacraments to a non-practicing Catholic, which is how the chaplain knew him. My father's last words to me were, "Go home. Watch the house."

I hurried to the car to bring a box of tissues for his use, but he was gone when I returned. Death was peaceful, swift, and painless. It was 11:30 p.m. Skupny Funeral Home would arrange his burial, I instructed the doctor who never left his side. Then distraught, I found a phone booth to notify my brother. It was comforting to have Helen and Irene Mayes with me during this stressful and another defining moment in my life.

We buried my father in his banker's gray suit that he bought for his retirement party. Christian burial in consecrated ground was assured by our pastor, Rev. L. Szok, who arranged a private funeral mass at St. Francis Hospital, with the hospital chaplain offering the Mass. This was after I spoke with our pastor about my father's faithful recitation of the Credo, his belief in following one's conscience, and his church attendance at Christmas and Easter.

My brother helped with all the arrangements. Mr. Skupny received the death certificate and released it to my brother. My mother's doctor was notified at the hospital and my brother decided that she would come to the funeral. Under heavy sedation, she sat emotionless in front of the open casket. The service at the funeral home, conducted by the funeral director, Mr. Skupny, was solemn, but brief. All mourners proceeded directly to the cemetery. The pall bearers, wearing white gloves, were men from the Veteran's Club on Caniff Street. My father frequently visited the club for card playing and camaraderie.

My mother's comment after the funeral was, "I did not even faint." But she did a lot of crying whenever we visited his grave in the following thirty years of her lifetime. She had conversations with him, expressing her sorrow over losing him, and living alone. Their married life together spanned just 22 years, followed by the separation of 15 years due to her debilitating illness.

My mother, brother and I missed my father, recognizing the positive influence he had in our lives.

There's a haunting melody I associate with my father. My mother also knew the song. It's plaintive, somber, brooding. The title, "The Song of Stenka Rasin," describes a Russian Cossack who freed the serfs along the Volga River and repelled the Persians in the 17th Century. My mother tried to translate the words from the Russian—floating down the Volga River was what she came up with. The translation by Mr. Brian Dumka, teacher of a course on Russian history at University of West Florida, gives a more accurate picture of what took place in that boat with Stenka Rasin and his Persian bride.

My father sang this song all through his life, particularly after a few beers. I wonder what memories, yearnings, stirred in his heart when he voiced this tune. Was he haunted, too, like my mother, by some long forgotten incident from that corner of the world he knew as a youth?

My father died on March 27, 1957, at the age of 67, before any of his six grandchildren were born. I hope they get a glimpse of him from these pages.

My niece, Charlotte, as a young woman, asked for a photograph of my father, her grandfather, regretting that she never knew him. She was born in 1967, ten years after his death.

From Behind the Island Into The Open Waves (Sten 'ka Razin)

From behind the island into the open waves of the main river channel, sharp-prowed, gaily painted boats fly.

Merry and intoxicated from his wedding, Sten'ka Razin sits in the front, embracing his princess bride.

With lowered eyelids, the semiconscious girl listens to the drunken words of the Ataman.

Behind the couple grumbling is heard: "He has abandoned us for a woman . . . Only nights with her will matter now . . . He is becoming a woman himself . . ."

The terrible Ataman, hearing this muttering and mockery, wraps a powerful arm around the waist of his Persian princess.

His black eyebrows come together like gathering storm clouds and the veins in his temples throb.

Overcome with anger, he declares: "I regret nothing" and with a voice growing in power he addresses the distant shores:

"Volga, Volga, Mother of the land,
Volga, Russian river,
Don't refuse a gift from a Don Kazak.
So there will be no discord among free men,
Volga, Volga, Mother of the land,
I give you the Beauty."

With a mighty effort he picks up the beautiful princess and casts her out of the boat into the center of the river.

"Why so gloomy, Brothers?
You, Filka, you devil, dance for us.
Let's sing a bold ditty for the girl's wake."

Summer Jobs

St. Vincent's Orphanage held a summer camp for their residents at St.Vincent's Villa near Brighton, Michigan. I spent three summers, 1945, 1946, and 1947, as a counselor there. The girls—only camp was for K through 12 "orphans," who lived in a turn of the century gothic structure on East Jefferson Street in Detroit. During the school year, the nuns, sisters of the order of St. Vincent de Paul, cared for the girls and held school classes in the facility. In the summer, all the nuns and the "orphans" moved to St. Vincent's Villa.

The nuns wore a dark blue habit, floor length, and head gear that was a large starched white "Cornet" resembling a sail boat. Most of the girls had at least one parent somewhere, but for some reason could not live at home. Only one pair of sisters were complete orphans, i.e., without a mother or father.

The counselors were mainly school teachers, with the summers off, and college students. All the counselors had separate cabins. The campers, and their nuns-in-charge slept in a large dormitory and had their meals in a common dining room.

I was assigned to teach archery, lead hikes, arrange for campfires, and assist with waterfront safety. In order to qualify for the last duty, I enrolled and passed a Red Cross life saving course. The small private lake had a dock and a floating "barge" reached only by "experienced" swimmers.

Miss Genevieve McMillan was the head counselor for the three summers. She needed to be a disciplinarian with this brood of sometimes defiant youngsters.

It was a "cushy" camp counselor job. Our weekends were free. Genevieve drove me home on Friday night and picked me up on Sunday evening. When we opted to stay in Brighton, we could walk to Daugherty's for their famous hamburgers.

We were off duty after the evening meal which gave us time to play cards, go "skinny dipping" after dark, and read. Our counselor cabins had three bedrooms with double decker beds. A rustic living room and a bath room completed the accommodations for the camp staff. I remember the compensation was $100 per month.

It was a job that gave me exposure to group activity and repeated a pleasurable time I myself experienced as a youngster at Tau Beta camp. But this time, my 13-year-old brother and father were at home, shifting for themselves. There were some duties I carried out at home on weekends: laundry and housecleaning, grocery shopping, and meal preparations. I did not consider my presence in the home to have much impact. Any attempts I made to correct or discipline my brother were ineffective, so I felt discouraged, but gratified if I could bring some new knowledge and enjoyment to others outside my home.

Entering the Work World—1947

Bachelor of Arts, sociology major, philosophy minor. With those credentials I looked forward to working at the Wayne County Department of Social Welfare. While a junior at Marygrove, I took a Civil Service exam with a couple hundred others, and placed #83. There was no indication when an opening would turn up, so for the third summer I returned as a camp counselor at St. Vincent's Villa near Brighton, Michigan. It was June 1947, I was twenty one years old.

In the middle of July, a notice arrived from the Civil Service Board informing me of a vacancy at the Hamtramck office. I was pleased that I could refuse, but remain on their list of eligibles when another position opened up. I could not leave the camp counselor's job, I decided, but would wait for the next opening.

When September came and I heard nothing from the Wayne County Department of Social Welfare, I halfheartedly applied to be a Group Worker at a small settlement house operated by and called the Polish Aid Society.

Formerly a bank, the building was two stories high, located on the corner of Harper and Dubois, in Detroit's Poletown. The front lobby was now a large hall with an alcove that held an upright piano. Another room had kitchen equipment and tables for craft classes. The basement was divided into more small rooms for group activities. On the second floor, there were offices, a small kitchen, a music room with a piano, a meeting room and a bedroom for a resident housekeeper.

I rode the streetcar to the first interview with Miss Irene Mayes, director of the agency. My outfit was a black serge suit, black pumps with Cuban heels and a small black pillbox hat embellished with pink satin ribbon at the back. This ribbon I added for a touch of color and femininity. At the end of the interview I agreed to notify the director if I accepted the job. A week passed while I waited and hoped to hear from the Civil Service. When Miss Irene Mayes phoned asking for my decision, I accepted.

My hours were from 1:00 p.m. to 9:00 p.m., except for Friday when I came in from 9:00 a.m. to 5:00 p.m. The resident housekeeper would provide supper during the days I stayed till 9:00 p.m. Another full time employee was a case worker, Rita Slizewski, and a secretary/office manager/receptionist, Helen Marchlewski. The entry-level salary for group worker in a settlement house in 1947 was $1,950 per year, with 22 vacation days. The pay check was issued once a month.

I plunged into the work in this small agency serving a neighborhood with predominantly Polish residents. Some were second and third-generation Poles, many were recent arrivals, Displaced Persons, (DPs) from a number of eastern European countries.

Recalling Tau Beta Community House, the program here was similar. I initiated a Camp Fire Girls group, then a Golden Age Club for those 60 and older. For adult women, I found a knitting teacher. A piano teacher, Mrs. Hoekstra, came once a week for lessons given for a small fee. In the evening, twice a week, the Detroit Board of Education supplied a teacher for an English class, as a second language. My own piano playing came in handy accompanying the ballet class taught by a young high school graduate, Miss Betty Pendracki.

The resident housekeeper, Miss Theresa Pike, plump and gray haired, prepared the noon meal for the staff and then cleaned the offices when they left. I was the only staff member for whom she prepared supper. It became a "chore" for her, I surmised, as very often, when the others left the building, she would ask, "Can I fry you an egg?" When she spoke these words, her face and mouth had a pained expression. I did not have the heart to say no.

My father was aware of the Civil Service job I was hoping for and of the requirement to have a car. Late that fall he located a 1935 black Chevrolet sedan priced at $125. He purchased it for me and I imposed upon the current boyfriend, Sherwood (Brass) Kilander, to teach me how to drive this stick shift vehicle. He was a patient and effective teacher. But, when couple months later, we broke up, I did not know how to back into a parking space. The AAA offered driving lessons which I enrolled into, specifically to learn parking. I remember circling around a River Rouge Park parking lot, on snow covered pavement, practicing those maneuvers.

I passed the driver's test without a problem. Having "wheels" increased my mobility 100% I found out. I drove to Mt. Clemens, Michigan, in the early part of the winter to the wedding of our Marygrove senior class president, Pat Smith. With me were former college classmates, Helen Jedlinski, Vicky Zalenski, and Chris Cieszynski. We were spectators at a "mixed marriage" in a Catholic Church. The bride, a Catholic and the groom, a non-Catholic, exchanged vows at the side altar. This was the protocol in 1947. The reception followed, with cake and punch served, a modest fare, compared to the spreads offered at Polish weddings.

Friends, Eleanor Jasinski and Dolores Wójcik came along on a trip to Sylvania, Ohio, to visit Irene Skoney who was a postulant at the religious order of sisters of St. Francis. It was mid-winter. On the return trip, snow began to fall. This old car's windshield wipers stopped moving so the accumulation of snow had to be removed by hand with the side window lowered. It was just the first of many malfunctions in this vintage vehicle.

In the early part of 1948, I was again informed of a job opening in the County Welfare office in Hamtramck. This time, even possessing a car as required, I turned down the offer and asked to be removed from their list. I was "bonded" to the group worker responsibilities and was fearful of the "unknown."

The small staff at the Community house made for a cohesive group. Friendships formed and activities followed engulfing other family members of the employees. The three Marygrove alumni, Irene Mayes, Rita Slizewski, and I held a "fund raiser" in the building auditorium. Music, dancing, refreshments, and "parlor" games were part of the Saturday night event. Donations were solicited resulting in $100 raised for the college. Attending were mainly our friends and family members.

On the professional level, this agency was a member of the local and national Federation of Settlements and Neighborhood Centers, the Michigan Welfare League, Catholic Charities, and the Metropolitan Council of Social Agencies. Staff members were encouraged to attend meetings and become active on committees. The three social workers were given a small budget for attending National Association of Social Workers Annual Conferences. The case worker, agency director, and I drove to Atlantic City one year and to New York City another time. I learned what turnpike driving involved going through Pennsylvania, and gained a lot more confidence on the road.

"Miss Betty" (Pendracki), the ballet teacher, injected a flamboyant element into the staff. Spirited, upbeat, with a flair for the artistic and unconventional, she was a breath of fresh air when in the company of the practical, sometimes stodgy social workers.

After a year at this job, my salary inched upwards a bit. Only with a masters degree could a social worker command a higher pay rate. A stipend from the United Community Services would cover the cost of tuition and some additional expenses. My father encouraged me to continue to study. I applied for the stipend for the Group Work program and was granted $150 per month for the four semesters of classes. In return, I promised to return for a two-year stint in a United Community Services agency. I already started taking a couple of classes, part time, at Wayne State University, School of Social Work in September 1948, graduation would be in June 1950.

Getting a masters degree in social work meant earning 48 credit hours over four semesters of class work and "field" work. Although I could have attended the U. of Michigan in Ann Arbor, or even the Catholic U. in Washington DC, I continued to stay at home and commute daily to classes at Wayne State University. Finances and a strong sense of responsibility worked to keep me close by. WSU was a public secular institution where student unrest, leftist leanings, and even rumors of Communist cells on campus gave me cause for concern. I met with Rev. Arthur Krawczak, assistant at St. Stanislaus church, a block from the Polish Aid Society address, to discuss my decision to attend Wayne State. He was very approachable, and a recent recipient of a masters degree in social work from Catholic U. He reassured me that my faith and religious integrity would not be harmed by studying at a secular school. I had sixteen years of education all in private schools with religious teachers.

In January 1949 I left the Polish Aid Society to become a full-time student at the Wayne State University School of Social Work. Classes were held in a brick bungalow residence at 451 West Kirby street. My field work placement was at the Detroit Orthopedic Clinic where after school, groups of handicapped children and teen agers met in a two-story structure on Ferry Street, within walking distance of the class room building. One day each week I took a bus to the Sigma Gamma Hospital School in Mt. Clemens (now Harrison Community Hospital) on Ballard Road. I stayed overnight, breakfasted with the youngsters, and returned by bus to classes later that day. Many of the young patients were recovering from effects of polio, cerebral palsy, and orthopedic surgery. During six weeks of summer school my assignment was at a "Day Camp" for very disabled youngsters. A male group work student drove a small van with the "campers" and me for an all-day "outing" at Belle Isle Park. The little bodies, in heavy leg braces needed assistance to move from one spot to another. Often I rubbed my banged shins and flexed sore muscles at the end of the day. Since the "campers" could not be left alone, I learned to "train" my bladder to postpone emptying until we returned safely to the Ferry street location late in the afternoon.

The second-year field work placement was at the St. Peter Claver Community House, on Eliot Street near Brush, in Detroit's "Black Bottom" neighborhood. Miss Hazel Braxton was my supervisor—a very skilled black social worker with a lot of "presence" and enviable control of the groups of children. She was the assistant director of this settlement house. The director was Miss Theresa Maturen, a white woman, dedicated to improving the lives of the predominantly black residents living just north of the downtown district. Some Brewster Housing Project dwellers sent their children to the popular agency nursery school.

The supervisor in my first year field work placement was an older woman whose previous experience was at the Meninger Clinic in Kansas with the renown Dr. Karl Meninger. I bristled and gritted my teeth under her direction, often irritated and perplexed at her "interpretations." Miss Hazel Braxton, a very controlled and gentle personality offered a lot more kinder direction. Both placements were indeed learning experiences.

My last semester master's thesis was written with the guidance of Dr. Fritz Redl, a cigar-smoking, rapid-talking, German-accented expert on group therapy. His "direction" was suspended before the thesis was completed and another faculty member filled in at the end. The most comprehensive direction I received was from Hazel Braxton, who carefully tried to steer me away from making any derogatory comments in the body of the research paper which described the Nursery school project at St. Peter Claver Community House. Parent participation was mandatory, and the parents club was directed with a strong hand, by Therese Maturen, the white director.

I met all the requirements for the masters degree and graduated in June 1950. Personally, getting through the classes, surviving the field work and being exposed to the "secular" university-level education was extremely "trying." It was the most difficult experience I had to live through. Early allergies flared up in smoky classrooms. My "old world" upbringing faced challenges. I would never be the same.

I returned to the Polish Aid Society in July 1950, to fulfill my obligation for the stipend. The familiar aspect of the work and the friendly staff felt "safe." There were very few openings in other settlements with any attraction to me.

The black Chevy became inoperable when the radiator sprung a leak that could not be repaired. It was "cannibalized" and was abandoned on the vacant lot next to the Surdacki grocery. Only the lower chassis and four wheels remained. My brother Leonard had a hand in its demise, I learned, so it was back to riding the Baker street car to work until I could purchase a new car.

Living at home during graduate school, I was able to save $800 to use as a down payment on a 1950 Plymouth which I bought in August for $1,800. Miss Irene Mayes provided a personal loan of $1,000 for the balance which I paid off in $100 per month payments.

There was a three-car garage I could use, but it was quicker to park the car in front of the house. The car was never locked, until I found a folded newspaper on the front seat just under the steering wheel. An unmistakable "dent" in it could only have been made by a reclining human head. Clearly my green Plymouth sedan was a handy haven for a "street" person.

At the agency, a new staff was hired. Rita Slizewski left to pursue a Masters Degree in Psychology. Rita Cyman, Anthony Bandyk, and A. J. Utecht became part of the team. All became good friends, enjoying classes at the agency and get togethers in the community. The agency director, acted like a benevolent parent with the staff, entertaining them in her home at "theme" parties. Her sister, Helen, a nurse and a wonderful cook, delighted all with delectable dishes. I was in awe at her culinary knowledge.

The 2-year requirement passed quickly. Programs in the agency were appealing to many neighborhood children, adults, and senior citizens. The summer day camp was especially popular in this inner city area. "Miss Betty" had a brother Carl, a school teacher, who was hired as a counselor and bus driver for the summer sessions.

Changes continued as staff left for other jobs, marriage, and the military service. 1950 brought on the Korean War. My own brother was now in the Navy.

In my personal life, a number of failed romances and broken relationships recurred persistently. The biological clock was ticking. In my frame of reference, a career in the world was to be followed and/or replaced by a career as wife, mother, and homemaker. It was not happening. I faced another birthday (29) still searching for a permanent relationship. In 1954 a woman was considered an "old maid," at this milestone, an abhorred designation to me.

SISTER ALACOQUE WITH CHARLOTTE
AND ELEONOR—1954

In graduate school several classmates had been in psychotherapy as a way of coming to terms with "hang ups." My "self" searching was not successful. Could I be helped? I determined to try. It was another pivotal decision that affected the rest of my life in a most positive way.

Margaret Baima MD, a psychiatrist, had offices in the Maccabees Building on Woodward near Warren. She was tall, slim, dark haired, and smoked a cigarette held in a long ivory holder. I chose a female doctor and had a strong commitment to completing the process of "self-actualization." I set three goals for myself: to change jobs, leave home, and enter into a permanent relationship.

Seeing a "shrink" in the mid 1950's was a bit avant garde, (except in social work circles). And the cost was not covered by medical insurance. Again, since I was living at home, I was able to manage the $10 per session fee.

In 1955, Miss Irene Mayes left Harper Community House (renamed to reflect the more cosmopolitan neighborhood) to join another Detroit agency, the NSO—Neighborhood Service

Organization. The Board of Directors of Harper Community House, still calling their organization the Polish Aid Society, authorized my promotion to the Director's position. For the next two years (1955 to 1957) my responsibilities shifted to administration. My salary was now $5,000 a year. My father was quietly very proud of my climb up the short corporate ladder. I'm sure he confided this to his buddies at the Veteran's club where he made regular trips now that he was retired.

However, the size of compensation was commensurate with the size of the agency. Harper Community House was incorporated into the Catholic Youth Organization, where we were a small cog in the large wheel encompassing the entire Archdiocese.

Early in 1957, I received an offer of another job, with a considerable pay raise. The agency was Barat House, a residential treatment house for emotionally disturbed adolescent girls, operated by the League of Catholic Women's Youth Service Organization. The Director was Pat Dorsey Bebin, who also was a Marygrove graduate (class of 1946). Twelve teen age young women occupied an old mansion on East Grand Boulevard near Mack Avenue. It was a group work job, with work hours 1:00 p.m. to 9:00 p.m. four days a week, 9:00 a.m. to 5:00 p.m. on Friday. Two "house mothers" near retirement age, lived in. I was to have an evening meal at the same time the residents ate. Our cook was a genial black woman who loved to prepare "soul food," often buying collard greens by the bushel. I learned to like them doused with vinegar. My salary was $6,000 a year. When I first told my father, he was understanding but I think was disappointed.

My father's health, continued to deteriorate dramatically. He found out treatment was available at the Veteran's Hospital in Allen Park, Michigan and had himself admitted without telling me. I don't recall how I learned his whereabouts, but by the time I did and visited him at the hospital, he was scheduled for an orchiectomy to halt the spread of Prostate Cancer. He returned home a broken, dejected man who now needed some assistance with personal care. I purchased an electric razor and set up a comfortable chaise lounge next to the dining room windows for his use. Then I arranged for the upstairs teen ager to check on my father after she came home from school. My father continued to lose weight and energy as the disease took hold again, metastasizing to his bones. He tolerated the pain without complaining, but became very withdrawn.

My new job at Barat House became intense and all absorbing. I needed all my skills and techniques with these highly volatile adolescents. Sometime their behavior bordered on the psychotic. One young fragile blond resident had to be coaxed off the porch roof, after she crawled out the second-story bedroom window. Dr. Joseph Fischoff, child psychoanalyst, was a consultant, advising the case work and group work staff at weekly meetings.

One successful craft project used papier mache animal figures as a basis for a circus "diorama." The circus "tent" was a card table turned upside down with crepe paper streamer decorations. This production was displayed in the lobby of the League of Catholic Women bringing surprised reactions from spectators.

It was near the end of March 1957, I was two months into this job, and was wondering about leaving home, but reluctantly postponed any action due to my father's grave condition. On March 26, my brother's birthday, my father wondered if he might be coming home. He was attending St. Joseph's College in Rensselear Indiana. My father died the next day. My brother came home for his funeral.

Death of a parent brings on a feeling of profound loss to a child of any age, I discovered. I was freed from the responsibility of caring for my father and could actively search for a place to live, finally severing ties with my family of origin. But, leaving did not come easy.

My mother was released from the hospital at my brother's request, but he returned to college. My brother, no doubt was feeling a sense of loss, too, wanting to preserve a sense of "home." But I made it very clear, I would be moving out. My brother consulted our pastor, Rev. Szok, who advised that at age 31, I was free to leave. I did promise to take my mother to follow up appointments at the hospital out patient clinic.

Adjustment to life in the community was difficult for my mother following fifteen years of hospitalization. She had to learn to shop, cook, do laundry, and clean house all over again. Her first words after coming back to 3293 Trowbridge were, "Where will I get my meals?"

I considered where I would want to live, coming to the conclusion that ownership was better than just renting. I found the River House Cooperative at 8900 E. Jefferson, near Van Dyke. My choice was an eleventh floor studio, #1101 looking north. Waterview units were more expensive to buy and the rent was also higher. By July 1, 1957, I was moving into a 500-square foot apartment. I was approved by the Board of Directors following a personal interview. I emptied my savings account of $2,500 for the down payment. Rent was $83 per month. To start, I purchased an orange Castro sofa-bed, painted a folding chair white, and brought a folding card table for the kitchen. An apartment size stove and a refrigerator were included. Cabinets and a kitchen closet completed the eating area which was screened off from the living room with a sliding bamboo drape. The floor was a dark brown utilitarian vinyl tile, the two large windows in the living room had Venetian blinds. All the walls were freshly painted "off white" per my request.

Adjustment to living alone in what was essentially one large room became a challenge. I missed the basement, attic, front and back porches, even the small yard of the house on Trowbridge and the familiar haunts of my Hamtramck neighborhood. First I found a dry cleaner on Jefferson Avenue, then a shoe repair shop, a nearby gas station, and a new parish church, Annunciation. There were a couple of movie theatres on Jefferson as well and a supermarket farther east on the same street. But it all seemed foreign. I brought up the possibility of returning home in a therapy session but received support to continue with my decision to live at River House.

When I decided to leave Barat House, I chose a casework position where work hours left my evenings open. Early in 1958, the Wayne County Civil Service posted openings for social work positions which I noted with interest. An exam was no longer required with a master's degree. The Department of Social Welfare offices were in the Juvenile Court building at 1025 E. Forest. Medical Social Workers assisted medically indigent adults with discharge and posthospital plans: placement in nursing homes, purchases of prostheses, supportive services in the home, visits and consultation with doctors, nurses, patients and family members.

My decision to work for the Wayne County Civil Service was the best decision I ever made. The fringe benefits were generous, the compensation was fair, annual raises were assured, the position gave me more authority and power than I had in any other job, and finally, it led to my meeting my life's companion.

From 1947 to the present (2002) my work had been in private and public agencies. Currently as a PRN (as needed) social worker for the Covenant Hospice, I continue to provide the skills and intuitive insights in this agency's program. I push full retirement ahead to ? age 80?

Other Milestones

One book, one magazine article, and a conversation with a very perceptive social worker provided insight leading to my being able to change directions in my adult life.

The book was, "*Fight Against Fears*," author's name forgotten. The magazine article in the *Ladies' Home Journal* was by a staff person of the Family Service Society.

In the book, the writer, a woman, describes her long bout with sinus and allergy problems and personality hang-ups that were relieved through psychotherapy. (I had recurring allergy problems.)

The magazine article related the struggle of a young woman to break away from her family. With the encouragement and support of a "case worker," she set out to establish her "own nest." In fact she designed the house she would live in, hiring a contractor to carry out her plans. At the end, she developed a relationship with the contractor leading to marriage! Wow! Such a possibility was mind boggling to me. At the time, my hangups kept me tied to my "responsibility" of caring for my "dependent" father.

It was a casual visit by Virginia Traphagen that addressed this issue. She was a social worker in the Detroit Public School system, and also a teacher of a Child Guidance course at Wayne State University. We became friends after I had enrolled in her class in January 1953. I was home alone on a Saturday morning, in 1954, when she "dropped by." In her gentle way she asked some very pertinent questions about my role in the household. Yes, I did the housecleaning and laundry, but my father knew how to run the washer in the basement and did so on occasion. Yes, I shopped for groceries, but my father frequently made trips to purchase the kind of meat he preferred, made pots of soup, fried bacon and eggs, pork chops, and boiled his homemade kiełbasa. His home-brewed coffee was done in an open saucepan, which he warmed up several times during the day, not waiting for anyone to serve him.

How about the finances? My father paid the utility bills in cash, walking to the local office of Detroit Edison, and the Michigan Consolidated Gas Co., both on Joseph Campau Street. When I established my own checking account, my father allowed me to send a check for the taxes and the water bill. All his activities of daily living were accomplished independently and without my assistance. His personal health problems and social life were attended to "on his own." Friends and card playing buddies were always available at the local VFW hall on Caniff Street where he walked regularly after retirement. He never informed me as to his destinations and I didn't ask. When he was in a binge drinking phase, any local bar became a hangout.

Even before Virginia Traphagen departed, I came to realize that my strong connection to my father and my absent hospitalized mother was like a magnet. The strong sense of duty and responsibility, like a chain binding and holding me, began to loosen. I had the tight emotional ties and dependency feelings. Dad didn't need me. I needed him!

Virginia Traphagen spoke openly about her own psychoanalysis and its value in her development as an adult woman and in her professional life. It took several months for me to come to terms with the fact that I would need professional help to get "unstuck" from the tangle of hangups tying me down and preventing me from experiencing any personal fulfillment.

It was now 1954. My August 29th birthday would establish me as an "old maid." Four years passed since I earned my master's degree and now was working with a steady income. Some of my pay would be "invested" into this medical expense—paying a "shrink." I searched the Yellow Pages, finding a woman doctor with offices in the Maccabees Building about 20 minutes from the community house where I worked. I wrote the name and phone number on a piece of paper, slid it into my wallet, waiting for "gumption" to make the first phone call. The fee, I learned, was $10 per visit. This, too, was one of the best decisions I ever made.

Initially, I told no one about my weekly sessions with a psychiatrist. From the start I was determined to complete therapy.

In graduate school I knew of students who "shopped" for the right doctor, getting bits and pieces of self-knowledge, giving them an "at loose ends" personality. My sessions, mostly once a week, were characteristically tearful, introspective, and usually ended with a deep sense of relief. All three goals I set for myself were accomplished finally, after seven years. Some friends never knew of this meaningful chapter in my life, but did witness the growth, the changes and the developments over that span of time.

The agency director at the Polish Aid Society, Irene Mayes, was the first to learn about my therapy sessions. But this was about 6 months after I began my weekly drives to the Maccabees Building. About a year later, she confided that she began her own psychoanalysis with the esteemed Dr. Editha Sterba, a well respected and well-known analyst in Detroit.

Over the years, I became aware of the healing potential of psychotherapy for the "run of the mill" neurosis, and its limitations in treating and resolving a psychosis. My mother's condition was controlled with psychotrophic medications so she could return to society. She was never totally rid of the "demons"—the "voices" she heard, the delusional thinking, that plagued her from time to time when the effects of medication wore off, or some word triggered a disturbing memory. Her periodic visits to a psychiatrist, as an out patient, were to monitor or change medication. Haldol worked the best. I called it the "happy pill" as its calming effects kept my mother on an even keel, satisfied and able to enjoy life and often to smile and laugh.

Resume

Charlotte L. Cavanary, MSW, ACSW, LCSW, BCD
(Mrs. Edward J. Cavanary, Jr.)

Permanent Address: Destin, FL 32541-2909

Phone Numbers: (850) 837-6897
                          (850) 837-6902 (FAX)

Education: MSW-Wayne State University School of
                          Social Work, Detroit, Michigan—1950
                          BA-Marygrove College,
                          Detroit, Michigan—1947
                          (Sociology)

Professional Organizations:
          National Association of Social Workers
          National Registry of Clinical Social Workers
          Board Certified Diplomat #2759
          Licensed Clinical Social Worker, SW 4135 (FL)

Post Graduate Courses:
          Psychopathology, U. of Michigan (1979)
          Supervision for Field Instructors, U. of Michigan (1970)

Field Instructor:
          U. of Michigan School of Social Work
          Wayne State University Institute of Gerontology:
          Oakland University, Department of Psychology, Gerontology.

Work Experience:
          Current Position: Social Worker (PRN) "AS NEEDED"
          Covenant Hospice
          July 1998 to present

101 Hart Street
Niceville, Florida 32578
(850) 729-1800
Branch Manager: Karen Hughes
Position Summary: Professional social work services to Hospice patients, family members and/or S.O. by psychosocial assessments, counseling, and assisting patients and families during the period of death and dying.
Salary: beginning—$12.00 per hour; current (2002): $17.35 per hour
Previous position: Medical Social Worker (Part time)
October 1993 to June 19, 1998
Choctaw Valley Home Health
554 Twin Cities Boulevard
Niceville, Florida 32578
(850) 678-9262
Duties: Home visits to persons receiving home health care to assess and evaluate social and environmental factors.
Salary: beginning—$16.00 per hour; ending—$17.00 per hour
Reason for leaving: Agency closed.

Previous Position: Contingent Senior Medical Social Worker
January 1987 to July 15, 1993
Providence Hospital
6001 W. Nine Mile Road
Southfield, Michigan 48075
(313) 424-3113
Supervisor: Ms. Ann Hill
Duties: Evaluation of psychosocial factors and assessment of environmental conditions as part of discharge planning.
Final salary: $15.00 per hour
Reason for leaving: Retirement and relocation to Fort Walton Beach

Previous position: Medical Social Worker (Part time)
January1986 to January 1992
Home Health Care of Metro Detroit (ABC Home Health)
24901 Northwestern Hwy. Ste. 720
Southfield, Michigan 48075
(313) 354-2990
Administrator: Sue Vanderbrink
Reason for leaving: Agency hired a full-time social worker

Previous position: Adult Outpatient Therapist (Geriatric)
October 1, 1984 to October 1, 1985
Macomb County Community Mental Health Services
    (SW Center)
29600 Civic Center Drive
Warren, Michigan 48093
(313) 573-7575
Supervisor: Ms. Peg Peterson, ACSW
Duties: Outreach to adults 60 and over experiencing
    mental health problems; mental health consultant
    and case manager to nursing homes; facilitating
    admission to psychiatric hospitals.
Reason for leaving: Retirement (at age 60)

Previous position: Outreach Therapist
October 1, 1980 to September 30, 1984
NSO—Geriatric Screening and Outpatient Services
    (Neighborhood Service Organization) 16030 W.
    McNichols Street
Detroit, Michigan 48235
(313) 272-4050
Supervisor: Ms. Gail Salinsky
Duties: Outreach mental health evaluations and ongoing
    psycho-therapeutic services to older adults in the
    community.

Previous position: Social Worker—Supervisor
November 1, 1978 to June 30, 1980
North Central Community Mental Health Center/Adult
Psychiatric Clinic—Hamtramck Satellite Office
650 David Whitney Building
Detroit, Michigan 48226
2940 Caniff, Hamtramck, Michigan 48212
Supervisor: Mr. Del Brown ACSW
Duties: Coordination of the satellite clinic; intake, social
histories and treatment plans; after-care follow up.
Salary: beginning—$17,000 (.8 time); ending—$17,850

Previous position: Consultant on Aging (Case Worker III)
September 1, 1972 to October 31, 1978
Family and Children's Services of Oakland
50 Wayne Street
Pontiac, Michigan 48058
(313) 332-8352
Supervisor: Mrs. Muriel Steele, ACSW
Duties: Direct services to older adults; consultation and
education of agency staff and other community
agencies; home visits and outreach; assist with
adjustments to stresses of later life, mobilizing
community resources as needed.
Salary: beginning—$9,280 (.8 time); ending—$14,385

Previous position: Medical Social Worker III
September 15, 1967 to January 31, 1971
Henry Ford Hospital
2799 W. Grand Boulevard
Detroit, Michigan 48202
Supervisor: Miss Mary Ann Sweeney, ACSW
Duties: Direct services to inpatients and outpatients
afflicted with chronic and/or terminal illnesses.
Supervision of graduate students and participation

on staff meeting committees. *Salary*: beginning—
$5,000; ending—$5,565 (20 hrs/wk)
Reason for leaving: Illness and wish for a year's sabbatical

Previous position: Medical Social Work (Research Assistant)
August 15, 1966 to August15, 1967
Michigan Cancer Foundation
4811 John R.
Detroit, Michigan 48207
Supervisor: Mr. Ron Koenig
Director: Dr. Michael Brennan
Duties: Research Assistant, interviewer, and counselor for
a project aimed at evaluating the needs and services
available to cancer patients. This was an "in-depth"
examination of social, emotional, and financial
problems of patients and their families.
Salary: $4,500 (20 hrs/wk)
Reason for leaving: End of funding for research project

Previous position: Medical Social Worker I
April 15, 1958 to August 15, 1966
Wayne County Department of Social Welfare, Medical
Division
1025 E. Forest
Detroit, Michigan 48207
Supervisor: Miss Virginia Chester
Director: Walter J. Dunne
Duties: Assisting medically indigent adults of Wayne
County with discharge and post-hospital plans:
placement in nursing homes, ordering
prostheses and authorizing payment; supportive
services in the home; visits and consultation
with doctors, nurses, patients, and their family
members.
Salary: beginning—$5,330; ending—$8,520
Reason for leaving: Desire for part time employment

Previous position: Recreation Director and Group Worker
February 1957 to April 1958
Barat House—Youth Service Organization League of
        Catholic Women,
120 Parsons Street
Detroit, Michigan
Supervisor: Mrs. Patricia Dorsey Bebin
Duties: Planning and carrying out a program of leisure
        time activities and group work with emotionally
        disturbed adolescent girls in a residential treatment
        center. A case work-group work approach was used
        to facilitate personal adjustment.
Salary: $6,000
Reason for leaving: Desire for change to daytime working
        hours.

Previous Position: Social worker, Program Director, Director
July 1950 to February 1957
Harper Community House
5928 Chene
Detroit, Michigan
Polish Aid Society
6000 Dubois, Detroit, Michigan
Director: Miss Irene Mayes, MA
Salary: beginning—$3,000; ending—$5,600
Duties: The Social Worker I job classification for the first
        1-1/2 years involved case work with children and
        adults of the neighborhood. Short-term counseling
        and referrals to community agencies were
        frequently made. Problems of individuals in the
        groups were also handled as well as supervision of
        the group workers.

The Program Director's job for the next 2 1/2 years,
involved planning, organizing and leading groups, clubs
and classes. These leisure time activities were set up in

response to the needs and interests of the neighborhood. Responsibilities included keeping statistical records, arranging schedules for use of rooms by the various groups, and assignment of leaders to the groups of children, teenagers and adults that met in the community house. In addition, volunteers were recruited and directing a summer day camp was also part of the job.

During the final 1 1/2 years at the community house, the work as director required working with the board of directors, supervising the staff, preparing and administering a budget, recruiting professional and non-professional staff, attending board meetings and participating on agency committees.

Number of workers supervised as director: 2 full time, 9 part time, 3 students, 3 volunteers.

Reason for leaving: desire for higher salary, and a more challenging position

Previous Position:
September 1947 to February 1, 1949
Title: Program Worker, Polish Aid Society
6000 Dubois, Detroit, Michigan
Duties: Under supervision of the director, worked with groups as leader of informal activities, helping children and adults in clubs and classes to develop new skills and interests; prepare records, materials and care for equipment; attending staff meeting and institutes.
Salary: beginning—$1,950, ending—$2,575
Reason for leaving: To pursue a master's degree in social work.

CHAPTER III

Behind the Iron Curtain and

Other European Countries—1959

Early in 1959, I began planning a trip abroad. Eleonor Jasinski, still single like me, became intrigued with the possibility of visiting some European countries as well as meeting Polish relatives. From the middle of August to the middle of September 1959, we planned to visit Switzerland, Spain, Majorca, and Poland. Air France was our airline to Paris and TWA from Madrid would return us to New York.

I financed the trip through a $1,100 refund I received from the United Community Services Pension Fund when I left the job I had for ten years at the Polish Aid Society. I put an additional $100 away for souvenirs. Most of our accommodations included meals, so we didn't need much money for buying food.

The arrangements for visiting Poland and my relatives there got a bit complicated. Initially our travel agent, Mr. Lawrence, of Moorman's Travel Service, assured us that an auto would be provided for our use in Poland. However, when we arrived in Warsaw, the Polish National travel organization, ORBIS, sent a woman who steered us into a package tour of the country. In order to arrange time for visiting relatives, she told us that we could leave the tour early, and then travel by train to visit our respective relatives.

Poland was under Communist rule at that time. Movement throughout the land was very restricted, especially to foreigners. The bus trip was guided every mile of the way. We were led through

Warsaw, Kraków, the Wieliczka Salt Mines, Oświęcim Concentration Camp, Częstochowa and Zakopane.

In Warsaw we viewed the Cultural Palace, a skyscraper built by the Russians after they acquired the country following WW II. The saying was that the best view of Warsaw was from the tower as it was the only place in the city that you did not see the Palace!

There were very memorable experiences during this first trip abroad. I believe that this was a result of an agreement Eleonor and I had when we embarked on this adventure. We agreed that whenever possible, we would sit separately on buses and/or planes in order to get to meet as many different people as we could.

The flight from New York's Idlewild Airport to Orly Airport outside Paris departed at 4 p.m. and arrived in France at 8:15 a.m. the following morning. I had some concern about motion sickness, so after our in-flight meal I took a Dramamine tablet and shortly fell sound asleep.

Eleonor observed that one of the male passengers, who was traveling alone, changed into a dark red satin smoking jacket to be more comfortable during the long overnight flight. As I snoozed with my last thought hoping we would not run out of fuel during such a long journey, Eleonor embarked on a nightlong conversation with this gentleman.

During our breakfast of ham, cheese, and croissants, she announced that we would be double dating that evening with this man, Jean Tallot, and his friend, Gabrielle. They were both naval captains in the French navy. Jean was returning to his flat in Paris between assignments.

When the time arrived for our date, we drove in Jean's Citroen to the Left Bank where they treated us to a steak dinner before we continued to Jean's small, but exotically appointed apartment. We celebrated our newly formed friendship there with champagne. We learned that these captains spent much of their time in the French navy, sailing around the Pacific Islands where they were influenced by the music and culture. The next night we learned the extent of these influences.

Gabrielle invited us to his flat for dinner that he would prepare himself. Eleonor and I wore our dress-up outfits that included high-heeled shoes and fur stoles. It was almost dusk when we entered the narrow entryway, and stepped into an old fashioned open elevator with wrought iron sides and a sliding gate. Gabrielle opened the door to his flat to greet us wearing a South Seas Island wrap, that circled his torso from his waist to his knees. His legs and feet were bare, as were his chest and arms. Native music with heavy drum beats surrounded us as we entered the flat. After a scotch and soda, Gabrielle served the meal on the floor on a colorful tablecloth set with plates, tableware, glasses and napkins. We sat down on the rug and tried to look comfortable despite our tight skirts and high heels. I remember that it was an Italian dinner of veal scallopini, spaghetti with a light tomato sauce, and French bread. We drank rosé wine with this meal, ate cheese and pears for dessert.

The two world travelers told more stories. The islands of the South Seas left a profound mark, especially on Gabrielle who said he hoped to retire in Tahiti. As the evening wore on, Gabrielle confided that he learned about smoking opium from a pipe during one of his trips. He brought out some equipment and offered to demonstrate how opium was heated on a small spoon and how the smoke was inhaled. As he proceeded through the steps, I'm sure that my eyes became as large as saucers. I declined to partake of this new experience, but I did permit Gabrielle to puff some smoke into my mouth. I did not inhale! It had a sweet, cloying taste that I knew I could live without.

When Eleonor and I returned to the Metropolitan Hotel that night, we realized that our first weekend in Paris was not yet over, and we had already been entertained in a man's apartment, and learned about opium use. We pondered what other adventures awaited us on this momentous undertaking.

From Paris we flew to Brussels and then on to Warsaw on Sabena Airlines. As we circled for a landing at Okiecie Airport, both of us shivered a bit as we were going to be behind the Iron Curtain during this part of our Grand Tour.

A government-approved bus tour took us from Poland's capital south as far as Zakopane in the Tatra Mountains that border Czechoslovakia. We had a handsome, personable bus driver who resembled Rossano Brazzi, the Italian film star popular at that time. A romance developed between Eleonor and this man who dreamed of becoming an American citizen. As the relationship heated up, Eleonor had to let reason rule. I am guessing that she reflected on the adjustment, language, employment and culture shock that would be involved should the courtship cross the Atlantic.

We returned to Warsaw searching out the appropriate train to take, Eleonor to her country cousins west of Warsaw, and I to my uncle and his family in Elbląg on the Baltic Sea. Counting my nickels and dimes, I decided on second-class travel on the train. It turned out to be a bottom-class ride. The seats were wicker and the wooden floor worn and thick with dirt and grease. Arriving at 12:30 a.m., alone, after a six-hour trip, the small railway station platform was dimly lit. But there was no mistaking that those six people standing in line were waiting for me. My uncle John was at the head of the line, then his wife Mary, a short woman with her hair pulled back in a bun, then two, almost adult girls, Lilka and Teresa, and then, two teenaged boys, Stanley, 18, and Edward, 15. Uncle John announced that this was indeed a moment to cherish—the first meeting of relations that had never met before.

We proceeded on foot to their fourth floor walk-up apartment where a meal of hearty bread, sausage, fried eggs and cherry wine awaited. A bottle of cognac was also on the table. Hospitality, warmth, acceptance, and wonder permeated this visit. I quickly learned what their daily lives entailed in this small city. Lilka worked in a candy factory. Teresa was a seamstress for a lingerie company. The two boys were in high school. Uncle John was satisfied with having a job in a steel mill that made parts for ships. Aunt Mary kept house, struggling to purchase food from the poorly stocked shops.

As we sat reminiscing, Uncle John remembered letters sent by my father after his arrival in the United States. I knew he frequently asked about Josephine, John's sister, who was to become my mother.

But he also described America as a country of many races living side by side, something he surely experienced working and living in downtown Detroit. We talked about my mother's mental breakdown and subsequent years of hospitalization. Uncle John commented, "If she had remained in her native village, with her own people, she would have stayed well." Then I looked at a photo album. In it was a snapshot I sent on the occasion of 8th grade graduation. I am standing in front of 3291 Trowbridge Street, wearing a white eyelet two piece dress with a small corsage pinned to the right side. Letter writing stopped during WW II, but resumed at the war's end. I, particularly, felt it was important to keep my mother's brother informed about her status. Eventually, she resumed writing, not only to her brother, but reconnected with her two aunts and cousins.

The apartment building had no elevators, and tenants shared bathrooms. Cousin Lilka accompanied me to the next floor up where their bathroom was located. A long, dark room, it had a tub and toilet, and a hot water tank that stood over a small coal stove. Lilka stood watch outside the door as I washed up bending over the tub to get to the cold water faucet. She explained that it was not totally safe to be wandering about the building alone.

This family of two adults and four children were currently awaiting housing promised to them by the government. However, their present rooms, which they shared with another family (Aunt Mary's sister, Felicja Radziwanowska, her husband, and their two daughters) were clean and neat despite the crowded conditions. In fact, Lilka and Teresa gave up the bed they used for me to sleep in! The next day's breakfast consisted of cheese, rolls and butter, and a mug of hot milk.

They then showed me their city with its 13th Century St. Nicholas cathedral and a cemetery that once held German graves. (I noted machine gun bullet holes in the walls of buildings.) After the border shifted, it was again within the boundaries of Poland. Aunt Mary's brother-in-law was very proud of a motorcycle that he owned and stored in the basement of this building. He brought it out onto the street and gave me a ride on it. It was a bit tricky to straddle the seat wearing a dress, but away we rumbled around the streets.

My cousins presented me with two heirloom handwoven coverlets, one green and one tan, that I treasure. In fact, they inspired me to learn to weave when I returned home.

That evening, my cousins treated me to a movie. One showing from 5 p.m. to 7 p.m. was French with Polish subtitles. The theatre was Spartan by U.S. standards—plain and unadorned walls, a scuffed wooden floor, and well-worn seats. Silently, all the spectators filed in from the front entrance, and when the first feature was over, just as silently they stood and filed out row by row through a door at the rear.

I decided that I would not deprive my two cousins of their bed another night, so I arranged to take the train back to Warsaw late that evening. My uncle advised me to upgrade my seat to the first-class section. This was a compartment that accommodated six passengers, and it filled up readily. Shortly after the train started moving and everybody got comfortable, one of the persons suggested we turn off the lights, in order to sleep better. As I leaned my head onto the corner of the upholstered back when the lights were out, I was nudged by a need to scratch my neck. Indeed, others in the compartment were shifting and squirming, too. We turned the light back on and determined that is should stay on to discourage the bugs from biting!

Eleonor and I returned to our Warsaw hotel room about the same time the next morning. I told her the experiences on board the first class train and she told of the flies that swarmed all over the people and food at her relatives' farm.

We had a taste of life behind the Iron Curtain that was unforgettable! But there was more in store for us as we flew the Polish airline, LOT, from Warsaw to Zurich, Switzerland, which was our next stop.

When East Met West

The LOT airplane left Warsaw at 9 a.m. on Wednesday, Aug.

26, 1959, and arrived in Zurich at 12 noon. Shortly after becoming airborne, the stewardess leaned over with an invitation from the crew to join them in the pilot's compartment. The plane was not full, so evidently we were easily spotted, the two American girls traveling around Europe.

We made our way forward and soon were comfortably seated on benches behind the navigator, exchanging information about ourselves. I recall that we received Russian coins for our collection and were offered Russian cigarettes. We found their tobacco very strange and strong. The pilot, copilot, navigator, and radio operator were Polish but were fluent in Russian, as the schools in Poland taught Polish as a second language.

Our conversation continued, with great interest expressed by the individual crew members as to our lives in the U.S. They seemed amazed that we were able to afford to own and operate a car and to earn a salary that allowed travel abroad. Suddenly the Zurich airport was just below, and this airplane needed to make a fast descent to the runway below us. The control tower and the plane's radio operator made some quick exchanges regarding the imminent approach which was now being done much to the concern of ground personnel. Fire trucks appeared from nowhere, their sirens whining and lights flashing. The plane landed hard, one tire blew out, and a few tense moments followed as the pilot braked and came to an abrupt stop. Eleonor and I were still in the cockpit, in awe of the happenings. There was a danger of fire from this kind of landing. Everything was okayed for the passengers to disembark. We thanked God for a safe arrival and the crew for an interesting trip.

At the Hotel Butterfly in Zurich, we signed up to take a night tour of the city, again using our "sit separately" method during the bus ride. The neatly dressed man who took the seat next to me seemed about the same age as I was. Of medium height and weight, his tanned face, black hair and trimmed moustache had the look of the Middle East. Before we reached our first destination, I learned that this was his first trip to the west and that he was eager to practice his self-taught English. We exchanged information about our respective countries. I remember that he cautioned me about stereotyping his countrymen. They were not all swarthy, black-haired and brown-eyed. His wife back home had light brown hair and blue eyes, as did some of his five children. He was a serious, thoughtful, and philosophical man whose career was in the Iraqi army. He expressed some apprehension about the future of his career in that country's unstable political climate.

Our tour stopped at the Annual Garden Exposition. An unusual display of decorative grasses was featured. He observed that they were planted to imitate what one would find growing naturally in the landscape. Another stop was in a night spot, where music and dancers entertained this group of visitors from around the globe as we drank champagne.

He accompanied me to our hotel, leaving the tour bus, deciding that he could make his own way to his lodgings. We found the rooftop patio was almost deserted and continued our discussion on one of the outdoor wrought iron benches. The night sky was ink blue with a canopy of twinkling stars. The August air had a hint of fall. His protective arm circled my shoulder against the falling temperature. The next day our paths would separate as he planned to continue west to Germany and England, and our itinerary would take us to Lucerne for the day. That night we savored the exclusivity of the surroundings before returning to the lobby where the concierge addressed my escort, berating him for being in the hotel at that late hour. It was probably after midnight. He was visibly upset at the allegation of impropriety as he strongly defended my virtue and innocence. Without any further discussion, I turned toward the elevator and my companion left the building to catch a cab.

The next morning Eleonor teased me as she heard the vigorous tooth brushing that followed my return to the room the previous night. We had been warned by a fellow traveler in Poland about being careful who we kissed as we visited the different European countries. I was carefully following an oral hygiene practice after the parting good night kisses.

Two days later as we were about to leave for the airport, a bouquet of carnations arrived. The card had a message, and was signed, *Taha Al Madhi, Brigadier General, Bagdad, Iraq.*

Nice and the French Riviera

The Hotel Westminster was directly across the road from the beach. On a day trip by bus we toured the area, the small town of Grasse and Monte Carlo. In Grasse we bought the chief product, Cologne. In Monte Carlo we tried Roulette, but left without winning. There we saw croupiers, men in dark suits with poker faces.

The beach at Nice had rocks instead of sand, and a lot of topless females. Eleonor got as close as possible, to take snapshots of these bare bosomed bodies.

On the bus tour Eleonor and I once more took separate seats. Two uniformed men boarded the bus and took seats beside us. They were U.S. Air Force on rest and recreation from a base in Spain. So we were escorted by Lieutenant Colonel Dale Defors and Colonel Norman Anderson during our stay in Nice, enjoying the flirtation and camaraderie that go on between the sexes when they are thrown together in a strange place. We left Nice with a new view of U.S. Servicemen who were away from their families, but still appreciate the companionship of others. True, each of these two, well-seasoned, married career men would have accepted more than a platonic relationship, but they respected our wishes to keep everything strictly friendly.

The flight from Nice to Barcelona was short, and when we landed, we toured parts of the city in a limousine. Later that afternoon, we boarded the plane for the island of Majorca.

A full weekend near the city of Palma was filled with sightseeing, shopping, sunning, and enjoying the Spanish cuisine. Our stay was the American plan so we took advantage of all the scheduled meals. Majorca was the island where Chopin lived with George Sand and where the Mediterranean Ocean waves splashed up on the warm shore, and vacationers soaked up the sun's rays at every deck, patio and poolside. We stayed at the Mediterraneo Gran in Palma.

A movie was being filmed there. Belinda Lee, an English starlet was being romanced by an Italian count, Count Orsini, who perched on a bar stool at the outdoor café near the swimming pool. In the pool, Belinda Lee stood, the water up to her waist, and a long braid that glistened in the sunshine, hung down her bare back. She was not going to get more wet than that. The camera crew was adjusting the tripods, lights, and other equipment before the next scheduled shooting. We were intrigued with this tableau of film stars and their lives.

Our escorts here were a couple of British tourists, Peter and Roy, two young men who were on holiday from their jobs in a toy manufacturing company in Manchester. They each rented a small motor scooter and invited us to ride with them to town, where we searched the shops for mementoes.

All our meals were served at the hotel. The hotel owner introduced us to the golden liquid—Spanish Sherry—that was prized by the Spaniards in all its forms. He referred to it as bottled sunshine.

From Palma we flew to Valencia for a two-day stay. We toured the Lladro factory, which at that time was just beginning to be recognized for its beautiful porcelains. I chose a graceful and simple Madonna, which I still treasure despite the glue marks from an attempt to repair the figurine after a fall broke it in half.

In Valencia we had a boat ride through rice paddies, and learned to enjoy the saffron-colored rice, that was frequently served with chicken and paella.

We visited Madrid and its surrounding places of interest from Saturday, September 5, through Saturday, September 12, 1959. We stayed at the Plaza in midtown, and it had a rooftop swimming pool. Again, our travel agent in Detroit arranged the American plan, so we chose our meals from an extensive menu in the hotel restaurant. My skirts and waist bands began to bind and cut as the calories piled on and added weight began to strain the seams of my clothing. We rapidly adjusted to eating the evening meal about 9:30 p.m., although I remember once we looked for a restaurant where we ordered a hamburger late in the afternoon.

We toured the city, the Prado Museum, Toledo and its palace, and sunned and shopped. The climate and temperature in Madrid in September was still very warm. I found and purchased a sheer cotton blouse that felt more comfortable than the nylon and wool that was in my travel wardrobe.

At the Prado, our guided tour introduced us to Spanish painters and their works: Velazques, El Greco, Murillo, Goya, and Picasso. There was one very large salon with wall-sized paintings depicting the Blessed Virgin Mary in scenes from her life and death. They looked like giant holy cards that we received throughout elementary school from the nuns and priests at holiday time and other special occasions. The figure of the Virgin was usually depicted in a heavenly blue garment that flowed over her body from neck to toe, her eyes raised heavenward or downward benevolently at the viewer. Her hands were folded in prayer or extended to the earth below, a golden halo glowed above her head. This was very reminiscent of the small holy cards that we found in prayer books that we carried to church. These were reminders to say our daily prayers, to ask favors of Jesus through his mother, and to have Mary as our eternal role model.

There were other famous paintings, many of famous saints: St. Anthony, St. Francis of Assisi, St. Sebastian, with arrows penetrating his torso and thighs. Women saints were depicted, too: St. Agatha, St. Cecilia, Mary Magdalene. They were all famous figures from grade school religion classes.

The work of Goya was disturbing, but informational about how one man can view life around him and preserve history using visual imagery that can be more impressive than a thousand words.

Eleonor took advantage of Madrid to practice her Spanish. One of the waiters, a blonde, blue-eyed native, arranged dates in the afternoon, so that they could go out on the town and converse.

Our return flight to New York from Madrid aboard TWA left at 10 p.m. Because of storms and accompanying turbulence, our in-flight meal was delayed for more than an hour. During this wait, I pictured the plane tumbling into the Atlantic and all my souvenirs either floating or sinking to the bottom of the ocean. The plane flew out of the rain clouds and we arrived safely the next morning at 7:25 a.m. at Idlewild Airport in New York City.

By 9:30 a.m. we left for Detroit, arriving at 10:55 a.m. Meeting us at the airport were Dorothy, Eleonor's sister, and my mother, who was wringing her hands, dissolved in tears, thanking God that we arrived safely. She had agonized over this trip, fearing that I would be harmed somewhere in strange surroundings. Later I told her of the warm reception and hospitality I experienced with her brother and his family, and showed her the handwoven throws they presented me. Fifteen years later, in 1974, my mother and I returned together, visiting John and his family in Elbląg.

Meeting My Life's Companion

It was October 1959. The days were getting shorter, the nights cooler, and the mornings had a crispness that is felt only in Michigan. I was settling into a work routine at the Wayne County Department of Social Welfare, where I was a Medical Social Worker. Memories of my Grand Tour of Europe were still fresh in my mind. It was hard to concentrate, after I saw "Paree" etc.

Mr. Tom Behnke, who worked in the Personnel Office down the hall, inquired about any snapshots or slides from my trip. His good friend had slides from a trip he made earlier this year to the New Orleans Mardi Gras. He invited me to his home, where we could view both sets of slides and exchange information about our respective experiences. Yes, I agreed, this would be an opportunity to see my slides on a screen and enjoy an evening of conversation.

I drove my 1958 black Volkswagen Beetle to the east side residence of Tom and Marie Behnke, about 20 minutes from my River House apartment on Jefferson Street. I remember wearing a two-piece dark blue wool knit outfit and, a crystal necklace purchased in Zurich. The other guest, Ed, wore a striped dark brown suit, tan shirt, and tie. There was a blue cast to his freshly shaven beard, and his gray-blue eyes steady and serious. Black wavy hair and gray sideburns gave him a look of sophistication and his quiet reserved manner hinted at worldliness I had not encountered in my other "dates." He was at ease in the company of his lifelong friend and the young family present. Tom and Marie's three children were in the comfortable living room, well mannered throughout the evening.

"Imagine, such an attractive handsome man still around," I mused to myself as I glanced at him when he wasn't watching, drawn by his silver sideburns below that black wavy head of hair and the blue cast of his shaved beard.

When the evening ended, Ed escorted me to my car, interested in its operation and unique features (the motor was in the back) then asked for my phone number.

The next day, back at the office, Tom stopped at my desk. After exchanging comments about the previous evening, I casually inquired, "What is his last name?" Tom wrote on a piece of paper, CAVANARY. I still had no clue as to his ethnic background, religion, or what he did for a living.

I was not free when Ed phoned the first time asking for a date. Another week or two passed before Ed called again inviting me to a stage play at the Shubert Theatre in downtown Detroit. Alfred Lunt and Lynn Fontanne were starring in "The Visit." This time I was free to accept. It was a dark and brooding drama, as I remember. But seeing this famous duo perform was a treat!

The Book Cadillac hotel had a bar popular with downtown goers on Saturday night. We stopped there for one drink and then drove to the Acapulco Restaurant on Jefferson Street and East Grand Boulevard for pizza and coffee.

More dates followed as we got to know each other and learned that we had similar tastes in music, theatre, and opera. I remember going to see "Fiorello" and "Cosi von Tutte" at Ed's suggestion. Sometimes we "double dated" with Tom and Marie Behnke.

I learned that Ed was an only child. He worked for a company that designed commercial interiors, did not smoke, was in the Air Force Reserves, and was a Roman Catholic. This was especially important to me as I had previous relationships with non-Catholics that I severed, believing that having the same religious background was very crucial to a happy life together.

Our courtship had milestones along the course. Introducing him to friends required caution and proper timing as it could be a "kiss of death."

Early in the summer of 1960, after several months of "keeping company" I received an invitation to the wedding of my former secretary, Helen Marchlewski. She was the receptionist and secretary at the Polish Aid Society, later the Harper Community House, during the years I worked there, from 1947 to 1957. All the employees who had worked at the agency and now were my good friends, were invited. Pleased that Ed accepted, we arrived at the evening reception held somewhere on the west side of Detroit.

Part of the evening festivities was held out of doors, I recall. Ed was wearing a lightweight midnight blue suit. As we all stood in the evening coolness, I was intrigued with Ed's smile. There was a small gap between his two front teeth. When the overhead light shined down on the surface of the front teeth, there was a luminosity, which I much later found out was due to fillings of gold that were used in the back of the teeth.

My friends, married ones and the single Mayes sisters, were all very cordial, but not at all intrusive. In that bustling crowd, with limited time for conversation, there was little opportunity for any intensive questioning. For this I was grateful.

That first summer of "getting to know you" was a round of Saturday night dinners at various east side Detroit restaurants and Sundays at the Metropolitan Beach and Kensington Park. Ed always came to the door of my apartment to escort me to his car, and led me back to my door—#1101 River House, 8900 East Jefferson, Detroit 14, Michigan. His car was a turquoise and white Ford convertible.

Another milestone, really a roadblock to a serious commitment, was announced by Ed during that summer of 1960. There was a recession that threatened his employment at a company that was family owned. Relatives would be retained but others may be "let go." So Ed announced that he planned to return to get a teaching degree that was offered at Wayne State University following two semesters of full time courses. He would quit working, continue to live at home during this school year, and could not take on any new "venture" until ?

The biological clock I heard ticking only speeded up. But we had not made any serious promises to each other. Gosh, I wasn't even "going steady." Crestfallen, disappointed, but still somewhat hopeful, I did continue dating others, albeit halfheartedly.

Happily, Ed continued the "courting" during his year of school. Then, after the formal classes were over, there was the application for a teaching position. Ed decided on teaching high school level art. After accepting the offer to teach at Seaholm High School in Birmingham, Michigan, he also announced that the first year of teaching required his full and undivided attention without any other "encumbrances." Again, I swallowed hard, prepared myself for a lot of patient perseverance.

ED CAVANARY—1960

A hiatus occurred in our relationship during the fall of 1961. Literally, "girl lost boy," following a disastrous trip to the Chicago wedding of my brother. My mother and I drove with Ed. Her actions and verbal outbursts disrupted everything and upset Ed so much that all communication and contacts came to a screeching halt. How could I face the rest of my life and now the Christmas holidays, without him?

True love never runs smooth, they say. But does true love prevail? You bet it does! Our love had grown over the months, was expressed in so many different ways including exclusivity. So Ed responded to my personally written Christmas greeting in which I summarized what the past year meant to me and how love permeated all my memories of what we shared. We resumed our dating on a regular basis.

I was attending a folk dancing class at the International Institute. After one of these sessions, Ed met me at the nearby Sapphire Lounge located in the Wardell Hotel on the corner of Kirby and Woodward. It was a cold March night, 1962. His demeanor suggested that he had come to some serious decision. Indeed, he asked if I wanted to go shopping tomorrow. I knew it meant an engagement ring.

We traveled to the downtown Detroit J.L.Hudson department store. Ed and I stood at the diamond counter, chose the solitaire, he put it on my ring finger and I considered that we were officially engaged. It was March 26, 1962. The salesman seemed just a bit surprised at this betrothal that took place in the aisle of the biggest department store on Woodward Ave. The box was put into a bag, but the ring stayed on my finger!

Serious talks followed about the wedding. Three months would be enough time to accomplish all that needed to be done to start our married life together. I loved those discussions of where we would live, who to invite to the wedding, where to honeymoon, how many children (2), how formal would the ceremony be, what kind of music at the reception, etc. We decided on Tuesday, June 26, 1962, at Annunciation Catholic Church, my current parish church, a luncheon reception at the Whittier Hotel for 35 close relatives and friends, and a cruise to Bermuda for the honeymoon. Eleanor Jasinski and Cy O'Connell would be our witnesses. Rev. Carl Mayes officiated at the Nuptial Mass.

Our first endeavor after the engagement was to notify our good friends, Tom and Marie Behnke. They were invited to a Saturday night dinner at my apartment. Ed already told his mother and father and I made a trip to Hamtranck to show my mother the engagement ring. Tom and Marie were elated at the news and said they would have an "engagement" party for some of our mutual friends.

Three wedding showers also were planned. My high school friend, Ann Tomas Dempsey, had a small luncheon at the Woman's City Club in downtown Detroit. Nada Davidovich, my neighbor across the hall in the apartment building, had an evening soiree for another group of friends, and Virginia Traphagen, a Detroit school psychologist and professional colleague, had a "His and Hers" Shower that concentrated on items for the well stocked bar.

Ed and I checked "Emily Post Etiquette" for non-formal ceremonies. A black dress suit for him and a street length dress for me was acceptable. Again the J.L. Hudson Co. had just what I was looking for in a wedding dress. It was off-white, linen looking, with short sleeves edged in heavy lace. A boat neckline also had a lace trim. The dress was floor length but was cut to street length and the surplus used to fashion a small hat with a shoulder length veil. I carried a single white orchid with trailing white stephanotis. My maid of honor, Eleanor's dress was a raspberry color with similar lines.

I met Ed's mother and father one other time before our formal engagement. It was an evening planned by Ed to listen to some of his records in his parents' loft (upstairs room used by Ed). He invited me and my neighbor, Nada, another single woman. It seemed that she was either intended as a "chaperone" or to leave the mom and pop uncertain as to which one was he really serious about. His mother made a cake that Ed served upstairs in his "quarters."

A newspaper strike was on so looking for a place to live meant driving along streets looking for vacancy signs. We did this after deciding to locate near Ed's place of employment in

Birmingham, 14 Mile Road and Cranbrook Road. Rentals were prohibitive in Birmingham, but adjacent Royal Oak was affordable, we discovered. On Leafdale Street, just east of Woodward Avenue and 14 Mile Road, we found a small two-story apartment building that had two bedroom apartments with a porch that featured a built-in outdoor grill! The Amber brothers had apartments in several locations around Royal Oak, and were eager to repaint the walls to our liking and install hanging book shelves in the den.

Our combined furniture and wedding gifts furnished those rooms very adequately. We purchased two walnut dining room chairs and a hanging ceramic lamp, to complete the picture. I savored the role of wife and homemaker. It required a new awareness—taking into account another's wants and needs. I had lived on my own for five years accustomed to a considerable amount of freedom to set my own schedule.

Ed's personality and character made it easy to accommodate him. What influenced me and attracted me to him was his intelligence and "rationality," as well as his excellent personal grooming and personal hygiene. We had many similar likes in music, drama, and use of leisure time. I had more leanings to physical activities and sports which Ed agreed to but in moderation. He was "city" and I was "country." But we "blended" these inclinations as time went on. Ed tried skiing. (My Christmas gift, of a pair of skis, was used for several seasons until I realized that the cold temperatures were barely "tolerated" by Ed.) We both liked square dancing, an activity that absorbed us for many seasons.

The wedding reception for 35 close relatives and friends was a luncheon with wine and a punch. Ed's father asked if the punch had a "stick" in it. We assured him that gin was added to make the fruit juices go down easier.

By 3 p.m. we changed into traveling clothes and drove to Youngstown, Ohio, for an overnight stay before driving to the port at New York City. I remember that Ed remarked after we were in the car alone, "I'm a husband now."

WEDDING OF CHARLOTTE AND ED

The honeymoon cruise to Bermuda, our first, was financed by Ed cashing in one of his insurance policies. The ship was our hotel in Bermuda as we toured the island, shopped, and enjoyed the sights of this unique spot in the Atlantic.

We settled into domesticity in our Royal Oak Amber brothers apartment near 14 Mile Road and Woodward. I returned to my job at the Wayne County Department of Social Welfare and Ed to teaching art subjects at Seaholm High School in Birmingham. Eventually we began to invite our friends to our new "home." Also, we continued to discover the beaches and parks of Oakland County. Then our friends invited us to visit them while they vacationed in various parts of the state and Canada. We traveled to Kettle Point in Ontario, where Tom and Marie took a cottage for their family every summer. Also three or four couples arranged a trip to Stratford, Ontario, to view the Shakespeare productions put on each year. Marie Behnke's brother and his wife, Frank and Joan Malje, and Joan's married sister with her husband, Ann and Claude Kinstle, and sometimes Bette and Bill Sallee were part of this congenial group. We also had parties to celebrate New Year's Eve, usually at the Malje home.

An interesting sidelight needs mentioning here about our "late blooming" nuptials. Ed was age 43 and I was 36. It was our first marriage. But the pastor at Annunciation Church needed more proof from Ed than just his baptismal certificate. Luckily, both his father and his mother were living and available. They accompanied him to the rectory, vouching for his "never married" status.

That first year, Ed's parents often invited us for Sunday dinner. Ed's mom made delicious potato salad and fried chicken. My mom, too, invited us for holiday dinners. She liked to serve ham and chicken soup. Ed's father was a happy retiree, spending his time around their small house and yard. We also exchanged visits with Ed's cousin Dorothy Cavanary, who was living at home, working at a downtown bank and also spent much of her free time caring for her aging mother and their comfortable brick house on Duchess Street. Ed's cousin, Norman Cavanary, lived in Wixom, Michigan with his wife and daughter, Melody. They owned acreage that was used as pasture for horses that Norman raised.

The first year passed quickly. I was looking forward to having a family and we both started to look for a house to own. Pregnancy did not happen—even after consultation and treatment by fertility and sterility specialists. It was 1963 by now, and in vitro fertilization and fertility drugs were not on the scene. Meanwhile, my close friends and relatives were having children. My best friend Eleanor, who married in 1963 had her first son at age 38, and then her third son at age 46! My brother and his wife have a family of six. Helen Hill had five children, Christine Keefe had five offspring, and Ann Tomas Dempsey also had a family of five.

However, this marriage was "otherwise blessed"—a faithful husband and a caring companion eased my disappointment at not having a child of my own. We became very involved in the lives of our nieces and nephews and the children of our friends and neighbors.

During this time, I reviewed my family history regarding childbearing. There were cousins and aunts that were "barren." My mother's aunt Bronia was childless. My mother's sister, Eva had a physically abusive husband who allegedly beat her because she did not produce an heir. On my father's side, there was cousin

Mary, and her two brothers, Frank and Joey, who had no offspring. (Many years later I learned that cousin Mary's marriage was possibly never consummated.)

I spoke with cousin Mary Deslippe when she was a patient in Ford Hospital and I was a medical social worker on the staff. Her name was on the admissions list one morning. She remembered me as Josephine's daughter. I told her how I admired her husband because of his striking looks, especially his wavy black hair that I remembered from their visits to our home on Trowbridge in the early 1930s. She then confided that her strict upbringing affected the marriage. Yes, her husband treated her as if she was on a pedestal, but he "had his women." So did this mean their marriage was never consummated, I wondered?" And was this the reason they never had children? I lost contact with cousin Mary who passed away several years later, in 1979.

What would have been my fate had I "connected" with my first love and began childbearing at age 21 instead of starting 17 years later? It remains my life's unanswered questions.

Buying the First House

On a map of Oakland County we drew a circle indicating a five-mile radius from Seaholm High School where Ed taught. Within the circle were the communities of Royal Oak, Berkley, Clawson, Bloomfield Township and Southfield, as well as Birmingham, the location of the high school. Before the snow melted, and after our first Christmas, we began to search the areas, on our own and with the aid of Realtors, for the house we could afford. Our requirements were: at least two bedrooms, 1 1/2 baths, attached garage, fireplace and brick construction. The Realtors consistently steered us to homes that did not meet our "guidelines" as to amenities and as to price.

It was a newspaper ad that led us to the house we were to occupy for the next 30 years. I found the street on the map, drove slowly looking at the neat red brick dwelling, and wondered what was wrong with it. The price was right $18,500. On an unpaved dead end street, it had a country charm.

Ed and I met the realtor at the house. It was sometime during the month of May 1963. When I saw that expanse that was the back yard, one and one-third acre stretching to the street behind, with maple trees and a heavy growth of cinnamon ferns beneath, I could not hold back my excitement. This was it! City water was just brought into this road, but there were no sewers. A septic system handled the waste water and sewage.

The owners, a childless couple who were planning to retire to Florida because of the man's recent heart attack, were a bit surprised when we signed a purchase agreement before leaving the premises. They told of the house next door being on the market for a couple of years before it sold. These owners placed their house for sale just six weeks before we came to see it.

The house proper was just under 1,000 square feet. It had a fireplace in the living room next to the corner windows, a dining EL, slate floor entry, two bedrooms, full bath, full basement. The house was connected to the two-car garage with a breezeway. There were four doors in the breezeway, one leading to the house, one opening into the garage, one facing the small west patio, and the fourth facing east onto the stone patio that overlooked the spacious yard.

The final agreed upon selling price was $17,900. We were approved for a 15-year conventional mortgage.

July 1, 1963 was moving day. Mr. and Mrs. Griffith gave us final instructions about caring for the ferns: piling leaves over them in the fall. Also, they showed us where their vegetable garden was located before they gave up putting one in due to Mr. G's health problem. The newly planted grass there was just coming up. We bought the rider mower that was kept in a small shed next to the double row of maple trees.

Many happy memories remain from those thirty years we spent at 28330 Ranchwood Road, Southfield, Michigan. The additions were to existing rooms. In one corner of the bedroom we installed a small vanity. That was to be our "half bath." In the basement there was room for a cedar closet for out-of-season clothing. Also many shelves were added along the basement walls for the "accumulation" of odds and ends we purchased over the years.

A big bonus was the fruit cellar in the southwest corner of the basement. The deep shelves, were ideal for home-canned items and preserves, as well as extra jars, bottles and food stuffs held in reserve.

The upright copper colored deep freeze stood next to the fruit cellar. Cherries from our own tree and raspberries from our own bushes and boletus mushrooms from beneath the white pine trees were stashed away for use all winter. Also, vegetables from the garden were frozen for later use. Italian green beans grew well in the long narrow garden on the south side of the row of maple trees. Carrots took longer to mature but were added to the store of produce in the freezer. When full, I could reach in for frozen soups, spaghetti sauces, bread, cake, and a variety of meats.

The enclosed breezeway became a second eating area, especially when company came. A small gas heater took the chill out of the air except in the dead of winter. A drop-leaf table easily accommodated eight persons, for eating only. Once seated there was only room for one lean person to move around to serve.

The long driveway was gravel and needed a fresh load of gravel periodically to fill in the low spots. The three tall white pine trees along the north side of the driveway shed their needles each year. These covered the driveway and had to be raked up, scooped into baskets and used as mulch around the flower beds. Late in August, beneath these mature tall pines, boletus mushrooms "popped" up through the turf. What a joy to gather a cupful each day, for a tasty garnish with a steak! Or to be blanched, frozen in small containers.

The "second" bedroom-den was also the guest room, library, office, and TV room. A sleeper sofa unfolded for use when my mother visited or nieces or other company came for an overnight stay. Thanksgiving weekend was the traditional time for two nieces to make the trip from Algonac. "Uncle Ed" and I enjoyed planning activities for all of us to partake in. In the neighborhood we had "toss the coin" hikes that ended at a restaurant or ice cream parlor. Visits to Christmas displays at Northland Shopping Mall were made, trips to the Detroit Institute of Arts, Greenfield Village, Cranbrook, ice skating at the Southfield Parks and Recreation and roller skating at a rink in Troy, all with the intention of "widening horizons" for my brother's family growing up "in the provinces."

Backyard Summers and the Swimming Pool

The "Esther Williams" swimming pool was partly in the ground and partly above the ground, encased in a redwood frame with a narrow deck all around and enclosed by a redwood railing which flared out slightly. The deepest section was seven feet deep. The rest of the water was three and a half feet deep. A swing-up stair case offered entry to the rectangular pool. Built-in benches were set in the long sides of the construction. The entire pool sat in the middle of the yard near the fence that ran along the north side, between us and the Johnson's next door. The golden delicious apple tree, mature size, was just in front of the pool, partially obstructing it. The tree was removed about the second year when it concealed "midnight" dippers that sneaked into the water after dark, after scaling the railing. Ed and I arranged a "surprise" raid one night after hearing splashing through our open bedroom window. When floodlights were turned on, I rushed toward the pool yelling and swinging a broom. Three agile male figures leaped onto the grass, each grabbing a pile of clothing, then dashed into the darkness between the houses behind our yard. Another time a younger group of boys "invaded" the pool in the dark, confirming our decision to remove the apple tree, and plant a "screen" of bushes and trees along the back edge of the yard. That ended the "skinny dipping."

The backyard with its swimming pool, vegetable garden, and cedar deck against the garage was our focus most of the spring, summer, and fall. Since our house was not air conditioned, a jump in the pool provided instant cooling off. This was especially welcome after work where oscillating floor fans moved the humid air around. (No air conditioning, either, at the Juvenile Court Building where I worked from 1958 to 1966.)

Ed "checked" the pool daily: skimming the surface for leaves, flower petals, and insects, vacuuming the bottom and sides and adding chlorine when indicated. The redwood deck, sides, and railing needed regular re-staining. Because of the meticulous care, we enjoyed the sparkling water from about the second week of May to the second week of October.

Invitations for a cookout usually included "bring your swim suit." The green "shed" was emptied of the rider-mower and a rubber backed bathroom rug was placed on the red brick floor. A beaded curtain was hung in the large opening. Then a length of green canvas hung from the rafter for more privacy. This was the "changing room."

The first grill was for charcoal. Eventually it was replaced with a gas grill that had a rotisserie. The surface of the grill was large enough for an "Indian" corn roast. (Fresh corn was soaked in water for a half hour, then "steamed" until the outside husks were dry and scorched.)

This became a favorite of my brother's children. In 1997 during a visit to niece Charlotte's home in East China, Michigan, I reaped the reward of those cookouts: the first course was "Indian" corn!

The rotisserie was used for chickens or a small turkey. "Centering" was crucial in order to keep the fowl turning. The results were usually very satisfactory: a crisp outside and a moist juicy inside.

It was the expanse of an acre and a third that appealed to me initially. There were trees and bushes, evergreen, and deciduous, in the front yard and some in the back. Three fairly large white pines grew on the north side of the long driveway that made a curve just before the garage doors. That remained in place and was not changed during our entire stay in that house.

The bridal wreath spirea and the althea bushes stayed in the location where they were originally placed. The snowball bush outside the east bedroom sent out shoots that were transferred to other locations around the perimeter of the back yard. Shoots from the red and green barberry bushes were also dug up and used as a fence line along the boundary between us and the Stocktons to our south. Mock orange shrubs were also sending up small shoots. These grew after being transferred and provided much fragrance and many bouquets. The most prized bushes were the lilacs! Deep purple, white, pink, and pale lavender blooms gave off their distinctive scent every spring, and also were used in vases throughout the house.

One of the teachers in the art department at Seaholm offered some Bittersweet seedlings when she was clearing out a part of her yard. These thrived and "exploded" all over our backyard, requiring constant vigilance. One vine was "encouraged" and maintained at the post holding the clothes lines. The other post had a flourishing trumpet vine that attracted humming birds and yellow jackets.

We also "nurtured" ground cover near the house and under the evergreens. The blue flowered periwinkles spread just behind the curve and under the three red maples. I weeded out the grass diligently to give no competition to the spreading shiny dark green leafed carpet.

Married life developed and flourished in that small ranch house in Southfield. In 1969, we planned our second cruise. From New York, a Greek line ship sailed to St. Thomas and then to Aruba and Curacao. It was a 14-day trip during the Christmas holidays. And memorable it was!

During an annual physical exam that fall, Dr. Gustafson discovered a palpable lump in the right side of my lower abdomen. I reacted in disbelief and denial, requesting a second opinion. The second doctor offered his opinion after similar "poking"— contradicting Dr. Gustafson. Happily, I continued to plan for the cruise which would have to be cancelled if Dr. Gustafson's plan was to be followed: surgery, of an exploratory type to determine the nature of the lump.

There were no symptoms, except for some small twinges in the lower abdomen, no doubt, I thought, brought on by the approach of menopause. There was a diminution in the days of the monthly cycle, which also could be a sign of cessation of menses. But when I next appeared for my annual physical in October 1970, Dr. Gustafson, again located a lump in the same area and recommended a D and C. The report from this nonthreatening procedure sent me once more into denial and disbelief. Cancerous cells showed up on the right side of the scraped uterus.

I phoned the medical director of the Oncology Department at

Ford Hospital where I was working as a medical social worker. Dismayed, I asked him to have this test repeated to make certain the results were as reported. He kindly talked to Dr. Gustafson and then assured me that a report would not be indicated. I was then scheduled for a hysterectomy and an ooferectomy, in two weeks—November 1, 1970.

I was discharged home, spending the next two weeks coming to terms with the big C and its impact on me, my husband and our future as husband and wife.

On one Sunday afternoon, our friends, Tom and Marie Behnke and Dr. Frank Malje with his wife Joan, stopped by to offer hope and encouragement. Ed and I agreed to be open about this catastrophic condition and discuss its treatment. At this point, surgery. Possible follow up, radiation and/or chemotherapy.

When I checked into Beaumont Hospital in Royal Oak, Michigan, and got settled into a two-bed room, I learned that Dr. Gustafson requested "consults" from several other GYN-OB staff doctors. I counted *seven* "pokes"—each definitely confirming the presence of a "lump" not only in the lower abdominal cavity but also one the size of a pea in the right breast. A separate surgeon was to excise the growth in the breast.

My roommate was a young married woman, experiencing GYN-OB problems that possibly would require surgery and affect childbearing. Hers was an exhibited distress as she complained about having to eat hospital food and smoked one cigarette after another. Her husband and parents hovered and catered to her wish for a pizza and coke.

While she was eating, I walked out to the nursing station and asked for the Director of Nursing for that unit. I confided that I personally felt compassion and empathy for this roommate facing a possible loss, but I was facing surgery the next morning and was concerned about recovering in a room where cigarette smoke would surround me. The nurse assured me that when I came back from surgery, I would be in another room. (In 1970, smoking was still permitted in hospital rooms.)

My roommate's visitors left, she had her last cigarette before turning out the lights and I had time to reflect on my life until now. I had been married eight years. There were no children that may need raising should this become a terminal condition. I loved my role as a wife, homemaker, aunt, neighbor, daughter, social worker, friend.

Would all this stop? I thought of my husband. Who would replace me to meet all his needs? Those "unremarried" female teachers at Seaholm? Naw! And yet I may have to accept finality to existence of this mortal flesh. I decided "I'M NOT GOING!" No one else I could think of would be able to replace me in my husband's life!

Dr. A. J. Utecht and Ederina visited us before my going to the hospital bringing a small glass vial of water from Lourdes. I drank half. The other half I gave to my roommate, when I learned she was a Catholic.

I awoke from the surgery in a bed with the side rails up. The bed was in a different room, now next to the window. Leaning over the bottom rail of the bed were my husband and my brother, both serious. Leonard (my brother, the surgeon) visibly distressed, saying that before I awoke, I was moaning as if in pain. Indeed, I quickly became aware of the raw wound, stitched up and stapled down my lower abdomen, the effects of the anesthesia wearing off slowly.

My first concern was about the stiff and hard round cover taped over the right breast. Was the breast gone? The lump, pea sized, underwent immediate testing to determine if it was benign or malignant. The surgeon shortly reported that the "pound of flesh" removed proved to be benign, no further surgery was required. I was greatly relieved; grateful I would continue to have TWO.

Dr. Gustafson, also gave his report. The uterus and both ovaries were removed. Each ovary, enlarged to the size of a lemon was considered to be cancerous. He consoled me by revealing he did not remove the appendix, which is usually taken out during this type of abdominal procedure.

My first reaction was to withdraw. I curled up into a fetal position, turning toward the wall, away from my roommate, crying softly. I remember my statement to the nurse, "I know the implications." (The previous four years I worked with cancer patients being treated at Henry Ford Hospital.)

The first "comfort measure" offered was by a nurse who brushed my hair. Later I was given alcohol back rubs, but the initial hair brushing had a very therapeutic effect. Then, I was "shunned" by the staff until I voluntarily turned my body to the right to face my roommate and the door, as well as the staff coming in to offer their services.

I asked for permission to attend Sunday Mass in the hospital chapel, calling my husband to be here with me. Tears did not stop flowing as he rolled me in the wheelchair to the elevator and then to the floor where the chapel was located. I was still reeling from the realization that I was diagnosed with ovarian cancer and would require radiation treatments following discharge from the hospital. Cancer was a treatable disease, like many other conditions. Only antibiotics could assure a cure. Heart problems, diabetes, arthritis, etc. were all "treatable" illnesses. Many times I repeated this information to patients I served at Ford Hospital. Now I had to believe it applied to me as well.

About the third day, I had a visit from Ed's father. He drove to the hospital by himself, from his east side of Detroit address. As usual, he was impeccably groomed: white shirt and necktie, suit and his silver gray hair neatly combed. At 79, he was still living independently and driving his own car. He appeared grave over this turn of events. He never mentioned missing having grandchildren during the past 8 years of our marriage. His main concern during this visit was about the help I would need after coming home, wondering if my mother was going to come to help out during my recovery.

Dealing with my mother required the utmost finesse. I had to tell her that I needed an operation. The news plunged her into despair and worry. I did not want her visiting me in the hospital, seeing me droopy and weak. When I phoned her, speaking in the strongest voice I could muster, I assured her that I was recovering, that everything went well, that I would see her when the doctor gave the O.K. for travel.

I was very touched by another duo who visited me at the hospital. My godson Lenny, age 8, and his sister, niece Ann, age 6, waited in the visitors room for me. The parents, my brother Leonard and sister-in-law Arlene brought them, concerned about the seriousness of my condition. Their other, younger three children remained at home. I was pleased and happy to be able to make an appearance, walking into the room on my own, reacting and unwrapping the gifts, wondering about their understanding of my condition. Since both parents were doctors, all the family members heard a lot of "medical talk" at home. I think they were relieved to see me "in the flesh" after learning of the surgery I had and the diagnosed life threatening illness.

My smoking former roommate was relieved when her condition was downgraded to an inflammation, not requiring surgery. She presented me with a small crucifix blessed by the Pope which I still keep in my jewelry box as a reminder of that stressful period in my life.

Upon returning home, Ed and I found a package on the small front porch. A whole fully cooked chicken awaited heating for our dinner that evening. A short time passed, and at the back door stood neighbor Ruth Stockton, carrying a freshly baked pie. The meat was dropped off by Betty Bandyk, not knowing when I would arrive. I felt fortunate and grateful for such caring friends and neighbors at this time of crisis.

The first radiation treatment took place on the morning of my discharge day. Twenty-four more treatments followed with blood tests interspersed to monitor the white blood count. Because of Ed's work hours, I recruited Ruby Simpson (across the street neighbor) to drive me to the radiation therapy for the first three weeks. After that period of time, I was allowed to drive myself to the 4 p.m. appointments.

Our hide-a-bed couch was put to use during my convalescence. It was in the den, where both Ed and I watched TV as we stretched out on the opened bed. He left to sleep in the bedroom, allowing me to rest without fear of his knee or elbow bumping my healing incision.

Chemotherapy, a once per week injection of Depo-Provera, followed the 25 radiation treatments for the next four months. Another neighbor, Mrs. "Billie" Kirkpatrick, a former RN, agreed to administer the hefty dosage to the buttock, after I obtained the hypodermic needles from my brother's clinic. Ford Hospital's

Oncology clinic mailed the prescribed dosage every week. The site of the needle prick remained tender and sore for the entire week. I determined to alternate "cheeks" allowing one side to "calm down" before the next trip to the Kirkpatrick's house.

I decided to terminate my medical social work at Henry Ford Hospital. It was, for me the ideal schedule: a full 8-hour day on Monday and Wednesday and a half day on Friday, for a total of 20 hours. And I wore a starched white Lab coat, as did all the other medical staff. Every Tuesday, I drove to Algonac to assist my mother with various chores, e.g., banking, shopping, etc. In return, she often had a stack of potato pancakes, still warm, waiting on a plate on the stove. I had been at Henry Ford Hospital almost four years, enjoying and feeling fulfilled by the various aspects of the position. I was qualified to supervise students in social work from the University of Michigan, an assignment I appreciated.

The current role of full-time wife and homemaker was one I had not experienced yet since adding MRS. to my name. The second summer came and restlessness led to considering work nearer home. It had been an 18-mile trip from Ranchwood to Henry Ford Hospital. A shorter drive would be welcomed. The Family and Children's Services of Oakland County had an office in Berkley, on Twelve Mile Road. I was hired as a Consultant on Aging, specializing with older adults aged 60 and older. It was September 1972.

Traditionally, social workers did not belong to unions. School teachers did get union representation and were benefitting by being able to negotiate contracts and annual pay raises. Having union representation became an issue about 1975, after three years of no pay raises for the staff at the Family and Children's Services.

A.F.S.C.M.E. (American Federation of State, County and Municipal Employees) would help the social workers of this agency after we voted to have them represent us at the "bargaining table." During the formation and organization of the staff, I was the Recording Secretary at all the meetings. The first one was held at our Ranchwood address, kicking off events unionizing the "line staff" and beginning a struggle to improve the pay scale.

Of course, union membership was chosen by my father and by my husband-teacher, and now I was proud to promote it for my fellow social workers. I recall driving to a social worker's home when her car broke down on the crucial election day, picking her up, and bringing her to the office so she could cast her vote. (She was one of the lowest paid workers on the staff.)

It was interesting to observe the polarization occurring. Any supervisor was considered part of the administration and therefore ineligible to vote. During this time, three social workers were promoted to supervisors, reducing the number of staff voting.

The agency director, Robert Janes, and his wife, also on the staff, resisted the changes after the staff voted to become part of A.F.S.C.M.E. Negotiations took weeks, with stalling techniques used repeatedly. It was a learning experience for all, especially for me. Mr. Janes left for a larger agency in Buffalo before the year ended.

Health care and follow-up. Dr. Gustafson was scrupulously meticulous in scheduling a three-month, then six-month, and finally an annual checkup after my surgery and treatment for ovarian cancer. The five-year anniversary brought a guarded sigh of relief, as there was no guarantee another "primary" source of malignant cells may not surface. Indeed, in later years, skin lesions on my arm, leg, and back were excised and found to be basal type lesions.

We faced another bout of treatment for Ed's bladder tumor, which was found to be malignant, was surgically removed and then treated with two different chemical agents. Each series of treatments, in 1985 and 1986, at William Beaumont Hospital, was scheduled once a week, over a six-week period. These were experimental drugs, prescribed for a number of elderly males having the same diagnosis. Ed continues with six-month check ups, via a cystoscopy, now done in the urologist's office.

We both believe in the value of early detection and both agree that cancer is a "treatable" disease. Since we are "survivors" of this dreaded condition, we are supportive and encouraging when we hear or learn of anyone, especially friends, who are faced with this illness.

Our good friend, Betty Bandyk, is a survivor of ovarian cancer. Her treatment did not include radiation, but was closely monitored by her family and four minor children. Both Betty and I are enjoying our "golden years" and now deal with age related conditions, none so devastating, or life threatening as cancer.

SILVER ANNIVERSARY, 1987, ED AND CHARLOTTE

CHAPTER IV

1989

With a heavy heart I drove alone from our Southfield home to Mt. Clemens General Hospital, a distance of 30 some miles. My mother, age 92, lay mortally ill in the Cardiac Unit.

The phone call from brother Leonard came earlier that June 26, 1989 evening. Husband Ed and I just returned from dinner celebrating our 27th wedding anniversary.

It was dusk when I parked the car, entered the hospital and headed for the CCU. In a cubicle, isolated by a drawn curtain, my mother lay on a narrow Gurney, an IV taped to the top of her hand, an oxygen mask over her face. Her eyes opened, fixed their gaze on me in recognition, then closed again. She said nothing.

A tall white-jacketed female resident-doctor stood on the other side, a stethoscope on my mother's chest. I told her I was "the daughter" and asked how she was doing. The answer, "She's dying," gave me a jolt and I squelched a sob. Her tone had a finality to it and the voice had no compassion.

My senses shifted into DENIAL. How many times before this we faced life-threatening hospital stays: an abdominal aneurysm, GI bleeding, renal failure, heart failure, a fractured leg, fractured vertebrae. A number of admissions coincided with our planned vacations.

Each time stabilization followed, sometime a short-term nursing rehabilitation stay brought my mother to a return to her former level of functioning. This resident did not know my mother's recuperative powers, I concluded. My mother would respond once more!

When I sought out my two nieces, Rachel and Charlotte, now young women in their early 20s, my emotions erupted. Sobbing, I grieved her possible demise. One on each side, they lead me down the hall, consoling and comforting me.

Just two days earlier, Sunday, I wheeled my mother in her wheelchair around the block next to the Abby Convalescent Center in Warren, Michigan, admonishing her about her refusal to take medications. She was adamant about the medicine "not helping." I was just as adamant, insisting medications would not help unless she took them. (The nurse on the floor told me they would not force her to take the meds—and that she had been refusing them for almost a month.) This information shocked me, since I knew that with a bit of coaxing my mother usually came around.

Now the task was to plan for post-hospital care. Hopefully, skilled care would assure closer monitoring of her chronic heart failure and escalating blood pressure. The hospital social worker agreed to a transfer to the Mayberry Chronic Care facility in Mt.Clemens. Mrs. Antonina Bierzynski, the wife of my brother's godfather, was a patient there after a leg amputation. Before my mother became wheelchair bound, we visited Mrs. Bierzynski periodically at her home for several years. My brother also agreed that this would be a good plan.

The plan was complicated by a scheduled three-week trip to Poland Ed and I had been arranging, that was to start on July 1st, just 3 days hence. I made daily visits to the hospital, attempting to feed my mother small amounts of ice cream. She would look at me but never spoke.

While my mother was still at the Abby nursing home, she knew of our travel plans. As many times before, when we would be going away, her response was, "What, again?" I could have cajoled her into believing that we would take her along despite her bed bound and total care condition, as she hoped. My pragmatic, practical response, just angered her.

At all her previous hospital stays, at Providence Hospital, at Harrison Community Hospital and now at Mt. Clemens General, she received VIP care, sometimes in a private room, the nurses and aides, doting on "grandma." Brother, Dr. Leonard Kasperowicz, was on the staff of Mt. Clemens General, available to assist with discharge plans, so Ed and I decided to go ahead with the July 1st trip to Poland.

On July 17th 1989, Ed and I visited Zakopane, a resort city in the Tatra mountains south of Kraków. We returned late to the flat of cousin Halina Pietkiewicz. A phone call from my brother notified me of my mother's death. She was to be discharged that morning to be admitted to the chronic care facility, instead she passed away peacefully in the night.

I cried out in shock, stifling tears so I could speak. Her funeral had been prearranged. She had chosen her burial outfit several years before, it was in a box at my brother's house. The dress was pink chiffon, her favorite color. I asked my brother to take a photograph of my mother in the casket and to notify some of her close friends of the funeral date. Then I told my cousins and my mother's aunt Albina Bielawska, age 91, who was living with Halina. Sadly, they did not get to meet my mother in 1974, when we visited Poland.

I remember cousin Halina's daughter, Ela, offering a shot glass of cognac, a palliative and numbing treatment for my grief. I asked Ed to hold me close as we shared a narrow bed that night, telling him I would miss my mother and needed time to cry over my loss. His comforting arms encircled me and provided the warmth of human touch.

On the day of her funeral we were at mass at the Polish shrine of our Lady of Częstochowa. Our final stop was Elbląg, where my uncle Jan lived with his wife and daughter. He was my mother's youngest brother. He sighed, noting, "I'm the last one remaining," when I advised him of his oldest sister's death.

In August, a memorial Mass was conducted at St. Ives parish church. In October, after the headstone was in place next to my father's, some family members gathered at the cemetery for a grave site service. I brought a zip bag of Polish soil which was sprinkled on my mother's grave. We listened to an audio tape of her favorite folk songs and presented short readings—memories of "Busia."

All the clothing belonging to my mother was now in a black plastic bag, removed from the nursing home. I determined to send the newest items to her widowed aunt, Bronia, age 93, now a resident of a retirement home in Poland. She and my mother exchanged letters over their lifetime. My mother regularly inserted money along with the latest information about her health and family.

The response and thank you note was penned by Bronia's niece, Teresa Sarosiek-Porębska, who was certain that she and I were related. The clothing was graciously received by my mother's aunt, but her eyesight was failing, so she asked Teresa to respond.

Because of this exchange, I learned of several other branches of my maternal side of the family (Sarosiek) still living in different cities across Poland. In 1993, following repeated invitations, I met and traveled with Teresa, finally reaching Gibulicze, in Belorus, where my mother and father were born.

Poland and Gibulicze—1993

All factors came together a bit hurriedly for this trip. Ed and I sold our house in Southfield, Michigan and made the big move to Destin, Florida, in July 1993. When the boxes were unpacked and personal items put away, I set to make arrangements with Four Seasons Travel in Warren, Michigan for the flight to Warsaw. From September 8 to September 30, 1993, I would meet and stay with various family members in several cities throughout Poland. Cousin Teresa Sarosiek-Porębska would assist with travel to the ancestral village of Gibulicze, where my parents grew up.

Letter contacts were made and a schedule worked out. I had invitations to visit and meet two cousins that I discovered after sending my mother's clothing to her aunt Bronia in 1989, after my mother died. Aunt Bronia's niece wrote a thank-you note, and remarked that we must be related! This niece was Teresa (my cousin, the doctor) Sarosiek-Porębska. She would meet me in Warsaw and at the end of my stay would fly to the U.S. with me. I also would meet Józef Sarosiek, Teresa's uncle and his wife Barbara.

The first leg of my flight was to Chicago. Beata, daughter of Teresa, met me at Chicago's O'Hare airport, presenting me with a single red rose and letters that I was to deliver to various family members. Beata was the most recent émigré from our scattered extended family to move and settle in this country. Small and slight, she had high cheek bones, almond-shaped hazel eyes and dark brown hair. (Tatar influence?) With her English speech noticeably accented, we exchanged greetings before I moved onto the International Concourse.

All the passengers were on board when I arrived at the check-in counter about 5:15 p.m. As soon as I was seated, the plane began to move, taxiing and taking off promptly at 6 p.m. Actual flying time to Warsaw was 8 hours, 30 minutes.

LOT Airlines uses Boeing 737 planes that are comfortable when NOT filled to capacity. Drinks, including cocktails, were served and were free. A tasty supper was served next: smoked fish, salad, breaded chicken, potato, asparagus, a small Polish pastry (piernik) and cheese and crackers.

By 8:35 p.m., we were over Nova Scotia heading for the Atlantic. It was a smooth flight, conducive to relaxing and napping.

Arrival time was 9:30 a.m. Wednesday, September 8, 1993. The group around the baggage carousel was relatively small. One by one, individuals with their suitcases left the area. Soon I was the lone survivor, watching the moving platform, now empty. Teresa was somewhere else in the building awaiting me. We had exchanged photos to make identification easier.

But I needed to delay our meeting to file a missing luggage report. Exasperated, I finally located her explaining the predicament. I had a small carry-on tote bag with a change of clothing and cosmetics that would have to last until the errant suitcase caught up with me. Teresa had a small bouquet of fresh flowers that were a comfort, a delightful gesture that I experienced previously during the very first trip to Poland in 1959.

Teresa and I agreed to head for the farthest destination first: Grodno and Gibulicze. But our base would be Sokółka, in the same province, where we would stay with her mother, Józefa Sarosiek. A widow, she lived alone in a two-room apartment in the center of this small city.

Teresa, my cousin-the-doctor, was a woman in her mid fifties, slightly taller than I, with short cropped blond hair, lavender tinted eye glasses, and a wide smile. She was about the same dress size as me, wearing a trim black suit and low-heeled black pumps. She received her medical education in Białystok, a city west of Sokółka and Gibulicze. When she began her studies, her two children stayed with Teresa's mother in Sokółka, while Teresa's husband, Bogdan, continued to work at his job as an aircraft engineer. Teresa's specialty was gynecology. She appeared fast moving, decisive, efficient, and articulate in Russian and in Polish. This proved to be a godsend as we traveled into Belorus later in the week.

We hailed a cab that took us to Embassy Row where I applied for a visa that permitted travel across the eastern border into Grodno and the village of Gibulicze in Belorus.

Teresa had a strong opinion about the newly appointed workers in the Belorus embassy. I was interviewed in the hallway by a man in shirt sleeves who agreed to issue the document for $60 U.S. I could travel with this visa for a period of 30 days. This "casual" kind of business procedure received a spate of negative comments from Teresa. She held a low opinion of anything that smacked of the former political system she lived under most of her life, and from which she was released in 1989.

The cab which was waiting for us, now took us to the train station in Warsaw. For $5.00 each, we had a second-class seat on the passenger train that left at 2:30 p.m. and deposited us about 7 p.m. in Sokółka. On the way, the train stopped in Białystok. This was the actual birthplace of my mother and was where her family lived until their move to the small village of Gibulicze, when she was about five years old. Teresa knew that the train station, now in the process of renovation, went back to the time of the Tsars.

Teresa's mother lived in a first floor rear apartment comprised of two large rooms: a kitchen with sleeping area and another multipurpose room that was a bedroom, TV room, and dining room. The turn of the century tile stove was used for heating and cooking. The back of the stove, clad in white tile was part of the corner wall in the large bedroom. The tile, warmed by the wood fire, heated that room nicely, and a stout cord across that tile was used for drying small pieces of personal laundry.

In the bathroom, too small to hardly turn around in, a tub stood on cast iron feet. A toilet was jammed into a small space between the wall and the tub. It had an overhead water closet that was not working, and there was no seat on the fixture. To flush the toilet, a bucket was filled with water from the tub faucet, then emptied into the toilet bowl. The washbowl/sink served two purposes: that's where the dishes were washed and dried on a shelf next to the wall. A hot water heater hung above the tub on the back wall. This ingenious contraption only heated the water when the hot water faucet was turned on! My tote bag with a change of clothing and cosmetics now had to serve me until the misplaced luggage caught up with me. This took almost a week. It also necessitated daily phone calls to the LOT offices in Warsaw. These phone contacts were made by walking several blocks to the post office, where a switchboard operator placed the call, and when the connection was made, the small phone booth in the lobby was used for conversation. Then, the time and charges were presented and paid for.

I reasoned that my late arrival in Chicago was not within the three-hour recommendation for an international flight and that the luggage never got on that LOT airplane.

Sokółka is a small town with Christian, Orthodox, and Muslim influences. Each religion has its own worship facility. The Muslim mosque is the smallest. It is called Bohoniki, built of wood in the 18th century. Every August, Muslims from all over Poland, gather in this eastern city for a festival, prayers, and worship. Teresa told me that the Muslims who were Tatars came from Crimea to serve in the army of King Jan Sobieski. Many stayed on, living in peace and harmony with their Christian neighbors for the past three hundred years.

The Roman Catholic Church of St. Anthony of Padua was also built in the 18th century. At the entrance, above the doorway was "Matka Boska Ostrobramska," a two-dimensional depiction of Our Lady of Ostrobrama, (the original in the city of Vilnus). The structure was Romanesque, massive columns flanking the altars. The floor was made of small white tiles. A silver monstrance stood on the main altar, with vases of lavender asters on each side. Small stained glass windows were placed high on the walls near the ceiling.

Many of the worshipers were older women. Facial features often reflected the Tatar presence in this part of the country: black hair, high cheek bones and almond-shaped eyes. A nun wore the traditional habit of floor length black with a black veil and a red rope sash with fringes on the ends.

In the vestibule, a directory listed TEN priests serving in this parish. The daily mass was at 6 p.m., and was well attended on this Thursday evening.

This town had no traffic lights, only stop signs. The main

street is called Grodzieńska because it leads to the city of Grodno, about an hour away by car or bus.

Teresa and I took a bus to the village of Klimówka where the church had documents on the Sarosiek family. We already roamed through the cemetery in Sokółka where Teresa's father, brother, and sister are buried. Bilminy and Szymaki were villages in the same area and had families of the Sarosieks moving in and out of the locality.

The Szymaks were the gentry living in this area. The Sarosieks married the daughters of the Szymaks, according to Teresa. Being gentry, the Szymaks owned land. One, Gregory Szymak, founded a monastery on his own property, and became the first prior. Gregory's sister Victoria, founded the order of the Sisters of Saint Brigid in Grodno, called Brigidki.

Not to be outdone, the Sarosieks, Victor, and his brother Antoni (Teresa's grandfather), donated their land for the cemetery in Klimówka. They are both buried in this cemetery.

The church we visited in Klimówka was The Holy Trinity and St. Dominic parish. The pastor lived alone in the rectory next to the church in a simple frame dwelling. Teresa heard that a dependence on alcohol was affecting this man of the cloth, so that he was known to flub the words of prayers and be late for funerals. Today he looked "hung over" but was accommodating. He led us into the office where he brought the parish register of deaths. Each listing gave the age, survivors, their age, and cause of death. I was looking for a listing of my grandmother, Anna Wróblewska (m.n. Sarosiek) who died in 1937. To date there is no official death certificate to be found but several relatives declare that she is buried in the cemetery of the church of the Franciscans in Grodno. I decided to visit this church too, as part of my search.

These records were in several volumes that were kept on shelves behind glass doors. One wall of the office was lined with book shelves. The recording was done by hand, written in ink.

I copied one entry that documented the marriage of a daughter of the Szymaki family and Victor Sarosiek (who gave land for the cemetery). On May 8, 1936, his wife, Anna, died at age 55. Her parents were listed as John and Salomea Szymaki. Their children were: Honorata 36, Józefa 32, Jacob 29, Genowefa 27, and Anthony 20. Victor's age was given as 68.

The above Honorata, now age 90, was still living on the farm operated by her son, Zygmunt Filipowicz and his wife Marya. Teresa frequently visits this family, checking Honorata's health status, and today brought a bag of fruit: bananas and oranges, to this frail relative. She was homebound, meals were provided by the daughter-in-law along with minimal housekeeping. Honorata preened herself, fluffing up her hair and adjusting her blouse and shawl for a snapshot I took of her in her modest surroundings. Her house was separate from the one of her son, Zygmunt.

Two of his sons passed us on the road to the house. Blond, blue eyed, stocky, they appeared to be of very short stature. This I learned is a trait that shows up in the Sarosiek family line. Stella Landers in Florida (daughter of Bernice Sarosiek Gafkowsky) is short, as are her four daughters. My mother's height was under 5 feet, but her brother was tall and lean. Her mother's maiden name was Sarosiek.

Marya, Zygmunt's wife, was barefoot. Her stocky, sturdy frame, muscular arms were a testimony to the heavy farm labor required of her. She led us into a front parlor where two easy chairs faced a small TV on a table. A snack appeared shortly: bread, sliced spam-like meat, cake, cookies, and tea. This was followed by some sweet wine.

We were still in the village of Szymaki. We met with Wacek Rapucha, a distant relative of my mother, who previously was contacted by Teresa to find out if the relatives of my parents still lived in Gibulicze. After being directed to a potato field, where several workers were stacking potatoes on large mounds, Wacek came to the edge of the work area to talk to us. Short and lean, he brushed some dirt from his trousers and hands. His Polish had the characteristics of this region. He was frequently in Grodno where he served as an acolyte in the Church of the Franciscans, so did make a stop in Gibulicze to confirm that my letter was received, and I was expected.

Our bus ride back to Sokółka was mostly on dirt roads and unpaved country lanes. The missing suitcase was still missing.

Teresa and I determined to make the trip to Grodno and Gibulicze on Sunday, September 12. So the day before, Saturday, we made a trip to the local marketplace. The area had a bazaar like quality: farm produce along with second hand items and stalls with clothing and furniture. My purchases were some fresh fruit that I made into a salad for our dinner. Also I bought a Palmetto-like plant for Teresa's mother, who immediately repotted it, as a reminder of my Florida home.

On Sunday, the train to Grodno left Sokółka at 12:05 p.m. When we inquired about the schedule and ticket price the day before, we were warned not to wear any gold jewelry, especially earrings, rings or necklaces. In addition, Teresa's mother expressed concern about our personal safety, fearing the worst, including theft, abduction, and murder! We each carried a small overnight case and a snack to be consumed on the train.

The train passed through Kundzin´ where a small number of residents live by the name Białobłocki. This was my great grandmother's maiden name.

The first stop was the Kuźnica—Białostocka train station. Kuźnica was the birthplace of my maternal grandmother, Anna Sarosiek. When we arrived at the train station in Grodno we took a cab to the village of Gibulicze, 4 km from Grodno. It was almost dusk. There were 20 dwellings in this village, three of them recently built. Some houses had narrow sidewalks leading from the front to the rear gardens. The cement on these walkways looked fresh and new. The one-story frame homes were in various stages of repair. A dirt road with water standing in the low places, extended from the main highway to the end of the village. It looked like every square of earth was planted with fruit trees, berry bushes and flowers. Low picket fences surrounded each house.

I reflected recalling the spread of fields around Gibulicze, and before, the countryside, rolling, verdant, peaceful between the villages of Klimówka and Szymaki, looking like a landscape painting. "Yes," I sighed, "Now I understand my mother's longing to return to her homeland.

Knocking on the first door we asked for the family of Józefa Ciereszko, my mother's first cousin. Her son-in-law, a middle aged tall man, Władysław Orłowski came out of the garage on the other side of the road, greeting us as he pulled out my letter from his pants pocket. He said there was some difficulty in reading my writing and understanding my wording. Later I found out that the Polish language was not used much anymore, that Belorussian was widely used in this area even before 1990 when Belorus became an independent country. In fact, Mr. Orłowski confided, his native Polish language was a deterrent in getting a job in Grodno, where he worked as a chauffer.

We soon met the rest of the family: my mother's cousin, Józefa Ciereszko, her daughter Teresa Orłowski and daughter Alicia, age 16, a winsome high school student who loves cats. Józefa came down the village road leading their cow from the pasture. There was another project going on. Two deep kettles of just picked mushrooms were cooking on a stove in an outdoor field-kitchen. Józefa sat down beside the boiling pots, looking weary. High rubber boots were on her feet, a woolen cap covered her head and a warm sweater had the sleeves pushed up. She held a wooden spoon stirring the thick mass from time to time. The steam carried a woodsy, earthy aroma.

My feeling was that chores needed to be done, that our visit would not stop anything that was going on. A short while later, Józefa's other daughter and her two teenage girls, came out of the nearby woods carrying baskets of filberts.

I spoke with Józefa as she tended the cooking mushrooms. She remembered my mother and her sisters. She mentioned Paulina, younger sister of my mother, who married and relocated in France. She loved to dance the "Karowiczka" according to Józefa. Another bit of information about Paulina was about her inability to breast feed her baby, due to inverted nipples.

I listened with interest about how my grandmother lost the sight in her eye. She was picking cherries when a tree branch struck her. My mother never mentioned this, nor did it come up in conversation in my subsequent visits with my relatives, in 1959, 1974 or 1989.

Later, examining my grandmother's photo, I looked carefully. Yes, the right eye looked blank. The photographer, cleverly positioned her body so the right side was away from the light, slightly in shadow, obscuring the vacant eye. It took four trips to Poland before I obtained this bit of information.

I never met my grandmother, but my mother often praised her homemaking abilities and recalled sage advice she gave to her offspring. She pointed to the double-pane windows, and observed out loud, "The world is on the other side of the glass." Indeed, three of her five children, left the homestead and the village. Son Alexander's final destination was Hawaii, Josephine emigrated to America, and youngest daughter, Paulina, married and settled in France.

Józefa recalled my mother's brother John and how he tended horses when he was a young man. I also heard about my father's brother, Kazimierz Kasperowicz, who had a son Witek. Witek married one of the daughters of the Czekiel family. He returned to visit the village and may be living in Wrocław.

Józefa has a bedroom in this house owned by her son-in-law, Władek (Władysław) and his wife Teresa. They also own a small apartment in Grodno that is still not completely furnished. They hope to accomplish this before their daughter marries and needs a place to live. Both husband and wife have been working during their married life and complained about low wages. Teresa and Władek often spend free weekends at this apartment although their intention is to live out their final years in Gibulicze. Teresa was particularly nostalgic about the fragrant blossoming trees and flowers that greet the residents each spring.

But there were two other stops I made in this village this evening. Antoni Czekiel, related to my father lived at #10 and Bronia Bujko lived at #11 formerly the Wróblewski homestead, where my mother lived from age 5 to age 24.

Antoni Czekiel, a widower, lives alone in his own house. His son Wacław lives in Grodno, visits occasionally. Antoni was born in 1911, and remembers my mother and a special visit made by my father in 1921. Antoni relates that he was 10 years old and had a dog. This pet ran after my father, a stranger in the neighborhood, and grabbed the hem of his overcoat, tearing it. My father yelled at Antoni, who later received a thrashing from his father for not keeping the animal under control. Antoni recalled my grandfather, Antoni Gasperowicz, that he was a large man, but my father Andrew was bigger! The one photo that exists of my father in his World War I uniform shows him to be fleshy and well developed.

Bronia Bujko now lives in the ancestral Wróblewski house. I identified myself to Bronia, a small woman, wearing a head scarf and smiling with gaps in her mouth. She allowed me to step into the dwelling of two large rooms with a small passageway that held another large storage room. I noted the wooden floor and informed her that my mother told of the house being built by my grandfather with the first wooden floor in the village. Bronia scoffed, "This is a new floor, replacing the old one that was rotting." Oh, yes, that first floor must have been put in about 1901, surely needed replacing after housing three generations of families with children.

This house was left by my Uncle John in 1957, when he, his wife, and four growing children relocated in Elbląg. John's sister, my aunt Eva, and her husband Jan Bujko moved in. They had no children, much to the disappointment of the husband. When Ewa died, Jan Bujko remarried a younger woman, Bronia, and had a son. When Jan died, his widow, Bronia, and her son continued to live there. During my visit, Bronia was a grandmother. Her married son, with his wife and toddler son, continue life in this old house, sharing the two rooms. As I stood talking, the daughter-in-law was positioning her young son over a small, round chamber pot on the floor near the bed, in an early effort at toilet training. The outside of the building is unpainted, a weatherbeaten gray.

Like the other yards, this one too, had flowers, raspberry and currant bushes and cherry, apple, and pear trees. A gray wooden picket fence enclosed the small lot. I only had a glimpse of the second room that was separated from the front room by a door frame with a striped cloth hung across the opening. In the far corner was the tile stove that was used for cooking and heating.

What stories my mother told about that stove. There was a narrow loft above it that was used for sleeping in the winter months, according to my mother. I could not recognize it now. The double windows, I was told, were used by my grandmother to decorate the place. She arranged dried flowers setting them in the space between the inner and outer panes. I tried to envision this humble hut when my grandparents were raising their five children and living off the land. Their acreage was beyond this enclave.

My mother often mentioned the various activities that occupied all the family members. There was a pond with ducks and geese. I located this small pond, now looking stagnant and abandoned being next to the highway that was put in recently. This new road eliminated the one well that served this village. It also split off part of the community, so that it now lay on the other side of the highway. The dwelling that belonged to my father's family was gone, only the foundation remains and two old linden trees. Without a water source, all the villagers rely on bottled water for their daily needs. It was rationed carefully, a cup at a time for washing, brushing teeth, etc.

One wooden privy serves any resident that is willing to walk to the end of the road. It required "arranging" before Teresa and I were allowed to use it. In fact it was totally dark, and I carried some matches to illuminate the interior, and asked Alicia to accompany me down the path.

Alicia waited on the path while I opened the wooden door, lit a match to see what I needed to do next. In the center of the floor was an opening that held a metal pail. On the wall a nail held small squares of white paper. Also on the wall was an arrow indicating that the paper was to be deposited in a metal basket in the corner. I followed directions noting that the "facility" must have been swept and furnished with appropriate containers just before I asked about using it. Of course part of the procedure was completed in the dark as I needed my hands to adjust clothing before and after using this unique privy!

Teresa and I shared a narrow bed that was prepared for our use for this one night. We positioned ourselves like two nesting spoons, and did not move until morning, when we planned to visit Grodno, the church of the Franciscans and then return to the train station.

Władek, offered to drive us to the church, which we accepted. It was on his way to his work at the train station. At the church, a funeral was in progress: a wooden casket was being carried by several men dressed in dark clothing. We found a priest that informed us that no records were kept here, that during and after World War II, the records were destroyed, and any that were kept would be in Białystok. But I did tour the church where my parents were married in 1921 noting the elaborate side altars with precious metals used to enhance statues of saints and paintings.

Rain began to fall causing us to open umbrellas and avoid the splashing from autos driving close to the sidewalks. After leaving the church, Władek drove up telling us that he asked to be excused from work for the rest of the day, so that he could take us to lunch in the train station restaurant. This was on the second level of the building. The table was covered with a peach-colored tablecloth, marigolds were in a glass next to the samovar that sat on the table. Soup had potatoes and barley, the blintzes followed. Hot tea was served in a thin glass.

Our train for Sokółka left at 4:50 p.m. We had time to search for the apartment of my cousin Janka Czujko, whose address I carried, but could not give her notice of my visit. Władek encouraged us to attempt a surprise visit. The address was a high rise BLOK built by the Russians. We climbed the stairs to the second floor, found the number on the door. This door had no window, was padded with a heavy black vinyl. There was no answer to our knocking, so we left a hastily written note on a small piece of paper.

We returned to the train station to wait for our return trip. A group of "senior citizens" was also waiting for the train. They spent three weeks at a health spa in this part of Belorus. Teresa was familiar with this spa, telling me that Marshall Piłsudski made regular visits to this place: Drusgienniki.

Before we bid farewell to Władek I reimbursed him for his time and gas with $25. He looked at the bills smiling, saying that it was not necessary to do this, but he kept smiling so I felt that it would be appreciated.

The return trip held another "experience." For 1 ½ hours, the train stood at the train station in Kuźnica, as the Polish immigration officials walked through the aisles going into each compartment, checking documents and asking questions about what persons were carrying into Poland. Our compartment was full. Six adults occupied the space. The compartment door was kept open, so we heard the commotion and the questions given. At one point a woman passenger was asked to leave the train for further interrogation in the station. Teresa became impatient with this delay, venting out loud her dissatisfaction with the immigration policies. Immediately, the passenger closest to the door pulled it shut, cautioning Teresa to curb her comments so as not to get us into any trouble with the authorities. When we arrived finally in Sokółka, we learned why this man squelched any negative remarks that would call attention to us.

When the train came to a full stop in Sokółka, the nervous man next to the sliding door of the compartment, rolled up his pant legs and began pulling out cigarette packages that were stuffed in his knee socks. Then he unbuttoned his suit jacket and unrolled a band that was wrapped snugly around his waist and extracted a liter of vodka. There were strict limits as to each of these items. Only one liter of "spirits" and only five packages of cigarettes was the allowed limit. His carry-on duffle bag had the legal amounts but those on his body were being smuggled into Poland from Belorus for sale and a source of income.

A pleasant surprise awaited us at Teresa's mother's apartment. The errant suitcase had been delivered on Sunday evening. Now I was free to continue my travels to the other cities in Poland. In Wrocław I was to meet another cousin, the very elderly Joseph Sarosiek who is Teresa's uncle.

Teresa and I traveled by train together as far as Warsaw. There she would continue to her city, Bydgoszcz, and I would change trains arriving in Wrocław (Breslau) at 3:30 a.m.!

We gained an hour going west. The train left Sokółka at 4:30 p.m., arrived in Warsaw at 8:15 p.m. My train for Wrocław left at

9:30 p.m. It was not crowded which gave me additional concern. I did not want to miss my stop in the middle of the night. Several stops were made with one or two passengers getting off. When I got off at the cavernous depot in Wrocław there were very few people around. But Joseph and his wife Barbara were there to greet me and escort me to their apartment in this old university town.

I soon was riding a lot of city buses through graceful parks, along tree-lined boulevards, and across many bridges that crisscross the area. Barbara and her husband Joseph walk a lot, and use the city transportation daily. This city of 700,000 has university students that were conspicuous everywhere we went. Our first excursion was to the zoo, on Thursday, when admission was free.

Joseph, almost 80, was still vigorous and agile. Short in stature, he was quite lean. His silver white hair was thinning on top, his blue eyes twinkled. Fair skinned with rosy cheeks, he was proud of his "działka," the farm lot outside of town, where he had a thriving vegetable and fruit garden. Soon we were consuming wild strawberries, pears, raspberries, and huge beefsteak tomatoes. The tomatoes were picked and continued to ripen on their balcony. Joseph's wife Barbara had home canned beets that were served in borscht along with roast pork and potatoes.

Joseph and Barbara were visited a few years ago by Danielle Randall, his great-niece from the US. She is also a great-niece of Stella Landers of Bonifay, Florida. Danielle also sought her roots, traveling to Poland alone, visiting the Kraków relatives: Halina and Ela Pietkiewicz and Albina Bielawska. Stella had photos of this memorable visit. However, my later attempts to communicate with Danielle did not bring any response.

Joseph and Barbara were "citified" in my opinion. Barbara worked crossword puzzles and had a smattering of English and French words in her vocabulary. When she liked something, she would say it was "Bonboniere." They both lived in cities during their married life. Joseph's first wife died of tuberculosis leaving him with a young son to raise. This son recently died in another town. Barbara and Joseph also had one son, Christopher, who is married with three children.

Barbara told of her humiliating experience in the 1950's when she was imprisoned for"SUSPICION" of belonging to an illegal subversive organization. Joseph spoke of the harsh living conditions during WW II. He presented me with newspaper articles describing the horrors and mistreatment of that time.

I felt very much at home in their spacious three-room apartment. The front room had a huge fern that cascaded almost to the floor from its high perch on a pedestal. An interesting tapestry hung on the wall depicting a landscape. The TV stood here but Joseph preferred to get his daily news on the radio that was kept in the bedroom. The front room had a dining room table where we ate the evening meal.

On Friday, September 17, 1993, Joseph and Barbara took me to see "Die Fledermaus" (in Polish). This was very well presented: the main singers were young and good looking. The ballet was done all in white costumes, followed by a spirited polka done in red and white outfits. A lot of rhythmical clapping was done by the appreciative audience. I bought a T shirt with a stylized black bat on the front and the words, "Zemsta Niepoteża." (The revenge of the bat.)

On Saturday, my cousin Stanley Wróblewski arrived and was entertained with a dinner to which he brought Russian champagne. This was his first meeting with Joseph Sarosiek who is related to Stanley's grandmother, Anna Wróblewska (Sarosiek). Stanley was sporting his new auto, a white 1993 Lada (Russian). Joseph admired it, revealing that he gave his car to his son Christopher, who drove it to Greece on a work project. The employment prospects in Greece were a disappointment, so this son returned to Poland without much to show for this journey. Joseph did not know what happened to the car, but he suspected that it was sold to get fare for the return trip to Poland.

I would not be seeing Stanley anymore during this visit to Poland as he was teaching in Kepno, a city not too far from Wrocław. But I planned to visit his sisters, Teresa and Lilka and his brother Edward.

Stanley also brought coffee and candy. He gave me a jar of

ointment for his mother's rheumatism. (I would be seeing her, too, in Elbląg.) He was dressed in a dark blue pin stripe suit with a white shirt, looking like a successful executive!

The following day Joseph and Barbara and I traveled by suburban bus to their son's apartment in Jelczłaskowice, about an hour away. We were offered dinner and enjoyed talking to the three children about their interests and about the U.S. I asked in my letters what were the ages of these youngsters so I could bring some small toys. The oldest, a boy about 11, was presented with a black T shirt with a Florida palm on the front, the girl aged about 9 received a small board game that she immediately started to carry around in her pocket, the youngest, a cuddly three-year-old girl with curly blond hair, was given a small troll doll with orange hair that caught her fancy. She never put it down during our visit.

The three of us, Joseph, Barbara and I were escorted by the whole family who waved standing alongside of the train until it left the station.

Joseph determined that he would accompany me on the next leg of my trip to Elbląg. I had the feeling that he wanted to assure my safe arrival. Indeed, we were in a compartment with other travelers when we left by train. He insisted that our luggage should not be left unattended. So I left alone to get a beverage in the club car. Barbara packed a hefty lunch of bread, ham, and green grapes that we enjoyed during the six-hour trip from Wrocław to Tczew. This city was 50 km from Elbląg. My cousin Edward picked us up in his Polonez car, so that we did not have to change trains for the last 35 miles to Elbląg.

Joseph now met the rest of the family: Stanley Wróblewski's mother and Teresa, his sister. He stayed overnight with them until the next day when he left by bus, returning to Wrocław.

Tuesday, September 21, to Saturday, September 25, 1993, I "bunked" at the duplex residence of my cousin Edward. Ed and I stayed here when we visited in 1989, but this year I noted all the remodeling and additions. A full bathroom with real tiles on the floor and on the walls had been added. The fixtures were all new with an automatic washer in one corner. (The clothes still were hung outdoors to dry!) The master bedroom now held a queen-sized bed, chest of drawers, dresser and a bedside stand on each side of the bed. I could see the influence of cousin Edward's stay in the U.S. In the kitchen a double stainless steel sink dominated the long room which overlooked the backyard. All the painted floors were sanded and refinished in their natural knotty pine. Cousin Edward and his wife Wanda had me use this newly furnished bedroom during my stay. Wanda left for her job at the Hotel downtown each morning, but cousin Edward was on leave and available for transportation.

The following day, cousin Edward, his sister Teresa and I visited the cemetery where their father, my uncle, Jan Wróblewski is buried. On the way home we stopped at the Farm Lot (działka) to pick beets, carrots, parsley, and apples. Teresa, with the help of her brother Edward, and brother Stanley keep up this garden plot that was first "leased" by their father. Vegetables and fruit are "put up" each fall for use throughout the winter. The apples we picked were processed into applesauce by cousin Teresa and stored in glass jars.

Cousin Edward and I set out the following day for Bartoszyce, a small town near the Russian border, where cousin Lilka and her husband Jan Raplewicz live. On the way we stopped along the road where woods skirt the edge of the pavement to search for mushrooms. It was a good year for these tasty morsels. Edward was familiar with four or five edible varieties that we picked.

Bartoszyce: ul. Kościuszki 23, is the two-story residence of cousin Lilka and her husband, Jan Raplewicz. Their three children, Zbyszko, Ania, and Darius are adults. Only the youngest, Darius is single, currently at home, awaiting the first day of studies at the University of Lublin.

Lilka apologized for not having prepared a meal for us as she did not expect us this day. But she started immediately to hustle in the kitchen stirring up some food. Jan was expected shortly from his day work. He now travels by bicycle as the auto they owned is not operable. Lilka complained that her lot in life is not happy due to her husband's dependence on and overindulgence in alcohol. She related that for many years his weekly pay was cashed and a bottle of liquor purchased instead of some worthwhile investment such as books.

When Jan came home from his mediocre job making windows (in the past his training as an architect was used by a county department for constructing strip mall shopping buildings), I noted how wasted and neglected he looked: personal grooming and personal hygiene were slipping. His teeth were stained and needing attention. A stubble of beard indicated he had not shaved for a couple of days. But he was gregarious and talkative and made several references to celebrating this occasion with a "drink."

Edward and I were witnesses to a conflict over a form needed by Darius for a student loan. His father will wait until the last possible minute to provide the paper that shows this family is indigent, i.e., lives below the poverty line, which will qualify Darius for a reduction in the cost of his room and board at the University. We heard Darius explaining this requirement patiently to his father who agrees, in front of the company assembled, that he will comply with the request.

In subsequent correspondence Lilka wrote that all was taken care of, and Darius was now away at the University studying theology.

There was a fenced yard with a vegetable garden, chickens scurrying about and a rabbit hutch. Also, flowers: peonies, lilacs, dahlias, etc. Lilka supplements their meager income by selling eggs. Her hastily prepared meal was hearty: beet borscht, scrambled eggs, potatoes fried with onions, sliced tomatoes, hot dogs, cookies, and bread with butter. While eating, Lilka recalled magical moments in Gibulicze where she grew up: the pervading smell of pine trees that was there all year round. She was disappointed I could not extend my stay with her—a few days, or at least overnight. But my schedule was such that I needed to continue with the final week's stay in Bydgoszcz, where I was to be a guest at the apartment of cousin Teresa, the doctor, and her family: husband Bogdan and son Darius.

When cousin Edward and I returned to Elbląg, we learned

that the following day the Swedish King Karol Gustav XVI was expected to visit this city. Walking around the town square, we witnessed an entourage of limousines with police on motorcycles escorting the royal party. Later, on television we viewed the ceremony and reception held for this distinguished visitor.

Other family visitors were expected at "Hetmańska"—the apartment where cousin Teresa and her mother, my aunt Mary, live. Lilka's daughter, Ania and her husband Gregory Danilowicz, joined us for a dinner of Potato Pancakes and Ukrainian Borscht (made with beets, potatoes, beans, carrots, cabbage and cream). Tea, candy, and chocolates were served later. Ania and her husband live in Gdańsk, but visit her grandma Mary often. It is an hour's ride by bus from a Gdańsk to Elbląg.

We said our goodbyes as tomorrow, cousin Edward and his wife Wanda will drive me to Bydgoszcz.

It was a 3-hour trip from Elbląg to Bydgoszcz. With directions, we found the street and spotted Teresa standing in the parking area of her apartment building. We were treated to a banquet. Cream of vegetable soup, breaded pork chops, spare ribs, hunters' stew (Bigos), cucumbers, potatoes and HOMEMADE cheesecake.

Teresa, her husband and son live in a five-story apartment building that is one of 15 such buildings surrounding a large open grassy square. Their apartment has many doors that open to an inner vestibule-like area with floor to ceiling closets. The TV is in one of the small bedrooms that is next to the kitchen. One bedroom is definitely masculine, belongs to son Darius. The living-dining-guest room has a balcony and two massive black credenzas, with a lot of carved wood and mirrors. Next to the window and door to the balcony stood a grandfather clock. Prints of old cities were on the wall above the deep gold velveteen covered couch which had a hide-a-bed, and was for my use. Lace curtains above a wide window shelf screened some potted plants. On a ceiling track, hung heavy deep gold velvet draperies. On the floor was an oriental rug with a gold background. These were living quarters of a slightly more affluent family than those I visited earlier during this trip.

Teresa's husband, Bogdan, is a jolly, short, bald man who is very personable, likes to tell off-color stories. His nose had a definite dent across the bridge, a remnant of a plane crash he survived. He was now retired from flying and servicing aircraft. A diminutive Fiat car, older model, is his contact with the outside world. We drove in that small vehicle to a nearby national forest to pick mushrooms, when he heard of my interest in this activity. Then I helped string these morsels into garlands, so that they could be hung over the stove burners for a drying. I left before they were ready, but had enough to bring back to the U.S. from purchases and gifts.

On Sunday, September 26, a light rain began in the morning but did not affect our plans to visit cousin Teresa's niece, Gosia (Margaret) Szymańska. She lives at home with her father Ludwik and his S.O., a very attractive blond woman. We were treated to a snack of molded gelatin with shredded pork feet, sliced tomatoes, pickles, cucumbers, cookies, chocolates, tea, and coffee. Gosia is in her twenties, a quiet young woman with long, curly brown hair, blue eyes, and a quick smile. She was studying tailoring but is showing interest in physical therapy.

The following day, Teresa and I traveled to the Lot airline office in the center of town to purchase her airline ticket. The cost for a Round trip fare from Warsaw to Chicago was $840. We celebrated this occasion by ordering Tea and Torte at the "Hotel Pod Orłem" (Under the Eagle). I used a charge card for this purchase which totaled $3.80 U.S. Teresa commented about the ease of obtaining food and services without any cash.

Tuesday, September 28, was a cloudy cool day that did not deter the trip to the National Forest nearby to pick mushrooms. Teresa remained home attending to last minute packing and preparations for our flight to the states. Her husband, Bohdan, and I ventured with two pails in the back of his tiny Fiat on our search for mushrooms. When we arrived in the vast area of old growth hardwoods, others were already there with baskets and pails roaming through the leaf strewn paths. After filling our containers, I later identified the four varieties that we gathered as: Suillus Luteus (maślak), Boletus Edulis (prawdziwki), Armillaria

Mellea (opienki), and Macralepiota Procera (czarnełebki). Bohdan teased me about the amount of work I brought for him. He painstainkingly brushed each mushroom, then put a needle and thread through each one making a garland to be hung over the stove burners for the drying process. This takes a couple of days.

Mushroom gathering was an exhilarating experience! At first the uneven terrain looked like a blur of earth smothered with undergrowth of various grasses, small flowering plants, tender seedlings of pines and oaks. Acorns were strewn about and an occasional black squirrel scurried and hopped across the forest floor. Then as the eyes began to focus and fixate upon the ground, I identified a roundheaded mushroom. Bohdan knew the edible types by their common names. Later I wrote down the Polish names and searched the handbook of mushrooms that I purchased in Elbląg to get the Latin name. Back in the U.S., I owned another mushroom identification book with the Latin and English names.

As we separated in the woods, we stayed within voice sound of each other. I mused about this national pastime in this country and its implications for future tourist travel. Imagine a trip in the fall with the express purpose of gathering and drying mushrooms! What an untapped resource and treasure located in the old forests of Eastern Europe!

When Bohdan and I returned to their apartment, a photo was taken of me holding the prize of the day: a Boletus Edulis that measured six inches across! The rest of the evening was spent "processing" these tender morsels so that they could be suspended over the stove burners to dry out. The air in the apartment soon was filed with the earthy aroma of these fungi as they went through the drying-out phase.

Visitors came to bid farewell to Teresa and to leave letters, messages, and small gifts for relatives in the U.S. Tomorrow we would travel to Warsaw, stay overnight, and then leave on an early flight to Chicago. Teresa's son Darius and niece Gosia were to accompany us to Warsaw, planning to bunk with a cousin who had an apartment in that city. Teresa had the key to this lodging place that they would reach by public transportation.

After considerable discussion and inquiry, we decided to hire a private driver with a car to drive to Warsaw from Bydgoszcz a distance of 270 km. The cost would be $23 U.S. A real bargain, as the rate by taxi was quoted as four times this amount. The vehicle turned out to be a Mercedes that comfortably held four passengers and the driver.

On Wednesday, September 29th, the morning was spent in final frenzied preparations. Teresa fretted, worried about going through customs carrying a number of pharmaceuticals not available in the U.S., that she would use, that her daughter requested.

I began to "fuss" over the time of departure. Finally about 11:00 a.m., after phone calls were not answered, Darius was sent to investigate. He returned shortly assuring us that the driver was washing the car and cleaning it up for this momentous ride. About noon we loaded the trunk and took off.

It was a cool day, the temperature in the 50's. We made one stop late in the afternoon at a gas station with food service, where we ordered a warm snack before continuing to the Novotel located near the Warsaw Okiece airport.

My double room was reserved in the states before I left. Teresa and I would share it.

Darius and Gosia left to find the apartment of their cousin as we made ourselves comfortable in the room. But this duo came knocking on our door after an hour or so telling of reaching his address, trying to enter with the key which no longer unlocked the door. Phone calls were made to no avail. Finally, the decision was made. They would stay in our room. The couch had two large cushions that were placed on the floor adding a sleeping area for Gosia. Darius used the couch. Teresa and I got tucked into bed, but Darius kept the TV going all night! At one point I asked that he turn down the volume, but my rest was disrupted by this unexpected turn of events. It was very cozy with four adults in one room and our suitcases with some food stuffs Teresa carried for their breakfast in the room.

Thursday, September 30,1993, a clear day with a drop in temperature that set our breath steaming when we got outdoors.

We all hastily dressed as Teresa set out cups of water heated with an immersion heater. I was entitled to ONE buffet breakfast in the coffee shop where I hurriedly ate and carried what could fit into the two pockets of my jacket. Back in the room, we all shared the "loot," mostly small pastries.

We all traveled to the airport in a cab, having plenty of time before the noon departure. This was the first time Teresa left her family for such an extended period of time. She planned to stay a year in the U.S., living with her daughter in Chicago, and working as a care giver/aide/housekeeper. Her son Darius was visibly emotional over this separation. Her niece Gosia was a stabilizing force during this parting. They planned to take a train back to Bydgoszcz after seeing us off. We all lingered at the kiosk where coffee was available. They were all in shock when the charge slip was presented—four coffees—$5.00! I assured them that my experience in air terminals in the U.S. was not much different from here as far as cost of food and beverages was concerned.

The flight to Chicago, from Warsaw, took 9 hours and 30 minutes. Teresa and I enjoyed all the services, drinks, and meals. Getting through U.S. Customs meant that we used different exits. Teresa asked that I accompany her through the gate for non-U.S. citizens, and was very relieved when she was waved through without a glitch.

Her daughter Beata met us, greeting us with warm embraces and wanting to accompany me to my next domestic flight gate. With all of Teresa's luggage, I assured them that I would locate the proper concourse bidding them a fond farewell.

My husband greeted me with warm embraces when I finally reached Fort Walton Beach, tired, but happy to be home.

CHAPTER V

A Not So Brief Encounter Revisited

"Repressed memories will surface," I read and recalled how one surfaced in my past.

Great Expectations, a Charles Dickens book, was turned into a movie in the 1980s. My husband and I viewed it one Saturday evening at home, absorbed by the dark and moody story of a jilted bride and her ward who grew up in her shadow, unable to express her emotions meaningfully.

At the movie's conclusion I reacted unexpectedly. Something in the story triggered a response, uprooting a repressed memory from the unconscious regions of my psyche, resulting in my dissolving into tears. Retreating to the bedroom, I plunged on the bed, sobbing. My husband was puzzled over this outburst, certainly not provoked by anything he said or did. Many minutes later I offered an explanation, "I'm crying over something that happened many years ago." He accepted this revelation without asking for further details, for which I was grateful.

Forty years had passed since, while a freshman in college, I suppressed the romantic feelings rising after each encounter with my first real beau, the pen-pal-soldier-turned-suitor. I had squelched the expressed fondness and genuine interest shown by this hometown Romeo whose feet tramped the same pavement as mine. Initially I was puzzled over the sudden, unexplained, and abrupt end to our company keeping, but cherished and relived every moment we were together.

When the crying spell subsided, I accepted this as response to a loss brought on by the immaturity of an 18-year-old fearful of expressing the true emotions in her heart. Now it was time to turn my energy and commitment to the present, my life's companion and the tasks ahead.

But more repressed memories surfaced when I enrolled in a Writing Your Personal History class in 1996. One assignment was to recall your First Love.

One class member read an account of her 50th high school reunion where she knew her first love would attend. The account had a flashback describing their teenage romance, its dramatic cessation, and her preparations for meeting the man again, with a bittersweet conclusion.

I began to wonder, if I recalled those magic moments of each encounter experienced with Bernie Zacharias, after all these years, did anything jar his memory about our golden hours? Did he ever mention HIS first love, to anyone? What about that abrupt ending of our relationship? The failed romance had a long-lasting effect on me. It was buried so deep, only now, 50+ years later, I decided to untangle the jumbled heartstrings.

My plan was a phone contact to inquire, curiously, as an old "acquaintance" and a WW II pen pal, if he remembered me and what the fifty+ years brought to his life.

Many years ago, my close friend, Eleanor Woźniak (Jasinski) worked at a bank where the Zacharias family had accounts. From her I learned that Bernie married, had two daughters, moved to Livonia, Michigan. She confided that a younger brother also had those searing brown eyes, adding, "No wonder you were attracted to Bernie." Then the trail ended.

After the "Great Expectations" incident, my curiosity drove me to ride by the Zacharias address in Livonia on one of my home health social work trips in the area. The ranch, red brick house with evergreens and shade trees was not unlike my own home in Southfield.

The present possibilities were: he could be dead, she could be dead, he would not remember me, he would remember. How to start the conversation? "Is this the residence of Bernard Zacharias?" Very likely the wife would answer. I would identify myself as someone Bernie knew when he lived in Hamtramck: a Lottie, who lived on Trowbridge Street.

The possibilities grew. My husband and I planned a trip to Michigan in July. Perhaps, Bernie and I could meet, and over coffee find what the years brought to our lives. I wondered how he aged, got gray or bald, whether he gained weight, and did those velvety brown eyes still have that penetrating power? Oh, and I would definitely wear blue, as I did on our first date. He would see the silver threads among the blonde, and note how my weight had rearranged, but I think he would recognize me.

So, on the first Saturday of June 1996, I drove to the office, to deliver some paperwork, closed the door and dialed.

The rings—one, two, three, four, five (perhaps no one was home). On the sixth ring a female voice inquired, "Hello?"

I asked, "Is this the residence of Mr. and Mrs. Bernard Zacharias?"

A pause, and then a hesitation, "Who is calling?"

"I'm calling from Florida to talk to Bernie. I knew him when he lived in Hamtramck."

More hesitation, then an uneven response, "He died two years ago—TOMORROW."

"I'm so sorry to hear that," I gulped.

"What is your name?" she inquired.

"He knew me as Lottie. I don't know if he ever mentioned me."

"He spoke a lot about his high school days. He attended his 50th high school reunion. Were you there?"

"No, but I've wondered about Bernie. I knew he had two daughters."

"Oh, we had four daughters and one son. We would have been married 50 years this October."

I made quick calculations—so he married in October 1946, the year after our breakup, and he died June 9, 1994, a year after we moved to retire in Florida.

"I've also wondered about his sisters, Leona and Bernadette. I met Leona during the war. We attended a War Bond Rally at the University of Detroit Stadium."

"Leona recently celebrated 50 years of marriage."

"What kind of work did Bernie do?"

"He was a Plant Analyst—engineer, you know. He worked 40 years at the Ford Motor Company."

"What did he die of?"

"He had an infection. His heart could not fight it."

Any further questions to this woman, I felt, would be too intrusive by a total stranger. "Perhaps Bernie's sister Leona will remember me." The following day, the anniversary of his death, two hearts grieved, one that he claimed in marriage, the other, he captured 50 years before and broke, leaving a wound so profound that all those years did not heal.

Bernie's wife gave me Leona's address and phone number, also in Livonia. I phoned her during our visit to Michigan the following month. She did not recall our trip to the U. of Detroit stadium. I reminded her that at the time she was employed at the downtown Detroit Sanders bakery.

"Oh, that goes a long way back. Perhaps if I saw you—"

But that did not materialize. However, Leona did respond to a letter I sent inquiring about Bernie's education and interests. He graduated from the Lawrence Institute of Technology, earning a degree in Engineering. He loved to golf and fish. He and his wife Alfreda enjoyed Hawaii after retirement, traveling there repeatedly. Leona characterized him as having a "zest for life."

So what happened to stop that burgeoning romance in 1945? Bernie would not be giving his version. I reexamined the discussion with him about my decision to spend a week at a cottage with girl friends instead of staying at home. He was to have a week's furlough during the same week.

If he took hold of my shoulders and told of being disappointed with this decision and said, "Unless you cancel those plans, all is over between us," would I have reconsidered? Why did I not beg off from going to the cottage? There were four others to split the cost of rent. What did it mean to me to be "available" for the entire week?

Very likely insecurity and immaturity entered into the picture.

Then I considered Bernie's reaction. He may have felt deeply disappointed and then furious at being cut off from continuing our relationship by this deplorable and thoughtless gesture on my part.

Then I fantasied about what could have been if I had stayed put and our romance progressed. Would I have quit college to become Mrs. Bernard Zacharias? Would we settle initially in Hamtramck in one of my father's flats? Several of my close friends started married life renting small quarters on neighboring streets in Hamtramck. How would my situation with my mother in the hospital, and my father and brother managing without me, impact upon us newlyweds? What kind of relationship would I have with my in-laws and Bernie's eleven brothers and sisters?

I grappled with possible answers, none very satisfactory remembering the hangups restraining me during those late teens and early twenties. Perhaps some insight and coping methods could have been gleaned from my friends who entered matrimony and were succeeding.

Now, I was overwhelmed with a profound feeling of loss, grief, and mourning for this hometown Lothario and for what could have been. There was an acute awareness of the powerful love I sheltered that was never fulfilled. It was a non-sanctioned grief. It could not be expressed openly or discussed with anyone, in spite of its gravity and depth. It never became public. When tears welled up behind my eyeglasses, I explained them away as an allergy, or raced behind closed doors to release the heaviness of my anguish and sorrow.

Even non-sanctioned grief can have boundaries. Gradually, after a number of months, its intensity subsided. Getting the memories of that fateful heartbreak into print has been "cleansing."

Other disappointment in affairs of the heart occurred over the next 17 years, but none so devastating as the one I call my first love.

In June 1962, my life's companion and I walked to the altar to exchange vows joining us in matrimony. I cherish and appreciate my faithful spouse and delight in the mutually appreciated daily routines we established over the years. The role of wife and homemaker has been very fulfilling. One of the songs popular at the time of our wedding was, "Love is Better the Second Time Around."

June 26, 2002, we celebrate our 40th wedding anniversary returning to Michigan, and to the environs of Hamtramck and Trowbridge Street, my boulevard of broken dreams.

CHAPTER VI

Letters

Christmas card sent by Ed Cavanary, 1960.

MERRY CHRISTMAS,
Sweetheart
Because you are my
Sweetheart,
My Christmas wish for you
Expresses deeper meaning
Than other greetings do;
Because you are my
Sweetheart,
There's love in every line. And happiness in knowing
That you are truly mine!
This doesn't convey half what I feel!

Love,
Ed

— — — — — — — —

Christmas card and note sent to
Mr. Edward J. Cavanary Jr.,
5108 Chatsworth St., Detroit 24, Michigan,
postmarked December 22, 1961 bearing a
4-cent postage stamp

Christmas 1961
My Dear Ed,

A wonderful year will soon end—one with many memories of you.

Because Christmas is such a season of love and of sharing, it especially brings you to mind: you—willing to share experiences, hopes, joys, yes, even disappointments.

How my life was enriched all those months having you near!

This year began and now comes to a close with the same sentiment needing to be expressed:

I love you.

Charlotte

— — — — — — —

Letter Sent After Hearing of My Engagement to Edward Cavanary

Monday 9:30 a.m., March 26, 1962

My Dearest Sister Charlotte,

How very happy I am this morning—I can hardly think of anything else except what you told me yesterday—that in the summer you would be married.

I don't believe you realize just how much happiness the future has in store for you and Ed. Perhaps in my happiness I can tell you, not as eloquently as I would like, but so truthfully, that marriage to the right man for you is a truly full and meaningful one. To share with a loved one all your moments of joy and sadness gives something which cannot be put into words. You will realize, I am sure, just as I have, that sharing a lifetime with your love, gives each day deeper meaning.

That trust in one another and together, trust in God, gives you a glimpse of heaven.

I love you both,
Betty Bandyk

— — — — — — —

Dear Ed,

Charlotte's call yesterday, her excitement and happiness, I'm sure, is an example of your feeling about the future together.

Charlotte is a wonderful girl. I want so much to put into words so many things about her, things I'm sure you already know. Her goodness, her sincerity, her warmth, how lucky you are to have enkindled in her the love which makes her a woman.

How truly beautiful she had looked these last few months. I know without your love this would not have been possible. It is not only a bride who is beautiful, but a woman in love.

Take care of her always, her future is in your able hands.

Love and Happiness

A wish for the future

Betty Bandyk

— — — — — — —

Mayes
5026 Caniff
Detroit 12, Michigan

Dear Charlotte,

I had this impulse before, but when Betty called this morning and told me she had written I knew I had to do it too.

It's difficult to express the thoughts generated by your impending marriage, but I want to be sure that somewhere in your heart you will hold the awareness of my feeling for you at this time.

From the first time I saw you so properly and Mary -grovishly dressed for your job interview at Harper House, you have had a special place in my life. I have been inspired by your integrity, cheered by your sense of humor, uplifted by your courage, influenced by your thoughtfulness and sense of fair play, elevated by your sensitivity and kindness and encouraged by your deep and broad interests.

There has not been a crisis in my life since I have known you that you failed to give me faith and courage.

My hopes and expectations for you have always been great and the kind of fulfillment which is now to be yours is the greatest.

My wishes for your future are as deep and wide as my soul can reach. If anybody ever deserved peace and happiness, you do. I hope you have them as deep and wide as your soul can reach.

Love,

Irene

March 26, 1962

— — — — — — —

Mayes
5026 Caniff
Detroit 12, Michigan

Dear Ed,

There are few men in this world that I would admit are worthy of Charlotte's love. You are the only one that I know—I congratulate you on your good sense and good fortune in attaining it.

I have known many people in my lifetime, but never one with more integrity, sensitivity and talent for graceful and intense living than Charlotte has.

Her reputation for loyal friendship, professional competence, and responsibility toward others has been well earned.

She also has a special vulnerability common to sensitive people. Please be good to her.

I wish you both great happiness.

Love

Irene

3/26/62

— — — — — — —

HOLY FAMILY CHURCH
311 North Woodland Avenue
Phone 3-8233
Oglesby, Illinois

Rev. Carl Mayes, Pastor
April 23, 1962

Dear Charlotte:

It is nice of you to ask me to officiate at your wedding in June.

I wonder if the synod laws of the Detroit Arch-Diocese will permit me to accept? Would you please check with your pastor and see if he is willing to permit me to have the services. If he is willing, please let me know immediately so I can give you a definite answer.

We have been enjoying our family reunion, and the weather has been wonderful.

Hope you had a very nice Easter.

Sincerely,
Fr. Carl

— — — — — — —

4000 Gulf Terrace Dr. #250
Destin, FL 32541
March 16, 1998

Mr. and Mrs. Edward Jelonek
122 E. Hickory Grove
Bloomfield Hills, MI 48013

Dear Edward and Adele,

My maiden name was "Lottie" Kasperowicz. I grew up on Trowbridge Street in Hamtramck, Michigan. A very important family with six children lived across the alley from our house. They were the Jeloneks.

Recently I began writing my personal history which has some very important chapters about the various members of this family. I remember that Edward was the youngest and probably was my classmate at the elementary school of the Our Lady Queen of Apostles church. I chose to attend the Girls Catholic Central High School because Eleanor Jelonek went there first.

I could go on, but, I am wondering about what fame and fortune came to those wonderful people who played such a significant role in my young life. I especially recall Sunday nights in a darkened living room where we sat listening to the radio: the "Inner Sanctum" squeaking door and crunched on potato chips brought up from the bar downstairs.

So I would like to complete the story about the Jelonek family—where are they now? As for you Edward, if you are my age and retired, what was your life's work? Grandfather and father of how many?

I found the Jelonek name in the Marygrove College Alumni Directory. My year of graduation was 1947, so last year I attended the 50th Reunion. My husband and I stayed with Betty and Tony Bandyk the weekend she attended her 50th high school reunion. One thing led to another when I saw the Jelonek name on her program.

I'm hoping you can reply with some details about Nell, Philip, John, and the oldest girl whose name escapes me.

Sincerely,
Charlotte Cavanary (Kasperowicz)

— — — — — — — —

Sunday, March 22, 1998

Dear Lottie,

Your letter arrived as Ed and I were going to Q of A for a Lenten Fish Fry with Lillian and Ted Sejnowski (Ed's oldest sister.)

Ed and Lillian are the only surviving children of John and Mary. All died in California. Bobbie died at 54 years in 1978.

Lillian and Ted still live in Hamtramck on Mitchell Avenue. We see them often. They had no children.

We have four (2 girls 2 boys). Ed just retired in January 1998 and we spent 2 months at Siesta Key, FL. The weather wasn't the greatest!

I was an Immaculata and Marygrove graduate—retired teacher in 1990.

We have lived in a Bloomfield Hills condo for 20 years.

I remember Betty at our reunion—she had wonderful tales of her round-the-world cruise.

Thank you for the memories.

Adele Jelonek

Memorial Service for Josephine

Dear Father Lou,

Enclosed are some notes about my mother for your use for the homily at her Memorial Mass on Thursday, August 17, 1989 at 1:00 p.m.

My good college friend, Helen Hill of St. Michael's Parish has a son Matthew, who is studying for the priesthood in Rome—he's home for the summer and will be Eucharistic Minister and do a Scripture reading if that's okay with you.

My oldest nephew, Leonard, will act as server for the Mass.

These notes are the only copy I made, so I would appreciate your returning them.

Thank you for your interest and personal consideration in this matter.

Sincerely,
Charlotte

P.S. Please join us at the reception at our home, 28330 Ranchwood, following the Mass.

— — — — — — —

Josephine Kasperowicz was the second child, first daughter in a family of five children. Born February 15, 1897, in a small city in eastern Poland, she left at age 5 with her family, to live in a farming village nearby. She told of the father building a house for his growing family that boasted the first wooden floor in that community. This homestead survived two world wars, a couple of generations, and is still occupied.

As a young child, Josephine was surrounded by family and extended family as well as some other familiar residents of this village. Her father, Alexander Wróblewski, was the oldest of seven—

his brother and sisters, married, living with their families in the same area. Her mother, Anna, one of nine children, also had older and younger siblings who were frequent visitors and with whom Josephine socialized. Two aunts of Josephine, aged 92 and 94 still live in Poland and corresponded with Josephine regularly.

Life on the farm, caring for livestock and crops, absorbed most of the family's time and energy. Josephine related how flax was harvested, treated, spun into linen, and used to weave necessary clothing and household articles. The finest thread made cloth for shirts and blouses, tea towels and tablecloths. Coarser yarn was used for bed sheets and work clothes. The weaving loom was built by Josephine's father, and stood in a special anteroom where the weaving was done—usually during Lent since it was the season before outdoor chores began.

Mushroom picking was a fall activity taking place in the nearby forest where once a sleeping fox was startled by Josephine bending over to gather up a mushroom—she was so taken back that her bladder released much to her embarrassment.

Religion was an integral part of this life. The parish church was located several kilometers from the village necessitating walking down country roads carrying one's boots, which were kept out of the mud and dust and donned only when one got closer to the destination. Singing hymns, prayers, litanies, matins, etc., were routine. Holy days, feast days—with accompanying rituals—Josephine learned and carried with her to this country.

World War I devastated the countryside, bringing separations that scattered residents of that close-knit community. Josephine's oldest brother, Alexander, fled the country and its military conscription by crossing into Germany then on to the U.S., where he gained immediate citizenship when he enlisted in the U.S. Army. His photo in Army garb still can be found in an old photo album. Alexander continued westward to Hawaii, where he married and died shortly afterward, about 1922. Josephine remembered getting news of his death from Honolulu. Josephine's younger sister left Poland to work and then marry in France. Other relatives were taken to Russia, returning after the Revolution.

Josephine survived the occupation of her village by invading forces. She and other villagers were ordered to dig trenches. Her father was told to give housing to the soldiers. As a child, I would hear her talk of the whistling gunfire, of blasts, and explosions that tore up the village. Her young girlfriend suffered a shoulder injury from an exploding mine—later died of it.

Josephine, her mother, two sisters, and younger brother took over all the farm chores after her father was arrested, imprisoned and died in July 1918. The Germans accused him of having firearms. His wife was not allowed to claim the body for burial.

In the fall of 1921, Josephine married Andrew, a bachelor of 31 years, who was from the same village, returning after 12 years. He left Poland at age 18 to seek a better life in the U.S.. Indeed, when he came to claim his bride, it was with $3,000. Josephine tells of her mother calling her to come in from the potato field to get herself presentable as a suitor was waiting.

The marriage took place October 25, 1921. A trip by steamship, "The Aquitania" followed. Andrew had two half brothers, Xavier and Frank, who preceded him with their wives to the U.S. It was to these in-laws that Josephine and Andrew came—settling in a small apartment in what is now Poletown. Soon a house was purchased in Hamtramck, across the street from the Dickinson Elementary School. The house had two rental units that provided additional income through many lean years.

Josephine's first two children died at birth. She missed them and mourned this loss all her life. It was a tragedy, but could have been averted with current medical knowhow. A daughter and a son were successfully delivered by Caesarean section in Providence Hospital, after a wise doctor ascertained that it was needed. I remember periodic walks to Mt. Olivet Cemetery where the two infants are buried. It was an irretrievable loss that Josephine recalled all her life.

During the time her two children were growing up was filled with highly functional activities. The Great Depression affected all activities. Nothing much was wasted.

Duck and goose feathers were plucked dry and stored for use in making down comforters and pillows. Worn-out clothing showed up as strips in rag rugs, made for areas that needed covering. Bed sheets and pillow cases were sewn from unbleached muslin and were hung up wet to bleach out in the sun. Favorite dresses were carefully disassembled to form patterns for new ones. Josephine sewed on a shiny new Singer sewing machine purchased in the late 1920s. Hand crocheted curtains adorned the kitchen windows and hand-knitted socks and sweaters kept the feet, back, and chest warm in the winter.

Baking raisin-filled yeast breads was an activity to look forward to—the black loaf pans held the fragrant glistening dough—the bottoms were often burned—but the raisins could be picked off when no one was looking.

Josephine was a homemaker all her life. She liked to cook and help with meal preparation well into her late 80s. In 1957, Josephine was widowed. She continued to live in the area, moving to a small house purchased for her by her son in Algonac. For 7 years, from 1978 to 1985, Josephine lived in the St. Elizabeth's Briarbank Home for Aged. After a leg fracture, she began to use cane, later a walker. When walking became difficult, she was moved to the Abbey Nursing Home in Warren, Michigan.

Up to the age of 90, Josephine liked to read the weekly issue of the *Polish Daily News,* and to listen to the Polish news broadcasts on the radio. Proud of her U.S. citizenship, she registered to vote wherever she lived. She kept her voter's registration card next to her Medicare and Social Security cards. Handwork was her daily occupation. She continued to crochet afghans and doilies and runners until her eyes began to dim. Her hearing, smell, taste, and responsiveness to human contact never dimmed. The Sunday before her final hospitalization, she enjoyed a spin around the neighborhood in her wheelchair, commenting on the freshly cut grass, the sounds of the wind in the trees, the yapping of the dogs, and the splash of color from the flower beds.

Josephine kept in contact with her relatives in Poland—often expressing regret that she left that family circle for a strange and foreign land. Small amounts of money were sent to her brother whose large family was much younger than her own. In 1974, I arranged to take Josephine back to Poland to visit her brother who now lives in a small city near Gdańsk It was a momentous reunion; after gazing at each other, brother and sister agreed they had gotten "older." At that time, he was 70 and she was 77.

For many years, Josephine was followed medically at the Providence Hospital Clinic. The doctors repeatedly urged her to lose some weight so her back and legs would have a lighter load to carry. She insisted she was not overweight—just—"swollen"—this was a favorite story we told about "Busia."

There were other stories too. Her grandchildren remember that for many years she was a steady smoker. When reminded of this, she only remembered having a cigarette "once in a while."

A few years ago, she undertook learning to read and write English. She asked for books with the English alphabet and simple words that she could practice writing on a lined school tablet. Then she would ask me the meaning of some word that was not in her daily usage. A friend who taught 1st grade supplied just what she wanted.

Josephine was ready to join her Creator and her husband for some time. The many aches and pains and medicines that sometimes had adverse side effects led her to what she wanted.

When she died, peacefully, I was with her aunt and cousin in Cracow, Poland. On the day of the funeral, we commemorated the day at the Shrine of Our Lady of Częstochowa. At her cousin Halina's suggestion, we brought some Polish soil that we plan to sprinkle on her grave after the headstone is in place.

I will miss her, as will her son, Dr. Leonard Kasperowicz and his wife Arlene of Algonac, their six children—her grandchildren who sent greeting cards to her for special occasions and visited her often in the nursing home and hospital. Her oldest grandson was put to the task of transporting her for holiday get togethers. She did eventually lose weight so that he could carry her into the house from the car.

Death is a part of life. Her death has become part of our life.

Charlotte Cavanary, Daughter
August 13, 1989

Busia Josephine Kasperowicz

Grave Site Commemorative Gathering, October 7, 1989

Mt. Olivet Cemetery
Present: daughter-in-law, Arlene Mruk Kasperowicz; daughter and
son-in-law, Charlotte and Ed Cavanary, grandchildren: Leonard
Kasperowicz, Anne Kasperowicz, Charlotte Kasperowicz, Kim
Kasperowicz.

Songs My Mother Taught Me

Looking into a window of a small bookstore on one of the
tree-lined streets of Kraków, a book title caught my eye: "O
mój Rozmarynie"—a compilation of Polish songs from 1900
to 1930. Caught my eye, and rang a bell with reverberations
to the late 1920s, when my mother sang that song and others
in that book.

My earliest recollection of my mother is of her singing Polish
folk songs when we lived in a four-room upper flat at 3364 Norwalk.
The center room was a dining room with the "central" heat of that
time—an Isinglass coal stove that occupied the middle of the room.
It had nickel trim that gleamed and opaque "glass" openings through
which one could see the dancing flames and feel the glowing heat
from within.

It was in this kind of setting, before radio, before phonographs
(in our house at least) and before TV, that my mother's voice filled
the air and time in the household. Folk songs, church hymns,
Christmas carols, and wartime ballads my mother recalled from
her native country: melodies that sprang from their religion, their
daily life, their soil. The most poignant wartime ballad is the one
we hear and play today as we sprinkle some of Busia's beloved
Polish soil on her grave. May each grain of soil be like a note from
all those songs she sang. And "may flights of angels sing thee to

thy rest." The ballad's white roses are like the progeny here gathered at her grave, children, and grandchildren.

Rozkwitały Pęki Białych Róż
(Song of the Blooming White Rose)

White rose buds are plumping out into full bloom
Return, Johnnie, from this war, return
Return, kiss me as in days gone by
I will reward you with a rose blossom

I wanted to substitute a white rose
For your rifle
But before you left my door
The blossom fell to the earth and wilted

Johnny was gone—the fog came
Storms and winds subsided
Winter descended, all the blossoms
Fell from the rose bush
Johnny went away, his footsteps disappeared

Another season passed, the roses came
And faded again.
Summer is gone, winter is here
What shall I give Johnny if he
Returns to his sweetheart?

Johnny will not need any gifts
Because white rose blossoms are blooming for him
There—where he fell in battle—
Upon his grave—grew a white rose blossom

Translated by Charlotte Cavanary (1989)

Busia Josephine Kasperowicz's Favorite Song

Polish:

Rozłąko, ty rozłąko
Ty obcy kraju
Nikt nas nie rozłączy
Jak matka—wilgotna ziemia
Poco mamy roztawać się
Poco mamy łzy wylewać
Czy nie lepiej pobrać się
I długo, długo żyć

English:

Parting, oh, you parting
You foreign land
No one will every part us
Like mother—damp earth
Why should we leave each other
Why should we shed bitter tears
Would it not be wiser to join together
And live a long, long life

(Translated from the original Russian into Polish by Stanisław Wróblewski, nephew of Josephine. Given to Josephine's daughter, Charlotte Cavanary, during her visit to Poland in May 2000. Translated into English by Charlotte and presented to Josephine's grandson, Leonard Kasperowicz, who recalled hearing his grandmother sing this haunting folk song many times as he was growing up and she lived next door on Colony Drive.)

May 13, 2001

O Mój Rozmarynie

0 mój rozmarynie, rozwijaj się! (2)

Pójdę do dziewczyny, pójdę do jedynej,
zapytam się. (2)

A jak mi odpowie:—Nie wydam się, (2)
strzelcy maszerują, ułani werbują,
zaciągnęsię.

Dadzą mi konika cisawego (2)
I ostrą szabelkę, I ostrą szabelkę
do boku mego

Dadzą mi buciki z ostrogami (2)
I siwy kabacik, I siwy kabacik
z wyłogami.

Dadzą mi manierkę z gorzałżyną (2)
ażebym nie tęsknił, ażebym nie tęsknił
za dziewczyną.

Pójdziemy z okopów na bagnety (2)
bagnet mnie ukłuje, śmierć mnie pocałuje
ale nie ty!

Translation:

O my rosemary, keep unfolding! (2)
I will go to my girl I will go to my one and only
To inquire.

If she answers:—I will not reveal (it)
The riflemen march, the cavalry enlists
I will join the recruits.

They will give me a chestnut horse
And a sharp sword
To wear at my side.

They will give me boots with spurs
And a gray visored cap
With a plume.

They will give me a canteen
Filled with brandy
So I will not yearn for my girl.

We will leave our trenches
To face the bayonets.
The bayonet will pierce me
Death will kiss me But not you!

— — — — — — —

Read by Anne Kasperowicz
October 7, 1989
At the Grave Site of Josephine Kasperowicz

My earliest recollection of Busha was when she lived on Cardinal.
Rachael and I ran away to grandma's house. We hid behind the couch.
Mom and dad came looking for us, and grandma told them she hadn't
seen us. It was the first time in my young life that I knew I had a
friend that I could trust. We both decided to surrender so our trusted
friend wouldn't get in trouble. As we grew older, we moved to the
Colony as did Busha. There are numerous memories of lunches spent

in her house next door, sleep overs, etc. Then of course there are the times she spent splashing around in our pool with all of us.

Then the day came when she was taken away from us and placed in a home for the elderly, which, for a youth is hard to forgive the one who took her away. But despite the distance, we still were able to visit her.

Many beautiful Sunday afternoons were spent at St. Elizabeth's Briarbank and Abby Nursing Home with Busha reminiscing about Poland, Hamtramck, and Algonac.

Holidays were the best! Because we knew grandma would be there to share in the festivities. Charlie (schnauzer) was happy because she knew grandma always had a couple extra helpings to slip her under the table.

I miss you, grandma, the holidays won't ever be the same without you.

— — — — — — — —

By Arlene Mruk Kasperowicz
Read at Cemetery Grave Site
October 7, 1989

The Americanization of Josephine

I will always remember Busia as a friend who grew in our relationship to a grandma that I too never would have enjoyed without her. I knew Josephine for a longer period of time than either of my own parents.

We could discuss many things that we had in common—motherhood, children, surgery, death. Despite our language barrier that we had at times, we had an understanding that was within our hearts.

One does not get to choose your in-laws ahead of time, but if I did, I would have chosen you for your spirit, humility, determination and your love of God and family.

How difficult it was for you to come to a different country and live a life that was foreign to you. May you now have the peace with God and Andrew that you so deserve. God bless you, Busia. I love you.

Memories and Inventions in My Lifetime

Memories

Before moving from Norwalk Street at age 5, I listened to a neighbor's crystal radio set with the sound coming through earphones—I was about 3 years old. Shortly after this my father purchased a radio-Victrola combination that remained in use for the next 40 years. It was a piece of furniture about 5 feet high, on four legs with a small dial that lit up when the knob was turned to an "on" position. An electric record player was housed behind two doors above the radio.

Not too long after, zippers became a novelty, then a necessity. Electric refrigerators were in grocery stores, and freezers were in confectioneries where ice cream was sold, but our family didn't buy one until after WW II, about 1947. Long stockings, silk then nylon, were made with a seam going up the back of the leg, requiring straightening repeatedly. What a discovery—seamless nylons and then pantyhose!

The first Maytag washing machine was gray with the motor visible beneath the tub. An electric wringer swung above the wash tubs. Many household appliances and tools were soon powered by electricity: lawn mowers, chain saws, drills, coffee makers, egg beaters, toasters, can openers. My father's rough carpenter tools were all manually operated.

We replaced the Bissell hand sweeper with a Crosley tank vacuum cleaner. (The Bissell sweeper replaced a wire rug beater.) Then a telephone was installed in the dining room next to the radio. My father bought me an Underwood manual typewriter when I was in high school. I used it for more than 20 years. My mother's foot treadle Singer sewing machine is still functional, sits somewhere in niece Kim's basement.

Inventions

"Talkies"—sound and then technicolor movies
gas-fired furnaces
knit clothing—dresses, skirts, and shirts
45 RPM and LP phonograph records
sulfa and penicillin
electrically operated hair permanent machines
home permanents
safety razors
electric shavers
electric hair dryers
ballpoint pens
powdered milk
powdered eggs
oleo—margarine
automatic hot water heater
electric can opener
plastic surgery
orthodontists
Polaroid camera
molecular telescope
molecular microscope
kitty litter
filter cigarettes
latex paint
plastic
shrink wrap
Styrofoam
aluminum foil
polyurethane
synthetics: Teflon, Acrilan, polyester, nylon
fake fur
stainless steel
stereo, quad sound, surround sound
freeze dried foods

instant coffee, tea
frozen foods
sugar substitutes
Phillips screws and screwdrivers
air conditioning
three-way light bulbs
ATM machines
credit cards
color photography
smoke alarms
flash bulbs
microwave ovens
TV and microwave dinners
electrically amplified musical instruments
moog synthesizer
supersonic air travel
movie cameras and camcorders
multiplex cinemas
ultra-sound
MRI
radiation and cobalt therapy
quartz clocks and watches
battery operated anything
copiers
automatic garage door openers
facsimile (fax) machines
mobile and cellular telephones
saran wrap
tranquilizers and psychotropic drugs
birth control pills and the diaphragm
knitting machine
the atomic bomb
nuclear power
radar
velcro
fiberglass

electrolysis
daylight saving time
self-winding watches
automatic shift cars
digital clocks and watches
aerosol cans
automatic windows in cars
tape recorders
automatic lawn sprinkler
automatic lights that go on in the dark
plywood
telephone answering machines with caller identification
personal computers
pay at the pump and self-pump gasoline
scanner labels on products
home alarm systems
thermostats in everything
automatic dehumidifiers
automatic hand dryers
automatic toilet flushing
mothproofing of woolens

                          Viagra

CHAPTER VII

Readings by Nephews and Nieces at Charlotte's

75th Birthday Party, August 21, 2000

Aunt Charlotte

My earliest memories of Aunt Charlotte are from visits to her and Uncle Ed's old house in Southfield. The house offered an array of unique items to capture the curiosity and imagination of a small child. Aunt Charlotte always kept such a neat and tidy household, everything had a place and was in its place. She always drove little cars. During the winter months I remember sitting near the fireplace, burning pine cones to see the colorful flames, sipping hot cider flavored with a cinnamon stick and snacking on peanut brittle. Ice skating with Aunt Charlotte and a cross country skiing adventure are among memories I will never forget. After changing into bathing attire inside the cool changing shed with the beaded doorway, I enjoyed summer visits swimming in the crystal clear pool, lazy afternoons spent lounging on the hammock. Summertime snacks and lemonade were such a treat. How could I ever forget my favorite, marinated mushrooms? I am not sure, but I know we must have been on picnics together. God looked over us all that one summer afternoon when a windstorm caused a tree to crash down onto the outside porch where we all sat just moments earlier.

The holidays seem to be the times I remember best. Of course it was never just Aunt Charlotte who arrived. Uncle Ed always came too. It was always so exciting because they would bring neat gifts and share accounts of distant travels from their vacations. All of us kids were eager to entertain and delight Aunt Charlotte and Uncle Ed with laughter and playful antics. Vacations to the warm sandy beaches of Destin on the Gulf of Mexico were terrific. It was really great to finally return to Destin a few years ago and share a day of offshore fishing with Aunt Charlotte and the rest of the family.

As I search my distant memory to recall cherished moments spent with Aunt Charlotte, the thing that stands outmost in my mind is that Aunt Charlotte has always been a good person. She devoted a career to helping others and always treated me nicely. She never raised a hand to me or shouted at me. She always encouraged me to be a good person and take an interest in activities she enjoyed, and I am a better person because of it. The overriding message from Aunt Charlotte has always been positive. I can't ever remember hearing her complain about anything. Aunt Charlotte is a rare treasure and a loving sister to my father. She has set a fine and noble example for her family to follow and I am proud to call her my Cha-Cha (ciocia) Charlotte.

Leonard Kasperowicz (nephew)

— — — — — — — —

August 20, 2000

Emily and I went for a walk. As we walked, Emily talked a mile a minute. I tried, attentively, to listen to her every word. As we walked, our shadows followed us, shadows of a young girl and a woman.

Emily would pause now and then to catch her breath and to inquire about this or that.

She stopped in front of some flowers and asked what they were.

In that moment in time, our shadows were transformed, my shadow that of the young girl and the shadow of the woman, my Aunt Charlotte, as the words "Black-Eyed Susans" were uttered.

Ann Humes (Kasperowicz), niece

— — — — — — — —

The fondest memories of the time we spent together were in the summer glory of your home. Laughter and family were always in abundance. The lush landscape of your yard provided hidden treasures during our scavenger hunts and your pool provide hours of cool enjoyment. The most special memory was looking at Busha's face when she was surrounded by her children and grandchildren.

Kim Suzor (Kasperowicz)

— — — — — — —

My Aunt Charlotte

There are just too many memories to share, so I will write many short thoughts about my favorite moments with my Aunt Charlotte.

My favorite memory was a scavenger hunt Aunt Charlotte and Uncle Ed made up for us when we came to visit. I think it was during one of their marvelous grill-out parties. Man, I loved that roasted corn on the cob and Aunt Charlotte's homemade salad dressing and tossed salad. Well, back to the scavenger hunt. We got this list of cool things to find such as: pine cones, mint leaves, feathers, etc. We had to find them in their huge backyard that reminded me of a secret garden. It was full of all sorts of neat things. A rose garden, raspberry bushes, and numerous types of trees, shrubs and plants. Not to mention a really groovy pool house and a pool. I loved to swim when I went to their house. When we finished the outdoor scavenger hunt, we had an indoor scavenger hunt that taught us about the artwork and souvenirs they had. Once you found a piece that was mentioned, there was a clue to help you find the next item.

The inside of their house was as interesting as the outside. It was full of all sorts of collectibles from their many years of travel. Their walls were covered with masks, and all sots of artwork. There were dolls, cars and sculptures that decorated their shelves. And that crazy furniture—all slanty and chrome. I thought it was the funniest stuff I ever saw, but it was very comfortable!

I remember sleeping in their guest room and being a little afraid of all the masks on the wall. Thank goodness my little sister was there to save me! ha! ha! I remember playing beauty shop. Aunt Charlotte would take small sections of our hair and wrap it around her finger and slide a bobby pin over the tiny circle of hair or set our hair in curlers, so when we'd wake up we looked like Shirley Temple. Then, when we were looking beautiful, we would go to the movies, ice skating, or the museum.

I remember their basement was full of all sorts of old stuff, and Uncle Ed's art supplies. Down there was the best toy I ever played with. It was a cigar box that was converted into an ice cream parlor. Complete with a tiny doll, an ice cream counter, miniature ice cream glasses, and little stools. One day I'm going to replicate that box and give it to my children to play with. I also remember playing that old Scrabble game with that very tiny dictionary.

Not to mention your two cats, Me Too and Ginger, who were always retreating to the basement or to the outdoors for a little lounging in the garden.

I remember Christmas at our house. You'd always bring this big box of gifts with strings hanging out. We'd get to pick a string and pull out that gift. I use this idea at school at Christmas time when I buy gifts for my students. They love it as much as I did!

As a grown-up I can thank you for all those special gifts you gave me before you moved to Florida. I cherish them and hope my children will appreciate them as much as I do.

I also thank you for our visit to Destin, Florida. I loved our morning walks on that gorgeous beach, those swimming pools, and the water park. Not to mention those weaving and lace tatting lessons. What stands out most is our deep sea fishing adventure. I loved that you caught more fish than anyone else on the boat. Those men should have taken some notes. I can't help but laugh about the suntan lotion episode. Remember that young man with really fair skin who was too tough to wear sun screen? He was getting so sunburned even the tops of his feet were red. Finally, the mother in you couldn't stand it anymore, and you started rubbing suntan lotion on him. It was so cute, because he went from Mr. Tough Guy to Mr. Softie in about two seconds. Then you became his Aunt Charlotte too! I will never forget that!

I love you very much and hope you have a wonderful birthday and thanks for letting Pat and me borrow your birthday for our wedding day!

Charlotte Ogden (Kasperowicz), Niece

— — — — — — — —

Memories of Aunt Charlotte

As I sat down to write this letter I was faced with many warm and cherished memories spent with my Aunt Charlotte over the years. These memories are just not of my loving Aunt, but also of her loving husband of 38 years, my Uncle Ed. Thirty-eight years of marriage; I do believe this deserves a round of applause.

I have many memories of time spent with my Aunt Charlotte, from decorating Easter eggs to seeing slide shows and hearing stories of her recent travels, to splashing around in her backyard swimming pool, to picking fruit and vegetables from her garden, to going to musicals and plays, to visiting art museums, to ice skating, to trips to the Big Kahuna water park in Destin, Florida. There are too many memories to share with you all right now. But, there is enough time to share a few.

On one visit to Destin with my Mother, and a good friend, Aunt Charlotte and Uncle Ed took us to the Officers Club at Eglin Air Force Base for a seafood dinner. My friend and I got into an eating contest that left a tower of crab legs on the table that was on the brink of falling over with every downed leg of crab. After this impressive display of pure carnivorous feeding, my friend and I entered into a coma-like sleep, much like the one most of us experience after a good Thanksgiving dinner. Not to worry, we awoke hours later with a growing boy's appetite for more vittles. True to form, my Aunt Charlotte was hospitable and made sure we did not go hungry.

On another occasion, in 1993, I was tasked with the duty of helping my Aunt Charlotte and Uncle Ed make their final move from Southfied, Michigan, to Destin, Florida. I was to be a designated driver for one of their vehicles and a box mover for the items that the hired movers were not given. In exchange for my help, I could shack up at one of their condos free of charge. Being the astute businessman that I am, this was a deal I could not pass up. So, I hit the road with Aunt Charlotte and Uncle Ed. Along the Way, Aunt Charlotte and I engaged in many conversations, some about life in general, others about her and my father growing up. Having recently celebrated my 21st birthday, I was allowed to partake in an Aunt Charlotte and Uncle Ed tradition. Which, if I recall correctly is called "attitude readjustment." Sounding like a social experiment, I was up for the activity. As it turns out, the "attitude readjustment" is the consumption of some tasty alcoholic drinks from Uncle Ed's portable bar. Hey, who knew!!!

Whether visiting with my Aunt at her house in Southfield, Michigan, or at her condos in Destin, Florida, you could always count on the visit being eventful. Unavoidable, was the collection of art always there to embrace your intrigue, increasing in size after every adventure of hers on the road. Being of Polish descent, every visit was sure to be centered on a meal and indicative of her hospitable nature. Aunt Charlotte was more than willing to oblige. Working in the kitchen is where Aunt Charlotte would showcase some of her creative abilities by concocting food dishes from old or new-found recipes, often met with raised eyebrows from me and my siblings. These signature food dishes made my Aunt Charlotte legendary. So, it is with the theme of food and cooking that I am going to break the rules of the party and present Aunt Charlotte with a gift. Now, this gift is not much, but it is something that is very practical and I hope it gets put to good use.

Aunt Charlotte, I wanted to bring back something for you from my recent travels to Italy that could be added to your art collection and that you would always remember me. However, my wallet was a little short in being able to spring for the high-dollared work of the Italian artisans.

What I was able to bring back was this beautiful apron with a print of one of Michelangelo's most famous pieces. A namesake of mine . . . Michelangelo's David.

Aunt Charlotte, I love you, and I wish you continued good health.

David Kasperowicz, Nephew

Encouragement and Counsel To My Descendants

Re: Obligations to our country. Make it a point to VOTE in ALL elections. Grandmother Josephine was a registered voter in the various municipalities where she lived throughout her life. She considered the right to vote a serious responsibility and a privilege.

Re: Obligations to our church. Become familiar with the latest teachings of the Vatican on social issues. Learn about the great encyclicals of the past and present. Subscribe to the Catholic newspaper of your state.

Re: Obligations to your family. A Polish saying states, "Pilnuj siebie, będziesz w niebie." (Mind your own self and you will gain heaven.) Our first responsibility is to save our own soul, then, the Bible tells us, leave our mother and father and cling to the "spouse." When our parents become infirm, our obligation is to see that they receive proper care, not necessarily provide it. This means steering them to the appropriate services.

Re: Honesty. "To your own self be true." And KNOW what is truth and reality. Honesty is the best policy.

Re: Health. Eat to live not live to eat. "Nuff said."

Re: Diligence. Learn the satisfaction of carrying a project to completion, even if it takes twice as long as planned.

Re: Thrift. Live BELOW your means.

Re: In-laws. Treat them like you expect to be treated when you become an in-law. Be grateful your children can know two sets of grandparents if they have them.

Re: Art. Make a visit to your art museum and/or historical
      museum regularly. Revisit your favorite painting or sculpture,
      then tell your children why.

Re: Music. Learn to read music, play an instrument, listen to the
      masters, opera, musicals. Get your children to do likewise.

Re: Sports. Chose those with "carry over" value. You can swim,
      walk, bike, ski (especially cross country), canoe, square dance,
      kayak, bowl, golf, and bird watch into late life.

Re: Games. Join a bridge class, "get into" crossword puzzles.
      Explore chess. Get your children to do likewise.

Re: Crafts. Try a handicraft: needlepoint, crocheting, knitting,
      macrame, embroidery, quilting, basketry, weaving, rug
      hooking. I've known both men and women who do most of
      the above. Instruct your children.

Re: Judging others. "Judge not lest ye be judged." God is the
      ultimate and last judge.

Re: Company keeping (dating). NEVER with a married person
      who is a legal spouse until the divorce is final.

Re: Fidelity (in marriage). Enjoy the peace of mind assured by
      the vows exchanged and the binding contract both parties
      signed. Monogamy is the best policy.

Re: Marriage. Chose your life's companion carefully. It is the most
      important decision a person makes as an adult.

Re: Languages. Learn a foreign language as young as possible,
      then add Latin and/or Greek.

Re: Tolerance. Practice and teach tolerance of all races, classes and the physically and mentally challenged.

Re: Liquor. Be aware that alcohol is a depressant. At least one ancestor was a binge drinker. Savor each drink over one hour's time to avoid getting tipsy.

Re: Promises. Eliminate these from your dialogue so you can be free of the guilt, anxiety, pressure and tension brought on by trying to fulfill unrealistic obligations.

Rehearse being assertive without being aggressive.

Learn to "fight fair," i.e., avoiding blaming. Begin statements with, "I feel, sense, need, want, am of the opinion, will consider, etc."

Experience compromise in interpersonal relations.

Resolve and then begin reading one book every month. Include classic literature from all the countries of the world.

Lastly review and remember the following:

Be Careful

Be careful of your thoughts
For your thoughts become your words.

Be careful of your words
For your words become your actions.

Be careful of your actions
For your actions become your habits.

Be careful of your habits
For your habits become your character.

Be careful of your character
For your character becomes your destiny.

Who Am I?

1. I am a 53-year-old married female without children.
2. I am a wife to a teacher of art, lover of music, and theatre.
3. I am a homemaker, daughter, sister, aunt.
4. I am a lover of nature, the earth and all it can produce.
5. I am a person with many interests and hobbies.
6. I am an employed social worker specializing in serving the older adult.
7. I am a neighbor, in a neighborhood of mixed ages, diverse religions, different races, multi-ethnic.
8. I am a firm believer in a sound mind in a sound body.
9. I am an avid reader without enough time to read all I would like.
10. I am a dedicated gardener with limits and frustrations on how much I can do in the yard.
11. I am a weaver and handicrafter with many projects planned but not executed.
12. I am a health nut—food, exercise, sports.
13. I am a square dancer and folk dancer, interested in keeping up with "mainstream."
14. I am a friend to few or many—intense or superficial, depending.
15. I am an avid traveler interested in getting steeped in exotic cultures and countries.
16. I am a "saver"—doing it myself—growing, preserving, drying, taking the effort to "do it right."
17. I am a "kook" in some areas—doing the unusual, attending theatre organ concerts, interested in Eskimos and Indians, animals and plants, antiques and sci-fi.
18. I am an ethnic buff—comfortable and proud of being a bilingual, second generation Pole with roots in Eastern Europe.
19. I am anxious to please, organize, entertain, repair, mend, push for progress, socialize.

20. I am a conserver, an optimist, a supporter, a caretaker, an empathizer, a "driver," introvert, quiet, mousey, nonagressive but assertive when necessary.

1978

Important Things My Parents Taught Me

1. Mother: On economics—patronize your local businessman, help him earn a living (daj zarobíc).

2. Father: On achievement—study, learn, get an education— so you can pay someone else to do menial jobs, e.g., housecleaning, painting, etc.

3. Mother: When walking outdoors, seek out dirt paths to keep your feet from getting tired. Avoid concrete.

4. Mother: "do tańca i do róźanca"—be as proficient in dancing as in praying.

Most Frightening

1. The big fire of 1933 at 3291 Trowbridge Street.
2. My father's brush with death during kidney surgery about 1933.
3. A bloody nose that wouldn't stop at age 8 or 9. (Dr. Kłosowski packed it with gauze.)
4. Fear of a whipping after brother, age 3, broke his arm while in my care.
5. My mother's "nervous breakdown" in 1942.
6. Surviving an accident in January 1993—when my Escort station wagon flipped, landed upside down, and slid to a stop on I-65 near Shelby, Alabama.

Most Exciting

1. Christmas Midnight Mass and Easter Resurrection Mass at Queen of Apostles Church in the 1930s and 1940s.
2. WW-II romance—my first beau, Pfc. Bernard J. Zacharias.
3. Buying my first new car—a 1950 Plymouth.
4. The trip behind the Iron Curtain in 1959.
5. Meeting my life's companion, engagement, wedding, honeymoon, first apartment.
6. Mushroom picking in Poland's National Forests—1993.
7. Snorkeling at the Cayman Islands—1994.
8. Viewing the Pyramids at Giza and the Tai Mahal, December 1996.
9. Holding each of my brothers granddaughters, our great nieces, for the first time.

Most Comfortable

1. The lasting relationship and commitment of married life.
2. Old friends.
3. Walking barefoot on the beach.
4. Elastic around the waist.
5. Saturday nights at home.

The Brake Job

"Why would you do such a thing?" he shouted at his 16-year-old son, who fancied himself a budding auto mechanic. His sister's 1935 Chevrolet needed a "brake job."

Now the owners of the car with the crunched right rear fender just left. They were satisfied that the cost of repairs would be reimbursed.

The sister's car's brakes failed at the stop sign, the wheels rolled the auto on into the stream of traffic. She tried to swerve to the left to miss the oncoming car, but just nicked the rear fender.

The son explained, "I replaced the brake fluid O.K., using oil. That's what I thought it was."

This happened about 1948. For the next two years I used public transportation to get to work and then to graduate school at Wayne State University. When I saved enough money for a down payment on a new 1950 Plymouth, I initially parked it on the next block to keep it away from my brother. He was drafted into the Navy and out of the area for the next two and a half years.

All the repairs and service on this car, for the 8 years I kept it, were done at the Dealer's Service garage where a grade school classmate, Richard Rożański was manager.

CHAPTER VIII

What I Did on our July 1996 Vacation in Michigan

or

How to Become a Legend in Your Own Time

The Fourth of July picnic at my brother's canal home in Algonac, Michigan, was well under way when niece Rachel walked next door to the garage that stored her latest interest, a full-size Kayak. I was interested as a former canoeing instructor in summer camp. When family members heard this, the word passed around. "Did you know Aunt Charlotte was a camp counselor?"

Rachel's "hobbies" have been various since she reached adulthood. Barbells for weight lifting, a mountain bike, cross country skis, photography (that won prizes), dog sledding, and now, kayaking. She gave me careful instructions before I slid in and got a push into the calm surface of the canal.

With a few motions of the paddle, I'm on the way. When the kayak and I slide around the bend within view of the family members on shore, they move toward the sea wall. "Way to go, Aunt Charlotte!" How old did you say you were, 50? Cameras are lifted, snapshots taken of this phenomenon. I keep on paddling around the canals for a while, returning across the smooth watery surface to the point of origin.

Another story about my accomplishments was told by niece, Ann. Four days earlier, my husband and I arrived at her tri-level house in Marysville, about 20 miles north of Algonac, just south of Port Huron, MI.

We offered to "house sit" while Ann and her husband Michael took a short trip to celebrate their wedding anniversary. Their daughter Emily would stay with grandma, so we had the house to ourselves. The stocked refrigerator supplied plenty of food for our meals that we took in the kitchen, at their round table standing in one corner of the long room. I notice the scuffed dull surface of the pale gold linoleum on the floor. They moved here a year ago? Roaming through the garage, I locate two metal containers on the shelves. A floor cleaner and a floor "renewer" or polish. So I plan this surprise: a new and improved kitchen floor. I am determined that it will SHINE. According to the directions, a thin even coat should be applied on a clean dry surface—30 minutes between coats. A second coat may be needed on some porous floors.

With rubber gloves, a pail of warm water, a sponge, and cleaning solution, I attacked the project, a rolled-up towel under my knees. The first and second coats of polish also "disappear" into the pores of the linoleum. I persevere—that surface will have a shine. SIX layers later I am satisfied with the outcome. Ann and Michael return the next day, stopping in their tracks at the door that leads from the garage into the kitchen. In amazement they scrutinize all the areas of the kitchen floor. Ann questions me and gets directions as to the procedure used, and writes down the washing formula that I promote: a solution of water, vinegar and baking soda for washing the linoleum and preserving the shine. This was my "hostess gift" to Ann, "Six coats?" they repeat incredulously.

Our niece Charlotte, and my namesake, lives in a mansion according to her sister Ann. We were invited to stay at her colonial home after leaving Marysville. Charlotte and Patrick moved into this house last year too. It is just outside of Marine City in a town called East China, about 5 miles north of Algonac. A well-developed garden with shrubs, flowers, and trees came with this property. The back yard has no grass, just beds of flowers around trees. Brick walkways interlace through the yard separating different areas of vegetation.

Niece Charlotte asks that I help identify some of the plants that are growing that she is not familiar with, and will not remove until she is sure what they are. We tour the yard. My offer as a hostess gift is to do a weeding of her flower beds. The flowering annuals and the perennials will thrive and fill in if there is not so much competition from the CLOVER that wants to take over. Yes, my dear, that is considered to be a weed although green. So this day, wearing a new pair of garden gloves, I spend in the cool sunny breeze getting my "fix" of yard work.

Charlotte's yard will be cleared of weeds before the steak and Indian corn roast planned for the next evening. It is to be another gathering up of family members. My brother and sister-in-law will join us for the backyard barbeque.

However, the highlight of the Michigan visit was the arrival of Jessica, our third great-niece, born June 25th, a week old when we got to hold her at the 4th of July picnic.

Evacuation Urgencies

Husband Ed and I (his wife Charlotte), left our Destin, Gulf Terrace Condo Home at 10:00 a.m., Wednesday, October 4, 1995, heading for the Mid-Bay Bridge, Highway 20, and into a NNE direction. Clothing, food, drinks, maps, hobby materials, and magazines were in the car, enough to last for 2 to 3 days. My "fantasy" was that once we reached Opp, Alabama, about 80 miles north into the interior, some small motel could offer shelter from the elements. From there we'd return to Destin to assess the damage from OPAL, the hurricane headed for the Panhandle Gulf Coast of Florida. Swirling clouds, gusty winds, and slashing rain accompanied us along Highway 98 east past WalMart, Henderson Park, and Matthew Boulevard. A steady stream of vehicles approached the bridge, ahead of us and behind us. Trucks, camper trailers, vans, and cars single filed across the span over Choctawhatchee Bay. We were gratified there was no delay at the toll booth. A sign in the window, scratched hurriedly in pencil, announced, "NO TOLL TODAY." Easily we continued on to Highway 20, turned right, heading east for Freeport where a left turn would take us north on Highway 331.

Here was our first bottleneck. At the traffic light in Freeport, official-looking personnel in yellow rain slickers gestured for vehicles to turn left only under the red flashing caution light. Until then we considered continuing straight on Highway 20, but a radio announcer warned of backups on Highways 79 and 77. So left we turned heading for DeFuniak Springs.

This is the road I travel at least once every week when making home visits to patients needing Home Health Care in Northern Walton County. Often mine is the only car in this stretch of this two-lane road between Freeport and DeFuniak Springs. This morning, the headlights and rear red lights glow as far as one can see ahead and in the rear view mirror. The trip that usually takes 1 hour is taking twice as long. Ed announces that finding a rest room is the next important task. We pass the C.O.P.E. center building so it is only 3 miles to I-10 and a gas station that I know, the Happy store is just beyond.

Noting the urgency in his voice, I ask where is the enamel urinal that stayed in the car from past treks to the hospital for cystoscopies. "In the trunk, behind all the suitcases." I offer to locate it as soon as we find a side road to turn into and stop. Just ahead, what looked like a road was a bridge. We crossed the bridge and noted a section of woods on the right with just enough grassy shoulder to park. The emergency flasher was activated as the car came to a stop. Without waiting any longer, Ed ran out into the rain toward the woods and bushes. The stream of cars moved on at a snail's pace passing our standing Mark VIII. Ed's white nylon jacketed back could be seen in the rainy mist as he stood beyond a clump of shrubbery. All the gas stations we passed had lines of vehicles waiting to get gas. Our next stop would be at the station where I remembered the gas is $1.09 for mid-grade. It was another half hour of inching along before we turned left into the gas station driveway.

Just before getting to this point, both lanes of Highway 331 became one way, northbound, with traffic "monitors" in the familiar yellow slickers, directing traffic just before the lanes are divided with a median and the entrance road to I-10. Making a left turn into this gas station was tricky given the volume of traffic. A large canopy protects cars and passengers from the rain and sun while dispensing gasoline. So we stop at the pump, only one other vehicle was there, a blue pick up truck, whose driver, rushed out just as we approached, he glanced at the sign on the door that announced, CLOSED, but moved onto the side of the building, turned his back, his shoulders relaxing as he relieved himself then and there. (Another Evacuation Urgency.)

I remembered a Tom Thumb store that sold gas just a couple miles further. We returned to the steady stream of traffic with great difficulty but did succeed to reach the Tom Thumb store where one tank got filled and another two were emptied. Before leaving we purchased a large box of freshly popped pop corn for 53 cents that was to sustain us until we stopped for the night.

Highway 83 off Highway 90 was next on our route to Opp, Alabama. This was another familiar road I traveled frequently. Today it was strewn with leaves and branches as the wind and rain continued to make seeing and moving a strain on all the driving skills of this evacuating duo. Ed was driving now, concentrating on staying on the road, slowing down for standing water on the pavement and torrential sheets of rain on the windshield.

Radio station 88.1 from Pensacola and the one from Panama City were tuned in while we drove. We switched from one to the other setting to get the latest hurricane coordinates and directives to evacuees. We munched on pop corn and I planned, "The first Motor Court in Opp will be our target." Ed wondered if that was a safe enough distance from Opal's land fall. It was nearly 2:00 p.m. when we reached Opp's city limits. The first Motor Court was on the left. When we drove to the office door, the sign in the window declared, "No Vacancy." Ed went inside to inquire about any other motels with vacancies in the area and to use the bathroom. He returned to the car announcing that all the motels were full here as well as in the nearby cities of Enterprise and Greenville.

To add to the frustration, the room clerk informed Ed there was no public restroom in their reception lounge, directing us to the Hardee's further up the road. Again the restaurant was on the left. Rain, dark clouds, made everything hazy and indistinct. Ed took the umbrella, heading for the building housing Hardee's. As I got behind the wheel, I could see Ed walk past Hardee's to the next eating establishment along this stretch, Chick Fil-A. He gestured for me to follow him. Only light rain persisted, but the water was flooding the corner of the parking lot where I left the car. In order to get to the Chick Fil-A, I must walk around the end of a chain link fence. Before I realized how deep the water stood there, my foot, shoe, and ankle submerged, soaking the bottom of my slacks which I pulled up over the knee before proceeding. Ed's motions were letting me know that Hardee's was closed. That's why he was going to Chick Fil-A. I shook out my shoes and feet when we returned to the car aiming for Montgomery, the next city of any size with hotels and motels.

Radio news continued, now from Montgomery, giving locations of shelters in various Alabama counties: Bullock, Crenshaw, etc. In addition, we heard of traffic congestion and accidents on I-65 and I-10, and of traffic stopped southbound on certain roads. Pressing on, bumper to bumper, stop and go, we finally crawled into Brantley about 4:30 p.m.

The next town was Luverne, with 44 miles to Montgomery! That was the longest 44 miles I can ever remember driving! There was more of a flow, fewer cars, until we reached South Boulevard. A solid band of cars, trucks, and vans trickled past porched houses in every small town along Highway 331. Some family members sat on rockers outside watching this parade of escapees from nature's wrath just before Montgomery. Another "pit stop" was made at another open gas station. This was an old country lane filling station and quick food stop. Iron grates guarded the two windows. One lonely cashier, a weathered faced man of indefinite age, leaned over the counter watching the TV set in a doorway opposite his perch. The restroom was Unisex with a line up. I took my place behind a young woman. A barefoot toddler stood beside her. His only garment was a diaper drooping heavily. Both mom and child went into the bathroom. In back of me was a young man, restless, moving from one foot to the other, proclaiming, "I'm ready to pop."I moved aside to let him get ahead of me. As we waited for the room to be vacated, this weary looking youth told of his being in a supermarket where check-out lines were so long it took him one and a half hours to go through.

Finally we were on the last leg of our journey. Plans A and B now needed review. If there was "no room at the inn," we would spend the night in the car. It should be in the parking lot of a large motel so we'd use the lobby restroom. An Army blanket tossed into the car as an afterthought was now to be put to good use. A long line of motor vehicles was in the left turn lane at South Boulevard in Montgomery. We assumed they wanted the I-65 entrance ahead.

We veered away from that direction deciding to take a right toward a row of accommodations where we stayed earlier in the year, when we attended the Shakespeare Festival in this city. The Fairfield Inn next to the Courtyard Inn had no vacancies, but the room clerk learned that two rooms were still available at the Courtyard Inn next door. Quickly we rushed over on foot to secure one room and I went to locate the door while Ed returned to the car to unload it. Just as he stepped outdoors, a deluge swamped over him, soaking him to the skin. With an umbrella in hand it took several trips to get all the supplies inside.

Fear of the unknown persisted as we watched, now on Alabama channels, what damage was done to the Destin area. How long will power be out? What damage will we find when we return? What will the roads be like when we travel south? Just outside our room the sound of chirping birds grew louder and louder. A pear tree was full of shrill high-pitched sounding blackbirds. And I thought I was upset!

Interesting Persons I Have Met

It was a cold, damp, dark morning as several adult men and women shivered as they stood at the railroad siding in back of the 14th Street Michigan Central station in Detroit.

Another group of Polish immigrants was due to arrive to be "resettled" in this city. It was 1950, fresh with my social work degree, this was my new job at the Polish Aid Society. A steady stream of "displaced persons" or DPs, as they were to be called, were already taking jobs and finding living accommodations in the Poletown section of Detroit.

They were given information as to where English, as a second language, would be taught and where other services were available.

Not long after the above experience, which was repeated a number of times, the secretary at the agency asked me to talk to a young woman who needed advice.

I learned, she was 27 years old, 2 years older than I was that year. She walked with a decided limp. Round faced, with long curly brown hair and brown eyes, she seemed anxious to talk in her native Polish. I noted her loose slacks were a bit snug around the waist.

Indeed, she was pregnant, single, alone, but determined to go through with this pregnancy. All her family was gone. She would assure a continuation by this progeny.

Reviewing the community resources and eligibility requirements for financial support, I told her that the alleged father needed to be contacted.

Zosia confided that the man was another emigre from Poland, and he was the only one with whom she was intimate. She began to cry, saying that he lost interest in continuing their relationship.

A letter was sent to him giving him an appointment time.

Zbigniev was of medium height, with short, dark blonde curly hair, intense blue eyes, and a European arrogance that emanated from his muscular frame. I guessed he was younger than Zosia, the woman he impregnated and discarded.

He denied paternity (this was before DNA), suggesting there were "others" involved with this girl.

There was no way to extract any kind of support for the woman and her future needs.

The next time Zosia came to see me she learned from me of the Maternity Home at Providence Hospital where she could receive prenatal care, remain during the final days of her pregnancy, and receive assistance with discharge plans after delivery.

We soon learned twins were expected. The hospital social worker assured us a basic layette, and bottles would be furnished.

Our agency, meanwhile, used its meager petty cash fund to purchase two wicker clothes baskets that would serve as the first cribs for the two baby girls that arrived on a snow stormy day. Housing was obtained in a four-room flat that an elderly widow was willing to share with this new family. Finances for rent payment and support of this trio came from the Aid to Dependent Children program.

The case was closed at this point.

I continued to work at this agency for another 7 years. One sunny summer day, about 5 years after my encounter with this enterprising young woman, the agency secretary announced there were visitors asking for me. I went down stairs to the small vestibule where Zosia stood. Beside her, two little girls held onto her hands. Proudly she let them parade around, revealing crisp flowered dresses, red ribbons in the dark blond curly hair, and laughing deep blue eyes. Long white stockings and black Mary Jane shoes completed the outfit.

Zosia wore a thin gold wedding band on the ring finger of her left hand. She said the girls were told that their father was killed in the war. They would be going to school soon. Her living conditions were different now. She lived in the one story house owned by an elderly widower who was offering to marry her. She was his housekeeper and he was witnessing the growth and development of young life.

I don't know what she decided or what further developments occurred in her life, but I marveled at her determination, resourcefulness, and spirit to fulfill a goal she made. And I was glad to be part of the struggle to assure that life would go on, that this lone young woman now had her own family that would continue growing and multiplying.

Stories

Paradise Valley
(c. 1975)

It was a sultry August "Dog Day" in the Motor City. The Parkside Residential hotel, old, but no longer gracious, was still operating on the fringe of Downtown Detroit, known as Paradise Valley. Rooms $2.50 a day—$15 a week, a sign on the outside wall beckoned. After parking the car, I approached the stoop at the edge of the cracked sidewalk. Stale tobacco smoke attacked my nostrils as I entered the small lobby. Behind the short counter sat a black man with shirt sleeves rolled up reading a newspaper. On the wall behind him several skeleton keys hung on curved metal hooks. Identifying myself as the County Social Worker, I asked to see a George Washington Jackson. Would he take me to his room? He shuffled through the unlit corridor with dark varnished paneled doors on each side. A weak response to enter came from inside the room, after the room clerk knocked. Turning the round knob opened the door to a cubicle forgotten by time and periodic maintenance. Smoke stained walls defined the interior: a single bed, a wooden chair with articles of clothing draped over it, a small sink on one wall, a double-hung window with the lower half raised to reveal an inner courtyard, and a dark-green window shade pulled down partly and unevenly. Curled up on the bed, the thin ashen-faced man had his head on a sweat-stained pillow, his shoulders hunched under a wrinkled bed sheet. His eyes, bleary, seemed to strain to see us standing in the doorway. Next to the bed, on a faded rectangle of carpeting stood a galvanized metal pail. The stench reaching me from the amber liquid that reached half way up the rounded sides was unmistakenly URINE. Remaining motionless, I requested of the clerk, "Would you please get rid of that?" pointing to the offensive vessel. Without hesitation he reached down, catching the wire handle with one hand, he lifted, with the other hand under the bottom, he deftly directed the pail toward the open window.

Like a golden arch, completely clearing the window sill, the entire volume of fluid cascaded to the cement pavement below with an audible splash. The empty container was replaced on the floor. The room clerk left, leaving me to continue with my "assessment." Whatever followed is now a blur and anti-climatic to the entrance.

— — — — — — —

. . . . and Grandma Drinks a Little

It was 11:30 a.m., on a sunny April day, 1972, that I sat across the dining room table from Barbara, aged 76. I noted she was still in her bathrobe, nightgown, and slippers and that her silver gray hair was not combed. We were in her granddaughter's house where she moved after being widowed and selling her own home.

This granddaughter was divorced, had three sons all in elementary school. Barbara moved in to help her with these three boys.

A stroke hospitalized her and the medical history told of suspected alcohol abuse. There were minimal residuals from the stroke: her speech was slightly slurred and she experienced some one-sided weakness, but she was recovering the use of all her extremities and improving her balance and endurance.

What she told me was that recently her granddaughter allowed a boy friend to move into the house. Even before this, Barbara noted that her granddaughter, Alice, had a very relaxed system of discipline and behavior expectations from her three boys. The addition of another person into this household complicated all the relationships. So when evening came, Barbara often had an extra Scotch or two just to tolerate all the hectic activity.

Now alcohol was forbidden, she was on blood thinners, a blood pressure medicine and had regular doctors' appointments monitoring her recovery from the stroke.

In addition, she found her tolerance for the disruptive antics of three small lively boys very trying. Also, her granddaughter's lifestyle was grating on her system of values. With a fixed limited income, she wondered what she could do. She had disposed of all her lifetime possessions before moving in with Alice.

Initially, I recommended she start wearing street clothes daily after she got up in the morning. Learning what income she could expect each month from Social Security, I suggested she consider government housing for senior citizens available near downtown Pontiac, Michigan. All the advantages were described to her: some diversional and recreational activities, bus transportation, to shopping and medical appointments, and the best feature, only 30 percent of her monthly income would be used for paying the rent.

Her first reaction was that she would want at least a one bedroom apartment. Knowing that was what most new applicants desired, and that there was always a waiting list for this size unit, I strongly urged her to accept a studio, and then be placed on a waiting list for a larger place.

A couple of months later I learned that Barbara accepted a studio apartment and was adapting to the life in a high-rise building close to the heart of the city of Pontiac. She invited me to have lunch at her penthouse studio on the 6th floor. The door was ajar. I knocked and when I walked in, she greeted me in her pants suit and her freshly permed hair neatly combed. Three-fourths of a wall separated the living room from the bedroom alcove where a single bed was covered in a blue patchwork spread. In the living room, a love seat, covered in a sturdy cotton plaid, beckoned. We ate cold chicken salad and hot tea from a small drop leaf table set against the wall that had an opening into the kitchen.

Barbara seemed very relaxed and flourishing in this setting. She told of other residents on her floor that would peek in to say hello if she left her door open. She often took part in card games scheduled in the recreation room on the first floor. She did not feel the need to have a car as she had access to the building van available for residents. Nor did she feel the need to do any heavy drinking now that her activities of daily living did not stress her out the way they did when she was at her granddaughter's house. She completed a craft project—a latch hook rug that she hung on the wall in the living room.

She had some long term plans to save enough money to take a trip west, to visit a younger sister who lived in California.

She invited me to "drop in" whenever I was in the neighborhood, a sure indication that she did not need me in the same way as when she was struggling to extricate herself out of an uncomfortable situation.

— — — — — — — —

And He Was Gentle

Angelina was just turning 60 in mid 1970s when she came to the Family and Children's Services, distraught over financial developments that left a serious deficit, now that her husband could not work after suffering a stroke that left him partially paralyzed.

She and her husband had owned an antique store and a furniture refinishing business, on one of the busy mile roads in Macomb County. Now she was torn by the demands of the shop and the care needs of her convalescing spouse.

This couple was born and grew up in the Calabria region of southern Italy, coming to the United States with their families. Guiseppi was trained and apprenticed as a skilled wood worker. He was hoping that one of their sons would follow in his footsteps. In fact, the oldest son did work in the furniture refinishing part of their shop, but found it difficult to support his growing family on the earnings from this work.

The marriage of Angelina and Guiseppi was strained by the health problems of Guiseppi. He had high blood pressure, was a borderline diabetic and had a heart condition. He resisted any attempts to change his diet. He grew up and was weaned on wine and did not intend to change now.

This couple came to the office together only once, as Guiseppi complained that going down the six steps with a cane took too much effort, after the trip they made in their pick up truck. (Angelina told that the truck was used to transport furniture they found at estate sales that was taken to their shop for selling.)

Unfortunately, no additional financial help was available for this couple who owned commercial property, and in addition owned other vacant lots in the area as well as their home. Angelina determined to take her husband to the shop, and have him nearby as she operated the day-to-day business.

His condition worsened and he passed away after another stroke developed.

Grieving and mourning over this loss, she recalled their courtship and marriage. In this strict Italian family, Angelina had to take her two younger brothers along when she and Guiseppi went to the movies. Their marriage took place with both families agreeing to this match. Angelina revealed that Guiseppi did not go along with the practice of displaying the bridal sheet to show that the bride was a virgin. She said she was pleased over this, and that the marriage was consummated, "and he was gentle."

Again finances were strained. She had to manage on one source of income. Soon she found that part of their shop was rented out and this rent helped with some of the expenses.

When I made a visit to the home of Angelina, I saw that she had the table set with two place settings. She explained that with different people coming to the house, some of whom were strangers, she did not want it evident that she was alone in the house. In fact there was a man's hat at one end of the table.

We spoke of her sister-in-law who was also widowed, but who was very much involved in a number of social activities. They centered around the Venetian Club, a service type organization that sponsored dances and other events. I supported Angelina in attending these planned events that attracted other Italian Americans.

Lo and behold she made an impression with her flashing dark eyes, and soon was being courted by Renaldo, a widower. He told her that he spent the winter months in his house trailer in Florida, and that he would be leaving on October first. Obviously she missed his company. Phone calls, letters, and bouquets of flowers urged this courtship on.

Renaldo asked that she visit him in Florida. She hesitated saying that "my name will be mud if my family finds out that I'm going to be spending time with a man in Florida by myself." I carefully pointed out to her that if she was going to "get in trouble" she did not have to go all the way to Florida.

But Renaldo was sensitive to Angelina's system of values and worked within them. He found her a room to rent in the home of a nearby woman. This way he could continue the courtship, take her out, and finally decide to make plans for their marriage in January.

Renaldo and Angelina came to the agency before their wedding. A short man, he had all the charm of a continental gentleman. He announced that he had a physical and that the doctor told him he was in good shape for the coming nuptials. (He was about 15 years older that Angelina.)

Now the house was sold, Angelina lived in an apartment that Renaldo kept for his stay in Michigan and the winters they spent in Florida.

About 5 years later, I received a note from Angelina that Renaldo passed away. They had a good life together. She asked that I visit her at the Apartment she stayed at during the summer months.

Grieving and mourning over this loss, she recalled their courtship and marriage. This marriage was consummated, she remembered, "and he was gentle."

Life was a bit easier now. She had some of her favorite antique pieces of furniture around her. A late model Ford Crown Victoria stood in the parking space next to her unit. Her grandchildren were getting educated and were planning careers and weddings.

— — — — — — — —

One Sheep, Two Sheep

"Turn right at Amanson's Quick Stop" the directions began,

"continue to end of paved road, drive 5.7 miles, etc. This referral from the Home Health nurse to the Social Worker was to "assess and evaluate" the situation of an 87-year-old bachelor living alone on his farm. The nurse was threatening to close the case unless "something" was done to make the house safer for this post-stroke man. His house was easily recognizable, she told me. It was the most dilapidated structure still standing on that rural road.

Oh, yes, there was the problem with 100 sheep this man owned. During his hospital stay, then with limitations brought on by the stroke, the sheep were not being fed regularly. They were breaking out of the fenced area, roaming out onto the road, and were overdue for a shearing. In fact, their wool was so thick that when they got wet in the rain, the soaked pelt became so heavy it caused some of the sheep to fall over and not be able to get upright.

Another concern of the nurse was the flooring in the house, which was weakened by age and perhaps termites. The openings in the floor boards were wide enough for rodents and snakes to get inside. She cautioned me to be careful where I stepped.

On a sunny cool fall day, I drove to the area north of Crestview, Florida, located the unpainted weather-beaten farm house, parked the car and headed for the front door. The yard was strewn with cans, bottles, farm implements, and old bedsprings. Looking around to the back yard, I noticed a small wooden shed with the doors swung open. Spilling out from the interior onto the ground was a mound of grayish wool. More discards littered the area in back of the house. Clearly, there were priorities that precluded raking or recycling.

In response to my knock, a voice asked me to come in, the door was not locked. The front door was remarkably new compared to the rest of the structure. Inside, a center hallway separated two rooms. The windows of both rooms had remnants of faded red drapes hanging. The fabric had deteriorated and disintegrated half way up the window.

Hanging on the walls of the rooms, near the hallway were farmers' bib overalls on hangers, ready to be worn. As I walked, I noted the pieces of linoleum covering the floorboards. With each step, the floor sagged slightly. I became aware of openings between the boards, and the daylight beneath.

Mr. Morgan was sitting in an arm chair in the center of the middle room, with a fireplace against the outside wall. A TV stood in front of the hearth, and to the left, an oil space heater was blowing some warm air into the large square room. A coffee mug stood on the small worn end table to the right of the arm chair. A half grown gray striped cat sashayed around the table legs and the tin can, half full of tobacco juice. There were chinks around the fireplace bricks, with the outside light seeping in.

I pulled up a wooden chair next to Mr. Morgan and sat down. Yes, the nurse told him I would be coming to talk to him. He was wearing bib overalls and a plaid flannel shirt. With both hands on the arms of the chair, he looked like a sultan on a throne.

I explained, that our agency, authorized by his doctor, was hoping to see that he recovered, and that his surroundings were safe for his progress and treatment. He acknowledged that his physical therapy was coming along well. Some weakness persisted but he was very optimistic about total recovery. Taciturn, he answered questions, but did not volunteer any information. His drawl was as thick as Corn Pone.

I learned that a female cousin was available to deliver Meals on Wheels that had to be picked up in DeFuniak Springs. This same relative cleaned up a bit and did his laundry.

The floor, according to John Morgan, was going to be repaired in the next 2 weeks, by another cousin who lived in Freeport. Yes, he hoped to sell the sheep, but the one offer of $25 per sheep was too low. He expected $40 per animal. Meanwhile, another cousin was coming by to look after these animals.

Mr. Morgan, although accustomed to living a solitary life, was willing to divulge some information about his family. There were three brothers who left to seek their fortune away from the homestead. Two married, now their widows live outside Florida. John Morgan returned to work the farm and help his mother after his father passed away. He never married, continued to care for the land and the animals after his mother died. The property was left to the three sons. The two sisters-in-law, now widows, were urging John to sell and divide the proceeds. But he continued to live out his life here, accustomed to the "make-do" kind of existence.

When I rose to leave, I told Mr. Morgan I would return in 2 weeks to see how he was doing, what other services were available and to see if the floor was repaired.

On the way back to the office, I visited the Farmer's Cooperative in DeFuniak Springs. What price can a sheep herder expect for his flock? He should have taken the $25 offer, I was told. Also, the sheep, without proper attention develop parasites, and thus their meat is not desirable as food. This also affects the quality of their wool.

But there was another service that I hoped to provide for Mr. Morgan. The Tri-County Council on Aging had funds to install indoor plumbing where none existed. All one had to do is furnish proof of ownership of the dwelling.

I decided to contact one of the cousins, Judy Morgan, to enlist her help in obtaining the tax records of who was listed as owner of the property and who was paying the taxes. I was not prepared for the facts this relative gleaned from the county tax files.

Judy Morgan easily obtained county tax records at the courthouse. Yes, there were three owners listed on the tax rolls. But the third owner was a Rufus Green. Then Judy recalled what was behind this surprising bit of information. About 3 years ago, John Morgan purchased a pick-up truck with a loan for 9 thousand dollars. The vehicle was immediately stolen from in front of the house. Mr. Morgan still was responsible for the money, and according to the cousin, rather than go to jail, he accepted an offer from Rufus Green. Rufus would pay off the loan if Mr. Morgan gave him one-third interest in the farm.

So now John Morgan, no longer an owner of the house was, a "squatter," and could be evicted. In addition, he was no longer eligible for indoor plumbing!

Meanwhile the "skilled" home health services were to be terminated since Mr. Morgan was progressing, able to ambulate without a walker, and independent as far as self care was concerned. The house and the sheep were another matter!

So my next visit was to be the last one. Well, the floor was not repaired. Mr. Morgan repeated, that his cousin would fix it in the next 2 weeks. About the third name on the property, Mr. Morgan tried, feebly, to assure me that Rufus Green promised to return the ownership to him. But from the way he said it, I was not convinced that this would ever come to pass.

I determined to have my last say with Judy, his cousin. She agreed that his environment was "shaky" and bordering on "unsafe." He refused to move in with a married male cousin who lived in Freeport. I wondered how his personal habits would be accepted, but urged Judy to pursue this "long-term plan" with Mr. Morgan along with the male cousin.

About 6 months went by when I was scheduled to visit a Jim Morgan who lived on a small farm even closer to the Alabama border. I was driving by fields of cotton and behind trailers hauling mounds of peanuts that flew off the pile onto the pavement. I passed at least two flat bed trucks with freshly cut logs swaying on the narrow road heading to a saw mill.

Jim Morgan's farm was small: one cow, and several goats that belonged to and were the responsibility of his teenage son.

Casually, I asked if he was related to a Morgan who owned a sheep farm east of here. Yes, John Morgan was his bachelor uncle. He was eager to fill me in on what transpired in the past 6 months. John Morgan, needed to have his knee repaired. Following the surgery he stayed with the cousin in Freeport. A clean room of his own, inside plumbing, meals prepared, and the opportunity to drive around as a passenger in his cousin's truck appealed to John. He never moved back to his farm, finally freed of the responsibility of managing those 100 sheep. The sheep were sold and Mr. Morgan was adjusting well to his new surroundings and to life in a "double wide"(house trailer).

On one of these truck rides, the cousin missed a curve in the road, landing in a ditch. The cousin survived, but not Mr. Morgan. He had just taken a "plug" of tobacco, which lodged in his windpipe, asphyxiating him when he was tossed out of the cab onto the ground.

His freedom from responsibility was brief, but I hoped it was fulfilling. This nephew had health problems and was in dire financial straits and would now need my undivided attention and assistance.

———————

The Little Girl and the Cheetah

One afternoon a lithe and sleek cheetah lurked in the shade of the rubber tree waiting for the little native girl to come along carrying a shoulder bag full of freshly roasted coffee beans to her bedridden grandmother.

Pretty soon a sprightly native girl child did come along and she was carrying a full load of freshly roasted coffee beans in her woven sisal shoulder bag.

"Are you carrying those beans to your grandma?" leered the cheetah. The little native girl said, yes, she was. So the cheetah asked her where her grandmother lived, and the little girl told him: Beyond the paddock of ferns and just over the mound of abalone shells, then to the left of the banana plantation. Just then the cheetah loped off.

When the little native girl lifted the leather flap of the hut at her grandmother's place, she saw somebody huddled on the rope hammock. She approached and saw it was not her grandmother but the cheetah, for even on the hammock, a cheetah does not look any more like your grandmother than Juan Valdez looks like his trusty white steed.

So the little native girl took out her blow pipe and expertly placed it between her lips, directing it at the cheetah's cheek killing him with the poison tipped dart.

MORAL: Never underestimate the pucker power of little native girls that travel through the Amazon jungle.

(Little Red Riding Hood, South American Style)

———————

If I Had My Life to Live Over

My childhood attire and personal grooming would contain certain items longed for but not attained. My blond hair, fashioned into hanging Shirley Temple locks would reach the shoulders. On the right side of my head, a pink taffeta bow would hold my hair in place. The dress to wear: a pink organdy affair with a ruffle around the bottom of the circular skirt, and a shiny satin sash, plumped out into a bow at the back of my waist. More ruffles around the collar and at the edge of the short puffed sleeves. My feet would be sporting black patent leather "Mary Janes" over anklets matching the color of the dress.

In the warm Sunday sunlight, this outfit would take me to an age 8th birthday party at Josephine Jachim's house, under my arm a wrapped present. Ice cream and layer cake with buttercream frosting would be served on shiny paper plates with a selection of soda pop: cream soda, grape, strawberry, root beer, and rock and rye. The game—Pin the Tail on the Donkey—planned as an activity.

Somewhere in my house, there will be a window seat with a long cushion, upholstered in striped red and white velvet, to sit upon and read. My bedroom will have bookshelves with my own owned books and cupboards for the boxes of children's games and toys. The switch for the overhead light will be on the wall, and in addition there will be room next to the single bed for a bedside stand with a small lamp with a fluted frilly lace shade.

— — — — — — —

December

She pulls open the bottom drawer of the bedside stand. Easily she locates the small footed art nouveau silver jewelry box, positioning it on her lap. Lifting the hinged lid, she gropes for the solitary piece of jewelry lying on the black velvet lined bottom. Grasping the heart shaped rose gold locket with the silver Air Corps

wings on the top—gnarled fingers struggle to open it—failing—
she closes her eyes, remembering the cutout photo of his smiling
face, dark hair, serious dark eyes, she fitted into the oval shaped
interior. She cradles the cold metal heart in the warm palm of her
hand.

A tape is playing highlights from "Oklahoma." Only she hears
the singing through the head phones. She traces the edges of the
casette case in her lap. The soft flannel housecoat comforts her frail
wasted frame as she leans back in the Geri Chair, the silver hairs of
her head flattening against the cushioned back. The song is, "People
Will Say We're in Love." A tear catches in the corner of her left eye
and is flicked away dampening the side of her nose. Her right
cheek is stained by another tear falling—absorbed and disappearing
into the cloth of the long sleeve. Her teeth bite the lower lip to
stifle a cry, muscles in her throat contract in a spasm. From deep
inside, a low moan rises, her chin drops onto her chest. She
succumbs to the ache, the sorrow, the grief, the memories—her
bony shoulders rising and falling with each wrenching sob.

— — — — — — —

Healthy Aging Primer
Or the ABCs of Salutary Maturity

The single most important thing I have learned about Healthy
Aging relates to ATTITUDE 'BOUT CHANGE.

All our adult life is a preparation for the time when we become
"older." We form attitudes about our bodies, about our circle of
friends, intellectual pursuits, and about earnings that pay for the
activities of daily living.

Advancing years bring on a change in our physical functioning,
what friends and family remain nearby, what cerebral exercises we
maintain, and how a fixed income affects all of the above.

Since the only constant in life is CHANGE, it is crucial to
remember this when confronted by the different demands made
by our physical, social, mental and financial status.

Re: Physical Health. Maintain FITNESS. Walking costs nothing, can be done anywhere.

Re: Social Life. Make friends that are younger as well as older than yourself.

Re: Mental Health. If you always wanted to learn about the stars or raise llamas, why not now? Continue to pursue the three "R's"—reading, 'riting and 'rithmetic (valuable when balancing the checkbook).

Re: Finances. Meet the challenge of a fixed income. Or add to it via a part time job. It can be rewarding.

This is what I would like to share with future generations.

Charlotte Cavanary

———————

Destin Quartz

The couple, gray haired, and a bit stooped, stride onto the beach, hand in hand. A hovering fog envelops them like a soft flannel blanket. His longer legs move him ahead, his hands now in the white parka zipped against the brisk cool breeze. She shakes open a plastic grocery bag, pulls on a pair of knit cotton garden gloves and with a long handled "picker upper" in her left hand, begins to stroll slowly searching the silvery sand just in front of her for discards. Several terns circle overhead, swooping towards the plastic bag—accustomed to feeding from similar containers. A solitary willet darts back and forth, pecking intermittently at unseen tidbits in the wet glistening sand at the edge of the lapping water.

The distance between the two human figures increases—now his form is completely obliterated by the gauzy fog. Her progress is slowed by the stops she makes to lift bits of insulation, roof shingles, crushed beverage cans, assorted pieces of clothing, plastic food containers—remnants of Hurricane Opal and tourist visits just before.

Yesterdays downpour left the sand surface pockmarked. A sand snowman was fashioned with a smile pressed into the face, twigs for arms. Farther, a fort, patted with hands, a sand wall surrounding it. White foamy waves roll over in a steady din, blocking out any other sounds, further from the water one can hear pounding hammers. Tracks in the sugary sand are many: of bare feet—child size and adult, imprints of intricately patterned athletic shoe bottoms, small and big bird tracks—showing movement in all directions. What animal makes those four deep claw marks—a large dog? the Florida panther?

This is a good time to review activities great niece, Emily Humes, age 3, may enjoy when she makes her first trip to Destin next week. Yes, we'll be sure to call attention to all the highlights of the seashore. Maybe we'll have another fogbound morning.

When he turns around to walk back on the hard sand at the waterline, she joins him. She discards the bag of refuse in the container near the boardwalk. Now they will plan the rest of the day.

1996

Spring

(The sugar white sand on Destin beaches is not silica but quartz, brought down from the Appalachian mountains during the last ice age.)

— — — — — — —

Poem

One of the few poems committed to memory during adulthood

If thou of fortune be bereft
And in thy store there be but left
Two loaves
Sell one
And with the dole
Buy hyacinths to feed thy soul.

MAPS

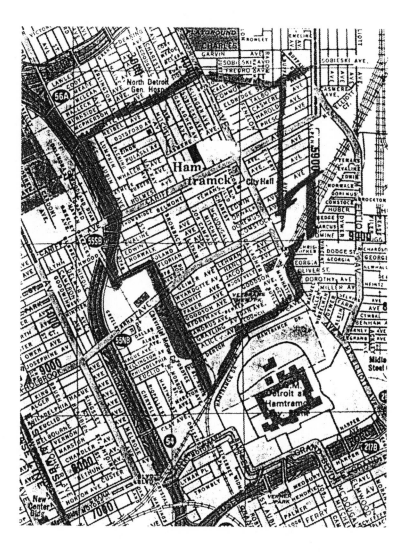

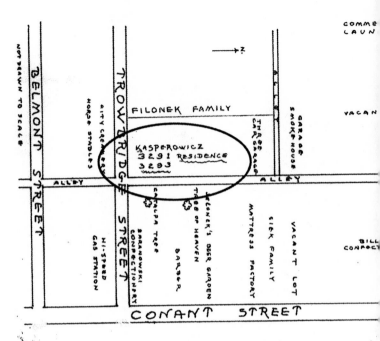

APARTMENT BUILDING

CLEANERS →N

KLINGER STREET

JASINSKI RESIDENCE

MORAN STREET

VACANT LOT

MILLER'S GROCERY STORE

JASINSKI SHOE REPAIR

JARA CONFECTIONARY

SKUPNY FUNERAL HOME

CANIFF STREET

CONANT STREET

CONANT STREET

NOT DRAWN TO SCALE

DOLORES WOJCIK'S FAMILY

FLORIST

FUNERAL HOME PARKING

JUDGE GRONKOWSKI AND FAMILY

MATTHEW LACEWICZ FAMILY

ELEONOR WIETNICK'S FAMILY

PRESCOTT STREET

RECTORY

HALL AND ELEMENTARY SCHOOL

OUR LADY QUEEN OF APOSTLES CHURCH

CANIFF STREET

HAROLD STREET

→N